CLÉMENTINE IN THE KITCHEN

SENLIS FROM A CROW'S NEST

CLÉMENTINE
IN THE KITCHEN

by Samuel Chamberlain
(PHINEAS BECK)

A NEW EDITION

Revised by Narcisse Chamberlain
(DIANE BECK)

Illustrated with Drypoints and Drawings by the Author

David R. Godine, *Publisher* · BOSTON

WALTER FRESE, founder and president of Hastings House Publishers, undertook the publication of *Clémentine in the Kitchen* in 1943 and kept it in print until 1985. His loyalty to this book for forty-two years is more than exceptional in the annals of publishing.   N.C.

Grateful acknowledgment is made to the Samuel Chamberlain Collection at the Essex Institute, Salem, Massachusetts, for the loan of original drypoints reproduced on pages 12, 75, and 102.

This revised edition published in 1988 by
David R. Godine, Publisher, Inc.
Horticultural Hall
300 Massachusetts Avenue
Boston, Massachusetts 02115

Library of Congress Cataloging in Publication Data
Chamberlain, Samuel, 1895–1975
    Clémentine in the kitchen

       Originally published: New York : Hastings House, 1943.
       Includes index.
       1. Cookery, French.   I. Chamberlain, Narcisse.
II. Title.
TX719.C4   1988   641.5944   87-8747
ISBN 0-87923-702-3

       Third edition
       Printed in the United States of America

CONTENTS

ILLUSTRATIONS

BY SAMUEL CHAMBERLAIN

THE VIGNETTES ARE BY HENRY STAHLHUT

CLÉMENTINE IN THE KITCHEN

THIS IS THE GASTRONOMIC DIARY OF THE BECKS, an American family in France, and of their most cherished possession, Clémentine, the faithful red-cheeked *cuisinière* who presided majestically over the Beck kitchen for close to a decade. It records how four well-upholstered Anglo-Saxons accepted the expatriate role without regret and reveled in the gentle way of life in the little French cathedral town of Senlis. The culinary keystone of this household was the alert, good-natured little Burgundian woman who is the heroine of this account. Through the peaceful early thirties and the dark days of Munich the industrious Clémentine gave us meals worthy of a *Cordon Bleu*. When black clouds gathered on the horizon in 1939 and it became apparent that we might be instructed to return to America at any moment, one thought reigned above all others — Clémentine must return with us. And return she did, under the quota and under our protecting wing, to begin life anew in the small American town of Marblehead, Massachusetts, and to wrestle with the English language. Her struggle with pounds and quarts and inches, with American can-openers, delivery boys, mechanical mixers, serve-yourself grocery stores, and dial telephones, and, finally, her triumph in adapting French cooking to the American scene constitute the theme of these pages.

PHINEAS BECK, 1942

2

FRUIT STORE FAÇADE, SENLIS

TWELVE YEARS OF LIVING IN FRANCE MADE THE transplanted Beck family blissfully, incurably conscious of good food. When the initial novelty of representing an American firm in Paris in the Roaring Twenties had begun to wear off, and as French schools, taxes, politics, red tape, and bicycle races began to puzzle us less, one towering realization dawned upon us: These French people know how to LIVE!

With great enthusiasm we had begun serving our apprenticeship at the art of graceful living in a Paris apartment in the Faubourg-St.-Germain. By the time we moved to the sleepy country town of Senlis in the Ile-de-France, where we had bought an eighteenth-century stone house, we were well along the gourmet's path, from which there is no turning back. And when the final blessing of a perfect French cook appeared to make our domestic picture complete, we became utter sybarites, frank worshippers of the splendors of the French cuisine. Now we would rather talk about a good *sauce béarnaise* than football, finance, or infidelity. Our French table has been the scene of endless gastronomic adventure and gustatory improvisation. Our library shelf of well-thumbed cookbooks has yielded secrets that have given us rapturous hours of research into "new taste thrills" altogether unknown to the advertising men who coined the phrase. Our kitchen is the most important shrine in the house, and our nostrils are instinctively strained in that direction any time after ten in the morning.

Much as we appreciate oil heaters, air conditioning, electric refrigerators, and other creative comforts of the American way of life, we admit, without shame, that we are hopelessly Francophile on the question of food. We will run a mile from ham and pineapple, jelly and lamb, sweet potatoes and marshmallows, but will warm right up to sweetbreads and peas, snails and Burgundy, radishes and butter. We like wine with our meals and think that beef steak and ice water is a barbarous combination. We don't think cranberry sauce helps turkey or that catsup is a

4

BURGUNDY HILLSIDE

necessary companion of well-cooked meat. We would rather have a few leaves of crisp lettuce, properly seasoned with olive oil and wine vinegar, salt, pepper, and a sprinkling of chopped chives, than any of the exotic tea-room salads that are rightly the targets of wise-cracking columnists. I hope our patriotism won't be challenged when the truth is told about daughter Diane, for example, who has all the qualities of a good American girl of sixteen, but who remains entirely indifferent to fudge cake, baked beans, pancakes, tomato juice, and corn fritters. But she's a fervent enthusiast of *tripe à la mode de Caen* (Hemingway or Faulkner would call it cowbelly, I suppose). She prefers the grey-green *portugaise* oysters of France, aromatic with iodine and sea water, to our placid Cotuits. She adores *cervelle de mouton au beurre noir*, those delicate little mounds of sheep's brains swimming in black butter. At one sitting she has eaten a dozen and a half husky Burgundian snails before being halted. Sweetbreads, calf's head *à la vinaigrette* (including the eye), head cheese, mussels,

rabbit stew — all delight her. She does weaken at eel, almost revolts at squid and octopus, and puts her foot down when it comes to blood sausage and *andouillette*, a Breton sausage the taste and texture of which lead to the blackest of suspicions.

Well, that's the kind of a family we are. I won't blame you a bit if you slam this book shut with impatience and dismiss us as a troupe of gastronomic Fifth Columnists. But if you are still with us, may I take you back to the month of May 1931 and to our kitchen in France where the estimable Clémentine, in all her culinary splendor, began her reign of many years.

We'll never forget when Clémentine came to us, out of the blue, as the result of a stray telephone number that Mrs. Beck had picked up at a Paris dinner party. She had just discharged the fifth cook in eight weeks and was scouting forlornly for a sixth. Clémentine sounded so good over the telephone that my desperate wife at once sent her fifty francs for transportation to our little town north of Paris. One look at the smiling, pink-cheeked Clémentine and we knew that she would be a godsend after the succession of indifferent cooks who had presided in our venerable cuisine. Old Amélie had been too cranky. Noëlie could prepare some toothsome specialties (her *cassoulet* still haunts us), but she was fantastically sloppy. Jeanne had made frequent and abnormal inroads into my wine cellar. But the fair, black-eyed Clémentine seemed to possess all virtues and no faults. She arrived on the five-o'clock local, a demure and smiling little person, and was busy preparing dinner within an hour. The Becks heard snatches of song coming from the kitchen and then sniffed the heavenly mélange of shallots, butter, and herbs browning in Clémentine's casserole. Our day of good fortune seemed to be at hand. And when we learned that our rosy discovery was a genuine *Cordon Bleu* and a resident of Beaune, the gastronomic heart of Burgundy, our joy knew no bounds.

The Becks had been in Beaune only a few weeks before and had reveled in the luxurious cuisine of that epicurean stronghold. Would our newly found treasure be able to duplicate the memorable Sunday dinner in Beaune, which we had enjoyed with the Bellon family, *par exemple*? We wondered. If she could, our reputation as Lucullan hosts was everlastingly made. Papa Bellon had spread himself on that memorable Sunday, and the enraptured Becks remembered every detail of the feast. A bourgeois dinner in Burgundy lacks finesse, perhaps, but it is glorious in earthy fundamentals. The menu of Papa Bellon's dinner was simply worded, but it made a more lasting impression upon us than many an ornamental menu of *la grande cuisine française* that we had sampled. *Le voici*:

Escargots de Bourgogne
Truite de la Rivière Nageante dans le Beurre
Coq au Chambertin
Petits Pois à la Française
Pâté en Croûte
Salade de Laitue
Fromage
Tarte aux Mirabelles
Café

Papa Bellon had ordered the dinner two days ahead of time at the leading restaurant in Beaune. From his confident air the Becks knew that auspicious things were in the offing. Besides the plump Monsieur *et* Madame Bellon there were with us two buxom daughters, a solemn son-in-law, and a strapping son of twelve. We sat down for the obligatory apéritif on the terrace while our host went inside to talk to the chef.

A clink of glasses, a few appraising glances at the townspeople walking home from church, and we were ready to go into the restaurant, where our table, decked with red-and-white checkered cloth, shimmering with glassware, and heaped high with crusty bread, had been set for ten guests. The prodigal plenty of that dinner saddens us now, when we think of the daily fare of the Nazi-held Burgundians. At each place were a dozen beautiful *escargots de Bourgogne* in their light ochre shells, very hot and very fragrant, exuding a heavenly aroma of garlic, parsley, and fresh butter. This rare comestible calls for specially designed platters, holders, and forks, but how well worth their acquisition! With the snails we sipped a full-blooded Nuits-Saint-Georges. Some people have the idea that snails, because they live in a shell, are closely related to seafood and therefore must be accompanied by a white wine. *Escargots de Bourgogne* are land

7

snails exclusively, growing fat on the leaves of the grape vines. They never get even close to the sea, and Burgundians prefer them with red wine.

The ancient waiter shifted plates and appeared with a massive oval, copper casserole containing ten handsome trout, deep in a prodigal bath of melted butter. *Nageante dans le beurre* was indeed the expression to use. The wine was a lighter gold than the butter, a clean, tempting Meursault Charmes of 1926. *Coq au Chambertin*, the *pièce de résistance*, could not have been more typical of Burgundy. It is doubtful if any Chambertin went into that delectable dish, which usually is content to be called *coq au vin*, but the sauce wasn't made from just any bottle of red wine, either. Then came a rich and fragrant *pâté en croûte*. Ham, veal, sausage meat, strips of fat, spices, pistachio nuts, and a symphony of herbs had been mixed and encased in a golden crust. This was served hot with a salad of plain green lettuce. We watched the headwaiter with fascination as he mixed the dressing on a flat plate — five parts of olive oil to one of strong wine vinegar, salt, ground pepper, and a generous daub of Dijon mustard. The wine was a lusty Pommard Rugiens 1926, which held over handsomely for the cheese platter, an impressive plank of Camembert, Brie, Roquefort, and Port-du-Salut.

Individual *tartes aux mirabelles* after this, accompanied by a rich Château Chalon poured from its distinctive bottle, then some very black coffee and a trio of liqueurs: Vieux Marc for those who could take it (*papa and son-in-law*), Armagnac for me, and rich purple Cassis for the ladies.

Well, it was quite a Sunday dinner. Do you wonder that we were enthused about the splendors of gastronomy in Beaune?

Would Clémentine, the native Burgundian, give us splurges such as this? Could our figures and my pocketbook take it? The answer, we soon found out, was magnificently in the affirmative. Clémentine was a *Cordon Bleu* in the best tradition. My son Phinney and I began to dream of fabulous banquets, and I began to recall uneasily that one gets gout in Burgundy. Luckily there were two deterrents to shield us from mad, headlong *gourmandise* — Clémentine's mastery of simple dishes, and Mrs. Beck's insistence upon a sane and healthy fare. Regardless of our curiosity about exotic dishes and our desire to sample all of Clémentine's sauces, our daily menu contained the same well-balanced fare that prevailed in countless conventional French homes. We had no huge dinners à la Papa Bellon. My unruffled wife saw to that. Our daily living was based, I suppose, upon no more than twenty-five classic French dishes, all of which Clémentine handled with the sure hand of a master. They are elemental dishes throughout France, as fundamental as bread, cheese, and wine. They vary, of course, from one family to the next. But the following list, taken from the most thumb-worn pages in Clémentine's notebook is typical, and eloquent, of the way a civilized French family lives.

EGGS
    Omelette aux Fines Herbes
    Soufflé au Fromage

LAMB
    Gigot d'Agneau
    Côtelettes de Mouton

FISH
    Merlans Frits
    Coquilles Saint-Jacques
    Turbot au Vin Blanc
    Moules Marinière
    Truite Meunière

BEEF
    Pot-au-Feu
    Boeuf à la Mode
    Boeuf Bourguignon
    Faux-Filet Rôti
    Entrecôte Béarnaise

POULTRY
    Poulet Rôti
    Coq au Vin
    Poule au Riz
    Poulet Sauté
    Poulet Cocotte
    Canard aux Navets

VEAL
    Blanquette de Veau
    Sauté de Veau
    Rôti de Veau
    Paupiettes de Veau
    Foie de Veau Meunière

PORK AND HAM
    Rôti de Porc en Casserole
    Jambon, Sauce Madère
    Saucissons aux Pommes Purées

Any one of these dishes serves as the *pièce de résistance* in numberless French meals. At lunch time such a *plat* would be preceded by an hors-d'oeuvre and followed by the classic *légume, salade, fromage, et fruits*. The menu varied little at the evening meal, except that it was briefer and began with a hot soup. It was accompanied, of course, by plenty of good crusty bread and an honest, substantial *vin ordinaire*. In view of the present plight of France, the use of the past tense is advisable and eloquent.

Clémentine in the kitchen! The bright-eyed little cook brought new significance to that part of the house, which had waited so long for a presiding genius. It was a neat and ample kitchen. Its red tile floor was worn down in spots but always beautifully waxed. Above the stove was our pride and joy, a shimmering *batterie de cuisine*, fourteen heavy copper pans, polished and tin lined, hanging against the wall in mathematical progression. They ranged from a huge fellow big enough to roast a duck to the tiny vessel just about right for poaching an egg. There was an

9

efficient stove, a commodious and rather ancient soapstone sink, a shelf for a library of cookbooks, from *Tante Marie* to *Ali-Bab*, a massive oak chopping board, and some well-balanced scales with a squad of neat little metric weights. A white marble-topped table stood in the middle of the kitchen, its drawer crammed with sauce whisks, wooden spoons, and a murderous collection of sharp steel knives. In a low cupboard was a mighty assemblage of seasoned earthen casseroles, some with handles, some with covers that could be hermetically sealed. On top of the cupboard was a husky stone mortar with a dark wooden pestle. Hanging near the door were the two invariable adjuncts of a French kitchen — a salad basket and a birdcage.

Here the cheerful Clémentine reigned, not as a despot (like a few French cooks we had known), but as a genial collaborator who, if coddled by the right amount of flattery, appreciated our insatiable interest and didn't mind our incessant intrusions into her domain. Her Burgundian good nature had to stand for a lot. Each of the Becks had a specialty. Diane interested herself (far too much) in the desserts. The young man of the house was absorbed in his vegetable garden and the possibilities for pecuniary profit that it held. The cheese, wine, and cookbook departments were indisputably mine. But there is no question, of course, as to who really holds the reins in a French household. It is *madame la patronne*, and our house was no exception. Once the authority and prestige of Mrs. Beck stood unquestioned, this family of incorrigible epicures went at a gallop, but in safe hands, down the road to gastronomic adventure.

12

EARLY MORNING MARKET, SENLIS

T HE MARKETPLACE IN MANY FRENCH TOWNS is a rather dreary affair, usually an open-air edifice of ornamental iron, covered with a tin roof and resounding with the hoarse shouts of local vegetable barons. Numberless early-morning sightseers have been attracted to Les Halles in Paris, of course, but they were looking for atmosphere and onion soup rather than architectural splendor. Even the sad events of 1940 do not dim the memory that most French markets are unlovely. But one notable exception to the rule is the market in our little town of Senlis in the Oise. Located in the disaffected medieval church of St. Pierre, this market is an absolute pageant of the picturesque. In its cool, white-washed nave the symphony of color caused by the vegetable and fruit stands and by the brilliantly costumed African Spahi orderlies, buying provisions for their officers, was something to delight the eye of an artist. Rare was the summer day, in fact, when an easel was not set up in some corner of the side aisles, with a painter working feverishly behind it.

The rich Gothic façade of St. Pierre looked down upon a small cobblestone square that, on market days, became packed with the umbrellas and stands of ambulatory dry goods merchants. Here sturdy peasant women from neighboring farms would buy strong black cloth with the proceeds of the sale of their *haricots verts*. And here would be stationed the inevitable unshaven accordion player, squeezing out silly, tinkling tunes while his wife tried hard to sell sheet music to a gaping circle of children and rustics from the outlying villages. And here also was our particular joy, the suspender salesman who had the marvelous technique of snapping a pair of suspenders into the air, using the principle of the slingshot, so that they hung on the lamppost, invariably bringing a laugh from the crowd—and, more often than not, a sale.

Market day came twice a week in Senlis, and twice a week the Beck family plunged into this animated picture with joy and abandon.

We came laden with market baskets and expanding *filets*, those wonderful nets, gathered together by a handle, that can carry an almost limitless amount of produce, depending only upon the strength of the shopper's arms. Our technique was to buy potatoes first (these filled the bottom of the net), then green vegetables, then fruit, and finally a few heads of lettuce, which could be crammed in at the top. The idea of a paper bag for each vegetable would have been utterly inconceivable. You simply piled your purchases into a given space, keeping the eggs, berries, and cheese on top, and sorted them out when you returned to your kitchen table.

Because of the weight-lifting problem, vegetable and fruit buying usually became my province, with the manly aid of little Phinney. The shrewder business of selecting meat, fish, poultry, and butter fell to *madame*, in earnest consultation with Clémentine. The venerable French custom of maneuvering for special privilege applies equally to the acquisition of a château, a seat in the Chamber of Deputies, or a mere cauliflower. I found a favorite vegetable woman and stuck to her, with the result that she would reserve her choicest produce under the table for the Beck family (and an appreciable *pourboire*). She was a memorable person with a fine moustache, a flashing smile, and more than ordinary displacement. In fact she bulged conspicuously over the chair that she always brought to market. "*Elle a de quoi s'asseoir,*" as I heard an interested observer remark.

Endive, leeks, artichokes, *cèpes*, and other mushrooms were cheap and plentiful. So was every sort of fresh herb. Parsnips, lima beans, corn on the cob, and sweet potatoes did not exist. Aside from these differences, the Senlis vegetable market ran very much the way it does in a small American town: potatoes, onions, peas, carrots, string beans, cabbage, tomatoes, cucumbers, eggplant, turnips, broccoli — with the fine distinction that all the French vegetables had been picked when they were young, tender, and not fully grown. Why did those vegetables taste so good on your last trip to France? That is the answer, combined with the fact that they were probably cooked in prodigal quantities of pure butter.

As for fruit, the neat mounds of apples, pears, peaches, apricots, and oranges in the side aisle of this ancient market certainly couldn't compare in size or pulchritude with the pyramids of gorgeousness we now see daily in Mr. Fred Popopulous's corner fruit exchange. But when it comes to *flavor*, the Beck family unanimously bestows its palm of excellence upon the small, unbeautiful fruit of France. I hope we don't sound disloyal. But too often the beauty of American "store" fruit is skin deep. Beneath its superbly tinted cheek frequently lies a wan and listless taste, a hollow texture. Under the peasant roughness of Normandy fruit lurks a Latin ardor, blended with a patrician subtlety of flavor, that our buxom Anglo-Saxon specimens often seem to lack.

The town butchers moved into the apse of St. Pierre on market day, lending one more note of color, this time predominately crimson, to the cool stone vaults. The owner of the *boucherie chevaline* was there (color note: a deep maroon), smiling under a golden horse's head and underselling all his competitors pound for pound. So was the genial *charcutier*, whose ham pies and aromatic *saucissons de Lyon* were the joy of the town. So was the innocent-faced Madame Goujon, all too ready to club one of her pink-eyed rabbits over the head with a wooden stick and then skin it for you. So was the sheepish Monsieur Tarreaux, *marchand de volailles*, the only merchant for whom the peaceful Clémentine regularly reserved a black scowl. It all dated back to the day he sold us a fat, hefty, and expensive duck. Proudly Clémentine brought it back from market, only to find upon closer inspection that it had been stuffed with a roll of wet, heavy newspapers. Monsieur Tarreaux will not soon forget the avalanche of vituperation that descended upon him the next market day.

Steeled by a few such experiences, Madame Beck and Clémentine approached the business of buying meat with great seriousness and knew the cuts of beef, veal, lamb, and pork by heart. This knowledge does them little good now, for the American way of parceling a side of meat is totally different. They also knew how to *marchander*, and this psychological knack of driving a good bargain is far from useless in our new home. The thing we miss most in America is young veal — really young, tender veal with hardly a blush of pink to it, such as sad Monsieur Lesage (the butcher whose wife ran away with the *garçon de café*) used to cut into paper-thin *escalopes* or magnificently thick *côtelettes*. But there are two sides to the picture. No economical French housewife in Senlis ever dreamed of possessing the whole sugar-cured ham that is a happy commonplace in an American home.

One transept of the sixteenth-century building was given over to tables piled high with sweet biscuits, macaroons, and *pain d'épices*. The other transept held the two rival butter-and-cheese magnates of the town: the oily Monsieur Dupuit, whom we distrusted, along with some of his butter, and the plump Madame Veuve Legendre, whom we adored. The perfect *commerçant* will always be personified in my mind by this neat and energetic little woman, surrounded by vast mounds of butter, baskets of fresh eggs, and a glittering terrace of cheese. She made absolutely no compromise with quality. Her prices were invariably fair. When she dexterously scooped off butter with a wire cutter she gave full measure, but no more. The independent Senlis housewives would wait in line for her,

but for nobody else — and she could keep four of them in conversation while waiting on a fifth. Madame Legendre had beautiful cheese. Fine, creamy, light-colored Roquefort was her specialty. Often she produced that rarity (even in France), a perfect Camembert or Brie. And her choice of other types, Pont-l'Evêque, Livarot, Coulommiers, Port-du-Salut, and Petit-suisse, was impeccable. We cherish the picture of Madame Legendre, her pouter-pigeon figure silhouetted against a cartwheel of Gruyère, although Wisconsin is helping us to forget.

The cool, sheltered cloisters of the one-time church provided a sequestered courtyard for the fish market, a noticeable convenience in the hot summer months. Here came iced crates of fish — English sole from Boulogne-sur-Mer, *merlans*, turbot, and tuna fish from Douarnenez. For the modest purse there were flat, ugly skates, which French ingenuity has made palatable in the form of *raie au beurre noir*. For the opulent there were fat *langoustes*, crustacean treasures well able to hold their own with Maine's choicest lobsters. In the right season great mounds of rosy shrimp, straight from Brittany, would be piled up on the marble-topped table nearest the exit. This was the final temptation for the Beck family, now heavily laden, and a kilo of *crevettes* would be stuffed into the *filet* before we emerged into the street.

Then came the incomparable moment to watch Gaspard. There are ingenious salesmen in this world, and there are great exponents of low comedy. We believe that Gaspard is a sublime combination of both. Gaspard sold corsets and cheap lingerie in the tiny paved court next to the dry goods store. His voice was hoarse, his manner compelling. With vast earnestness and eloquent gestures he would entreat the housewives to inspect peach-colored slips and pale lavender rayon panties, bordered with shoddy écru lace. Finally he would assemble a capacity crowd, and then would come the exquisite event for which we had waited. With Chaplinesque subtlety, Gaspard's every gesture suddenly became feminine. He preened; he assumed a languid hauteur. Then, with magnificent mimicry, he snapped on a corset over his street clothes. With delicate poise he stepped into the panties and then slid the gaudy slip over his head. He turned around slowly, so that the farmers' wives could admire, and then, observing an elaborate decorum, he removed slip, panties, and corset, one by one. Then only did he resort to the telling gesture that broke the tension and sent the housewives into roars of hilarity. He scratched himself vigorously in the midriff. And the well-merited sales scramble was on. . . .

The Beck family loves to go marketing in America, too. We think it is a *lot* of fun to push a two-decker baby carriage through an old theatre revamped as a serve-yourself grocery store. But without Gaspard, market day is never going to be quite the same.

17

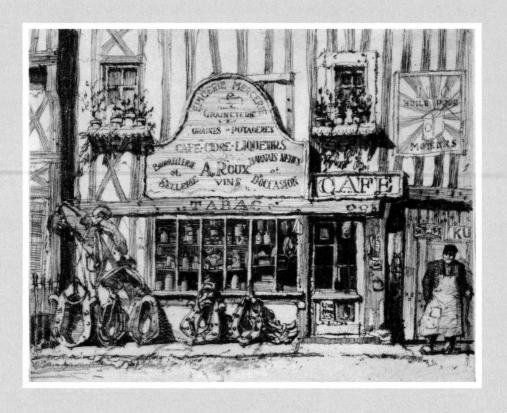

THE SHOP OF ARISTIDE ROUX

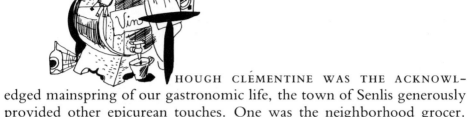

THOUGH CLÉMENTINE WAS THE ACKNOWL-
edged mainspring of our gastronomic life, the town of Senlis generously
provided other epicurean touches. One was the neighborhood grocer.
Another was the vegetable garden. And most memorable of all was our
ancient wine cellar.

Our grocer was a particular delight. Clémentine recognized that
perishables had to be bought in the marketplace, but she had her own
peasant ideas about staple groceries. She had a deep distrust of the gaudy
chain stores, which had sprung up in the twenties, and even the long-
established houses of Félix Potin and Julien Damoy could not dispel this
suspicion from her thrifty mind. When the Beck larder needed sugar or
salt, flour or rice, coffee or tea, Clémentine was convinced that there was
only one sensible way of obtaining them — by trotting around the corner
to the nearest independent *épicerie*. And thus the colorful Monsieur Aristide
Roux and his even more picturesque shop came into our lives. On a
timbered side street in our *quartier*, Aristide, a little gnome of a man with
a black skull cap, kept a shop whose varied stock satisfied the immediate
wants of a hundred or more neighboring families. Few Yankee general
stores can boast of greater variety than Aristide stored in his ancient house.
The faded sign over his shop window proclaimed that his was a grocery
store, a dry goods emporium, a tobaccc shop, and a café, all in one.

Finding farm life too strenuous, Aristide had come to town at the
turn of the century. His love of the farm had come with him, however,
and made itself felt in his merchandise. You could always find a good
choice of seed and grain in a far corner of Aristide's store. Dusty saddles
hung on the dark brown walls. In the back room was an aromatic assortment of used and new harnesses. Aristide had a particular specialty
— secondhand horse collars — which added immensely to the atmosphere
of his shop.

Of course, it's fun to buy dried peas and lentils and beans encased in cellophane, as we now do in our New England town. It's a great convenience to order by telephone — sometimes. It's nice to have a date on your coffee, a slogan stamped on your oranges, a chance to add twenty-five words or less to your soap wrapper and thus win a fortune. But we miss Aristide a lot, even though he growled a bit and wrapped everything in old newspapers.

Our vegetable garden was the particular domain of little Phinney, whose eagerness to exploit it for profit augurs well for his economic future. With a zeal patently lacking in his schoolwork, the youngster would begin to spade with the first early blush of spring. By May he was selling us the first fruits of his agricultural efforts, and by September his accrued profits amounted to almost enough to buy that coveted bicycle. Of course we all knew that the real mainstay of the vegetable garden was the genial and faintly simple old Monsieur Beaubernard, who spent three mornings a week there supplementing Phinney's efforts.

Our stone house was situated on the edge of the town, looking out upon open fields and a calm country road. Half a mile away, we could see a sprawling farmhouse framed in trees. Along the edge of this road was Phinney's plot of fertile loam, planted mostly in carrots, peas, string beans, and tomatoes. The outside of our high stone wall formed another boundary, and the two extremities of the plot were barricaded by a double row of assertive cabbages. Phinney's ambition led him to attempt eggplant, sweet peppers, and Brussels sprouts with fair success. He even started to grow corn, but being a sensitive child, gave it up when he overheard a very cruel remark which I quoted from *Le Rire*: "*Le maïs, c'est pour les cochons et les Américains.*" An ample space was given over to lettuce, chicory, and escarole, to the delight of the snails. Cucumber vines wove their way through the tomato plants. Against the inside of the garden wall, espaliered pear trees formed geometric patterns, troubled now and then by an enterprising pumpkin. Close to the wall, where they could get the maximum of reflected heat and sun, were the herbs — chervil, parsley, thyme, sweet marjoram, basil, and especially tarragon. Ah, those prodigal shoots of tarragon. How I wish we could make them grow that way in our new home! The soul of a *sauce béarnaise*, the aromatic secret of a fine vinegar, the fairest flower in many a *bouquet garni*, tarragon is a true aristocrat among herbs. We have never tasted anything better than the tender young chickens Clémentine used to prepare for us, stuffing them generously with branches of fresh tarragon and basting them incessantly until they were roasted a perfect crisp brown. The herbs were removed before serving, when their haunting fragrance had permeated the bird, with sublime results.

THE COUNTRY ROAD

Secure inside the garden wall were our chicken yard and rabbit hutch, both enclosed in a cage-like contraption resembling an aviary. Here some tender broilers passed their childhood, in company with a squad of ducks and a few seasoned veterans that had become permanent friends of the family. There was Alfred, the plump pet duck, who was skinny and forlorn when I first won him at the carnival, and Gringoire the goose, who resolutely refused to get fatty degeneration of the liver and thus always escaped the Christmas axe. Clémentine finished the careers of many of our ducks by the rather startling method of driving a pair of scissors through the tops of their heads, and then prying the scissors open. But Alfred and Gringoire always remained serene and unmolested. We also grew sentimental over Marius and Olive, the white rabbits, who finally became enormous, as did the cost of their upkeep. We found a home for all four of them when we left for America, but we worry about them now and then, the food situation being what it is just now in France.

Next to Clémentine, the most prized possession of the Beck family was our ancient wine cellar. In the Middle Ages our little town had been

22

an ecclesiastical stronghold behind whose battlemented walls thrived many a monastery, church, and convent. Thousands of people used to find shelter in the subterranean network of vaulted *caves* that spread under the town. Beneath our eighteenth-century house were the remains of the noble Romanesque crypt of a forgotten monastery. Five handsome Romanesque capitals were still visible, caked with dust and half imbedded in the walls. These cool, silent vaults had been transformed by a previous owner into a grandiose and richly atmospheric wine cellar, by far the most distinguished feature of our house. Whenever we wanted our visitors to be genuinely impressed, we gave them lighted candles and led them through these dim confines. A two-inch blanket of fine white sand covered the floor. The temperature varied but little from winter to summer, always remaining between fifty-five and sixty degrees Fahrenheit. There were no electric lights, nor any traces of a central heating plant. But the ventilation was good. It was a perfect place for a wine cellar.

Against the dim walls were tall wire racks, reserved for a variety of *ordinaires*, wines that I usually collected on pilgrimages to Bordeaux or Burgundy. There in the corner were some three hundred bottles of honest Beaujolais, husky and near-purple in color, equally good as a table and a cooking wine. I recall that I bought this *en fût* in a wine grower's booth at Dijon's *Foire Gastronomique*. A half cask would have done just as well, but my sales resistance had melted beneath the glistening smile of a Burgundian belle who, after offering many lovely samples of wine, proffered the order blank for an entire cask. Weeks later it appeared at the local freight office, and, after a little formality with the town tax collector, it was lowered by ropes into our vaulted cellar. There it lay on its side for six weeks or more, to permit it to recover from *les fatigues du voyage* and to regain its poise. Then on a clear day, when the moon was in the right quarter, Monsieur Archambault the *tonnelier* presented himself, accompanied by his droopy son and bottle washer. Their task of washing three hundred bottles and filling them from a spigot inserted at the bottom of the cask took scarcely more than two hours. The dexterous Monsieur Archambault never allowed the flow of wine to stop for an instant. The neck of one bottle was always waiting as its predecessor filled up. Before you knew it the three hundred bottles were filled, corked, and lying on the racks, ready for another period of rest, Monsieur Archambault had collected his modest fee, and the empty cask was taken back to the railway station, headed for Beaujolais. This procedure, which is followed by many French families, is certainly more complex than the simple business of going to the corner wine shop. But it is much cheaper, the wine is more reliable, and the thrill of the chase is there.

A fragrant autumnal Saint-Emilion and a vigorous Châteauneuf-du-Pape usually filled out our bins of ordinary reds. Annual pilgrimages to Chablis, for the dual purposes of tasting the *fondue de poulet à la crème* at the famous Hôtel de l'Etoile and of ordering wine, kept us bountifully supplied with a clean, crystal-clear little Chablis, a total delight with fish. From Vouvray we ordered half casks of a crisp, faintly *pétillant* wine that harmonized well with fruit and desserts and delighted our American friends.

Clémentine used the fragrant Beaujolais for a sublimated pot roast that I exhort you to try. Beaujolais is not essential to its success, however. A good California red will do handsomely. Here is the recipe, translated from Clémentine's old notebook. It begins magnificently:

L'Estouffat Lamandé

A morsel of beef, massive and tender (4 or 5 pounds, boneless, of rump or round)
A light *farce* of truffles, garlic, and bread crumbs, warmed in butter
A pound and a quarter of tender fresh carrots
One half pound of fresh mushrooms
One quarter pound of ripe green olives without pits
One fresh sweet red pepper, diced
Two fresh pig's feet, or a large veal knuckle, broken up
One bottle of Beaujolais
Salt, pepper, and a *bouquet garni*

Place the beef, after searing lightly in fat in an iron skillet, in a large earthen casserole whose cover can be hermetically sealed. Apply the stuffing of chopped truffles, garlic, and bread crumbs to the top of the meat. Surround the beef with the sliced carrots and mushrooms and the olives, pepper, and pig's feet. Pour in the wine. Salt and pepper your morsel and add the *bouquet garni*. With a long strip of flour-and-water dough, seal the cover of the earthen casserole and cook for six or seven hours in the slow oven heat customary for *daube*. Present in the casserole, which may be unsealed at the table, as is preferable.

This symphonic dish used to gurgle gently in our oven from noon until seven, making a soft sound like the bubbling of a spring. The fragrance of the truffle and the garlic seeped down through the meat as the wine reduced slowly. When the casserole came to the table and the crust was broken for the first time, the aroma that escaped perfumed the whole house for hours. And the morsel of beef, massive and tender, crowned by its light *farce*, could be eaten with a spoon.

Such a dish called for a noble Burgundy, and though the Beck family budget didn't permit many collector's items among wines, we had a few, locked in a corner of the *cave* behind a heavy wire screen. I had been lucky with 1929 Burgundies and treasured several cases of Corton,

Richebourg, Musigny, and Bonnes Mares of that extraordinary year. There were a few majestic bottles of Montrachet 1919 for particular friends, and a golden Château Chalon for sophisticates in search of something new. From Bordeaux, some Château Pape-Clément, Château Léoville-Las-Cases, and Château Haut-Brion had fallen into my hands. That was the beginning of a little library of vinous "first editions." Needless to say, it has not survived the events of 1940. Our hopeful cellar book, if it still hangs on the hook in the old crypt, contains mostly blank pages. But it was a humble start on a noble enterprise, and some day we'll start again.

Meanwhile, our *next* wine pilgrimage will be to California!

ITHIN A WEEK AFTER CLÉMENTINE CAME TO preside over our kitchen in Senlis, the Beck family realized what a treasure it had found. One cool evening, after her dishes were washed, we watched Clémentine take an exploratory stroll out to the garden gate, a rather picturesque bit of rural architecture with a steep tile roof. It had been a rainy day, and the ground was humid under her feet as she disappeared around the corner wall. Suddenly she came into view again, visibly excited. She rushed up to us wide-eyed, then gulped and regained her composure before breaking the news.

"Mais madame, vous avez des escargots dans votre jardin! Des centaines d'escargots!" This breathless bit of information came as a thunderbolt to the innocent Beck family, though we should have guessed what was destroying Phinney's young lettuce plants. We rushed down to the garden in the semi-obscurity. An incredible evening promenade of snails greeted us—dozens and hundreds of them. They had grown reckless, perhaps because of the long immunity our innocence had given them, and, deserting their daytime retreats in the deep recesses of the wall, they had come out in droves. The moist terrain doubtless made smooth and agreeable traction. They clung to the branches of our dwarf pear trees like baubles on a Christmas evergreen. They paraded over our newly spaded vegetable beds, carrying their ochre-colored shells lightly and leaving silvery trails behind them, intent upon devouring tender young green shoots. Some of them merely basked on the stone wall, apparently enjoying the moist evening air. With peasant enthusiasm at getting something for nothing, Clémentine plucked them up with joyful rapidity, and the whole family joined in the hunt. In no time at all we had a brimming pailful.

When, we asked, would we be able to feast upon our find? Clémentine looked surprised at our ignorance.

26

"Oh, not yet, Madame. First they must fast themselves. They should be kept captive for a week. *Then* we can prepare them."

To give the snails enough parading space to divest themselves of their impurities, Clémentine hit upon the idea of allotting a cardboard shoebox to each three or four dozen snails. For several days these boxes stayed unnoticed in a corner of the kitchen, securely tied with string. But Clémentine had not counted upon the disintegrating effect of snail moisture upon cardboard. And one memorable night the boxes softened up enough to permit a wholesale escape.

Our first intimation of it came at about midnight, when strange cracking noises arose intermittently from the kitchen. Philosophe, the family cat, usually a phlegmatic animal, seemed to be disturbed and made

restless sounds. When we finally padded downstairs in our slippers, a rare sight awaited us. Every one of the snails was on parade again, over the floor, the sink, the table, icebox, and gas stove. Many of them had loftier aspirations and were proceeding up the walls and across the ceiling. Here the traction was not so good, apparently. Snails had lost their grip and fallen to the floor, shell and all, making the peculiar cracking noise we had heard upstairs. It took an hour of ingenious acrobatics and cautious stepping about to contain this truant flight, but finally we had them all assembled, except for the cracked and fallen ones, in a well-sealed wooden crate. Clémentine was a trifle red-faced the next morning and hastily removed the traces of silvery scum from the kitchen. She had another bad moment when she began to wipe the breakfast dishes and found the dish towel alive with errant snails.

This variety of snail was the smaller *petit gris*, of course, and not the magnificent creature that deigns to live only in Burgundy. The *petit gris* is a forager, working hard for what he gets. The real Burgundian snail, however, leads a charmed existence until his hour of reckoning arrives. He is encouraged to gorge himself upon the lush, fat leaves of the Pinot and Gamay grape vines in the Burgundy valley, since he leaves the grapes strictly alone. The effect of such a mass attack on the leaves is very noticeable. Frequently only the dried veins of the leaf structure remain. Here the snail serves the wine grower well. By removing the body of the leaves he has opened up a path for the ardent rays of the September sun, so vital to the fruition of the grapes.

When it came time to prepare our *petit gris*, I was curious about the authoritative recipe and asked Clémentine if she knew of one. With a troubled look she brought out her green-baize-covered cookbook and gave it to me.

"It's in here, Monsieur, and it is very good. But I should warn you that the *monsieur* who wrote the recipe is long-winded and full of silly words. I think he's something of a *farceur*."

The recipe that greeted my astonished eyes is such a unique document that I can't resist sharing it with you. It is written by Georges Lecomte. With only a few deletions, here is a fairly accurate translation:

ESCARGOTS DE BOURGOGNE

"You ambush them in the morning, while they are parading nonchalantly on the humid leaf, when their slow, fleshy promenade makes one think of the throat of a voluptuous woman shuddering under a gross and clumsy caress. The snail, sticky and thick, carries its light shell with a facetious air and projects or contracts its horns, so lasciviously elastic, as the mood pleases him. He irritates you a little with his tactics of a gluttonous beast, rampant on his well-filled stomach and everlastingly on the same greedy quest.

"So, between two indignant fingers you imprison this shell, fallacious as a crinoline, and you pull, in order to disengage the adherent flesh from the leaf to which it is sticking. The beast beats the air in distress with its bewildered tentacles and then retreats glowering into its kiosk, like a much-teased maiden who rushes sobbing to her bedroom. But no pity! These melodramatic gestures no longer move the soul of a gourmet.

"You next cloister your snail in a cool cellar and, regardless of its own ideas on hygiene, you invariably nurse him for eight days on green and succulent lettuce, exactly as you stuff a nursing mother with lentils in order to have better milk, even though the good woman is refractory regarding such fattening fare. On such favorable tidbits our beasts are to enrich themselves. And what noble flesh it makes — rich, velvety, worthy of a princely banquet!

"From there on, cease to regard these slugs as living creatures. Like an ogre, with your cutlass in your teeth, you begin the bold hunt for these voluptuaries who lounge on their divans of lettuce. They would like to make you tenderhearted with their imploring horns. Ignore them. Place them at once in a *terrine* with salt and vinegar. *Ah, dame!* There will be convulsions, if not tears! With your hands you manfully move this seething mass to make it foam. Secretions that are too bitter or too listless

escape from tissues thus sharply attacked. Then you pour repeated torrents of water upon them to sweep away the scum. And when, upon the beasts thus purged, only a last crystal glaze remains, limpid as spring water, you collect your immobile mass of snails, cringing terrified in the corners of their shells, and you throw them to their final torture in an earthen crock bubbling with boiling water. You cook them for a half hour or so, until your instinct signals that you may exhume the rich meat from the shells.   29 Ah, since this last adventure, our beasts have ceased to be self-indulgent foragers, and their antennae, formerly so proudly retractable, are now very melancholy little things. But what of that? You have the ferocious heart of a fanatic now!

"Quickly drain these corpses, still in refuge at the far end of their dwellings. Then, without any pusillanimity, pull them from their retreat. If you are very refined, give them a supreme *toilette* in several baths of hot water. Having arrived at this paroxysm of murder, you have, of course, no further scruples. So, with the cold eye of a torturer, you contemplate these soft submissive snails and, as one possessed of a cruel frenzy, you strip off their green outer skins.

"All that remains for you is the delicate routine of an artist, a sumptuous chef. *C'est charmant.* In a radiant copper casserole you spread out this flesh that has ceased to suffer, accompanied by the traditional and poetic bouquet of bay leaf, parsley, and thyme. In order that the vegetable garden and the wine cellar may join in the festivities, you add a handsome golden brown onion, the sliver of a section of garlic, and the sunshine of a glass of cognac. Then you dilute this appetizing mixture with water and let it simmer over a calm, tranquil little fire for six or seven hours. And then, what aromas arise as you lift off the cover! Your snails are impregnated with all these fine substances. Let them cool peacefully, like a wise man not too impatient for his pleasure. Wash and wipe the shells as you would handle precious bits of porcelain. In each shell pour adroitly one unctuous spoonful of good *jus de viande*. As soon as you think the snails are cold, make a pious restitution to each one by putting it in a shell thus prepared. And when the animal, unaware of the fine nectar into which it is being plunged, reclines gracefully in the sauce, block up the opening of the shell with a thick layer of beaten butter, joyously sown with chives, shallots, salt, pepper, and chopped parsley. In a special circular plate place these little domes sheltering their savory preparations and heat them in a hot oven. May the butter melt and run, so that all these aromas will penetrate well into the meat.

"Then, your soul rejoiced, your eyes sparkling, you have only to regale yourself with this truly exquisite dish, despite the abominable animal that furnishes the pretext."

Clémentine, though very distrustful of Monsieur Lecomte's fine words, admitted that his recipe was worthy of the best Burgundian master cooks and followed it closely. She insists that six or seven hours is too long to cook them, but admits that the *ciboulette* and shallots in the butter are more subtle than garlic, which almost everyone uses. In any event, the result we tasted ten days after the discovery in the garden was utterly superb. My good spouse, who had shuddered on the brink of tasting a snail for almost five years, fell overboard with a vengeance after the first taste. We had to be stern to stop little Phinney at two dozen. I had known snails during the war—had gone to a snail party with a group of *poilus*, in fact, where twenty of us polished off some eight hundred snails they had prepared with loving care and magnificent dosages of garlic. Plenty of red *pinard*, bread, strong cheese, black coffee, and blacker cigarettes had gone with them. When I crept back into the barracks at midnight, my breath had been sufficient to awaken all of my slumbering fellow doughboys and to stir up a fine flurry of profanity. But I had never known snails like these!

Commercially speaking, the snail would seem to offer great possibilities for exploitation. I will never forget the lecture on the sex life of the snail that an English biologist delivered before a table full of rapt listeners at the Brasserie Lipp in Paris. Illustrating his points with sweeping pencil sketches on the marble-topped table, he divulged the startling fact that *all* snails have offspring, lots of them, and that in their hermaphroditic and individual way, each digs a little hole in the ground and lays about seventy eggs, which soon take their place in the snail world. You don't need a slide rule to calculate the phenomenal proliferation this represents, and something ought to be done to take advantage of it.

Clémentine is a little shamefaced about her snail recipe, I sense. She looked worried when she saw me making the translation, so, to atone for my indiscretion, here is a recipe of which she is visibly proud. It is her many-times-tested version of a formula devised by one Chef Pascal for *homard à l'armoricaine*, or *homard à l'américaine* as the scholars prefer it be called. Clémentine followed this faithfully, with absolutely sublime results. It is by far the best interpretation of this often-abused dish we have ever tasted. This time, you do not have to wade through word pictures:

Homard à l'Américaine

For six people: Cut the tails of four 1¼-pound live lobsters into sections and crack the claws. Melt 4 tablespoons of butter with 3 tablespoons of oil in a broad copper pan. Add the lobster pieces and stir and cook them gently just until the shells turn red. Remove the lobster and reserve it.

To the pan add 1 grated carrot, 1 chopped shallot, 1 chopped onion, and 1 mashed clove of garlic. Cook the vegetables until slightly softened and add salt, a good dash of pepper, a pinch each of saffron and curry powder, a *bouquet garni*, 3 tablespoons of tomato paste, and 1 teaspoon of meat extract. Blend all the ingredients well and add 2 cups of dry white wine.

Simmer this sauce, covered, for about half an hour. Return the pieces of lobster to the sauce and simmer all together, slowly, for 10 to 15 minutes. Warm 3 tablespoons of brandy, ignite it, and pour it over the surface. When the flame dies, stir in

3 tablespoons of fresh cream or *crème fraîche* and a few bits of fresh butter.

Serve the lobster with its sauce in a large, heated serving dish with a sprinkling of finely chopped parsley and other fresh herbs as a finishing touch.

Snails and lobsters! Unlovely creatures — or were they made to be sublimated by a good cook?

ALUES HAVE CHANGED SO RAPIDLY IN THIS headlong world that three years can be a long, long time. It seems almost incredible, as I write this, that only three years ago the Beck family was installed in comfort and comparative serenity in a little French town, secure behind high stone walls, well fed, thanks to the ministrations of their faithful Burgundian cook, and, save for a lingering foreboding following Munich, reasonably happy.

June 1939 — it seems distant indeed! Then we were free to fill our gasoline tank without complications or ration cards and to travel anywhere in France. Then an amateur photographer could set his camera on a tripod and take pictures without being questioned by *gendarmes* or sentinels. Then one could buy tweeds at Old England in Paris or crumpets and orange marmalade at Smith's Tea Lounge. June 1939 — when Chanel, Picasso, Molyneux, Maurois, and Lalique were significant names; when people thought about skiing and perfumes and Longchamps; when businessmen concerned themselves with foreign exchange, reservations on the Simplon-Orient Express, and *rognon flambé* Chez Lucas for lunch. They worried less then about the five-day week and (unhappily, as it turned out) about the lag in aircraft production.

June 1939 was beautiful, a perfect month of clear, crystal days, when Parisian families waited eagerly for the weekend and the early Sunday-morning sortie into the country. The roads from Paris were only moderately filled by such a peaceful exodus. Nobody thought of carrying a mattress on top of the car, but elaborate precautions were taken to fill the hamper with delicacies for the classic *déjeuner sur l'herbe*. And *madame* did not forget the Saint-Emilion to go with the cold bird or the chilled bottle of champagne to accompany the *fraises des bois*, which the children would collect in the forest before the *pique-nique* began.

Our little town presented a lively spectacle on a Sunday morning. Monsieur Rollet's *pâtisserie* was always thronged with shoppers at such a time, and his stock was often sold out before noon, leaving nothing but jars of Jordan almonds on the shelves. The *pique-niqueurs* were heavy buyers of his *brioches* and *croissants* and his magnificently sodden *babas au rhum*. The motorists liked his classic *éclairs*, *madeleines*, and *sablés*, but the townspeople, strolling back from services in the cathedral, went straight for the elaborate chocolate and mocha *gâteaux* and for his famous fruit tarts. The mystery of the crust of Monsieur Rollet's *tarte aux fruits* was unsolvable, even for our sharp-eyed and resourceful Clémentine. Crisp, tender, firm and flaky, all at once, his pastry shells were subtle and succulent containers for the glistening strawberries, cherries, apricots, or sliced apple that constituted the fillings. How he achieved them is indeed a professional secret.

Monsieur Rollet's *pâtisserie* was on the corner of the Rue St. Hilaire. It was a busy little street, dominated by the apse of an abandoned church. Next to the *pâtisserie* was the many-windowed shop of the shoemaker, and next came the spotless *charcuterie* of Madame Minard, the plump and immaculate little woman who made the best *pâté en croûte* in the region. Her rich ham and veal pies, flavored with herbs, truffles, pistachio nuts, and Madeira wine, were the ultimate luxury for the Sunday-morning sybarites. Eaten while still warm, with a good green salad, they could make any weekend a success. Madame Minard's game *pâtés* and *galantines* were nothing to be sniffed at either, but her most treasured articles of trade were a large *jambon d'York*, which she sold in very thin slices at a fantastic price, and a basket of truffles, which were given all the deference of a Cartier tiara. Her neighbor, the swarthy Monsieur Bouvier, merely sold butter, eggs, and cheese, and shared less in the general rush of trade, though I used to see passing motorists poking inquisitive fingers into his Camemberts. Next came the newspaper store, its doorway flanked by a dozen Parisian dailies, each neatly folded, and then the grocery store of Monsieur François, the butcher shop, the *confiserie* of the frilly Mademoiselle Durelle, and so on up the street. The Rue St. Hilaire was our rural Rialto, and it had thousands of counterparts throughout France. It isn't pleasant to picture the contents of the shop windows on the Rue St. Hilaire right now. First of all, a part of the street was destroyed by shellfire in the poignant days of May and June 1940. Secondly, the present food situation in France, where housewives line up at 5 A.M. before the *boucherie chevaline* to get their quota of *poulain*, hardly inspires agreeable thoughts.

But for those few radiant weeks in June 1939 life seemed full indeed. There was the fateful feeling of security behind the impregnable Maginot Line. Baron Edouard de Rothschild's stables were doing famously, and he seemed to have the best chance of winning the Grand Prix. The bicycle races had begun. Beautiful trout were appearing in the fish market. Straw-

35

RUE ST. HILAIRE, SENLIS

berries, those enormous, fragrant berries for which France is noted, were at their best. Tender young turkeys were ready to be turned on the spit. And Clémentine, inspired by this plenitude, was in the full flush of genius and good spirits. She sang from morning till night and became positively ostentatious in the dishes that she set before us and our visiting voluptuaries. Her contribution to our tranquillity was enormous. Brillat-Savarin contended that a balanced *gourmandise* is a vital factor in conjugal harmony. A celebrated Parisian lawyer has confided that he never had a divorce case where the wife was a perfect cook. Clémentine's culinary skill accounted for much of the fragile calm that reigned in our household during those last uncertain weeks. A tenuous Paradise it was — a moment when we could enjoy, with a perfectly clear conscience, such unpardonable luxuries as truffles cooked in champagne! *Truffes au Champagne* — how ridiculous, how indefensible it seems now, when the weekly bread ration is a matter of grave concern. The truffle has become a symbol with us — the symbol of an era that was too good to last.

It was Madame Minard who introduced fresh truffles to the Beck family, shortly after we came to live in our little town. In her window was a small basket of mysterious objects that looked like black walnuts powdered with cocoa. Each sat pompously on a pillow of cotton, like a very precious thing. My curiosity took me inside at once. After learning that they were *fresh* truffles, shipped directly to the enterprising Madame Minard from Périgord, I came out poorer by ten valuable francs, but richer by a magnificent black nugget. This was proudly displayed to the entire family and then, by inadvertence, allowed to rest on top of the piano all night. If you have ever entertained the idea that a truffle is just a lot of black texture added to *foie gras* and *galantine*, but pretty tasteless and odorless by itself, just leave it overnight on your piano. Our whole house smelled like a deliciously dank cellar for two days.

We raced through our cookbooks until we found an enticing recipe, *sauté de truffes noires*, and then raced back to Madame Minard's *charcuterie* for enough truffles to make half a pound! Clémentine washed, brushed, and dried the truffles, according to directions. Then, with a sharp knife, which had been rubbed with garlic, she cut them in slices about a quarter of an inch thick. On a brisk fire she put a casserole with a few tablespoons of olive oil, salt, pepper, a piece of garlic the size of an almond, a small glass of white wine, a spoonful of brandy, and the juice of half a lemon. The truffles were sautéed in this savory liquid, once it had reduced. Care was taken not to overcook them, and the result was pure ecstasy. The Becks became ardently truffiverous at once. Thereafter, whenever the budget permitted a little extravagance, it took the form of these "black diamonds of the cuisine," which Escoffier preferred to call "pearls of Périgord."

The origin of the truffle is obscure, though not so shrouded in mystery as Brillat-Savarin believed when he wrote, ". . . we find them, but we don't know how they are born, or how they vegetate." They grow, of course, on the roots of a certain type of oak tree and are detected by the keen snout of a certain type of pig, who appreciates them as much as does a certain type of gourmet. Everyone has his own mental picture of how a truffle-conscious pig is exploited. When he begins to dig at the base of the old oak tree, does his master yank him aside by the chain around his neck and stake the pig down while he digs for the "subterranean

Empress?" Does the pig get discouraged? Is he given one truffle for every five that he discovers? I really don't know. But I would rather have a grove of truffle oaks and a pack of keen-scented pigs than all the foxes and hounds in Warrenton, Virginia.

There are several varieties of truffle — black, grey, blond, violet, and the white Piedmont variety that grows in Italy. But the truffle universally claimed to be the best is the black one from Périgord and the Lot. The Romans loved the red and white truffles from Libya, which proves that they are not just a passing fancy. Medical authorities have pronounced them a rich but healthful food. Their firm texture, their color, and their magnificent earthy perfume, which is imparted to everything cooked with them, distinguish truffles from anything that grows. They have become an inseparable partner of all the preparations of *foie gras*.

Brillat-Savarin found a *dinde truffée* to be a marvelous thing, "*un objet de luxe qu'on voyait qu'à la table des plus grands seigneurs, ou chez les filles entretenues.*" This magisterial dish, a classic for the New Year's Eve

37

feast in France, is dominated by the haunting fragrance of truffle. Thin slices of the black nugget are placed everywhere under the skin of the bird, so that with some stretch of the imagination she resembles the ten of clubs. The stuffing is a rich and fragrant mélange of sausage meat, chicken livers, truffles, chestnuts, herbs, and a moistening of Madeira wine. Accompanied by a noble, full-chested Burgundy, such as a Corton or Richebourg, this turkey becomes a towering achievement. Clémentine had no difficulty climbing to the heights with such material, and she only regretted that her surgical skill was not sufficient to achieve an even rarer dish — the same truffled and stuffed turkey, but completely boned. It can be done, of course, and the host can enjoy the ultimate, the supremely proud moment when, before the eyes of his guests, he begins to carve the bird. After removing the legs in the conventional manner, and then making sure that all eyes are upon him, he takes a very sharp knife and cuts directly across the bird, slicing it like a loaf of bread. Then, to the general stupefaction of his guests, he presents each with a thick slice containing white and dark meat, and aromatic stuffing, all in one.

We boiled truffles in champagne, which would seem to be a Lucullan climax, and we steamed them in a potato steamer over a vapor of white wine and *eau-de-vie*, but neither of these approaches was as grandiose as the method prescribed in a recipe from Dijon:

Truffes et Marrons en Cocotte

Take equal quantities of well-formed truffles of Burgundy and massive, handsome chestnuts from Luc. Simmer the truffles for fifteen minutes in white Meursault, butter, salt, and spices. Grill the chestnuts lightly in the oven and peel them.

Have prepared a good concentrated juice made with lean beef, chicken wings, and a knuckle of veal. Chop up the truffle peelings and some *foie gras* and chicken livers into fine dice and add them to the juice when it has been reduced and strained.

Moisten the truffles and chestnuts with this juice and cook them gently in a *cocotte* for about 45 minutes, adding a Bordeaux glass of brandy, two tablespoons of thick cream, and six tablespoons of old Madeira wine. Serve in the *cocotte*.

Then there was the recipe I had obtained from Monsieur Rouzier, of the famed and fabulously successful Rôtisserie Périgourdine in Paris. Whole truffles, baked under live coals, were one of his regional specialties. It is the simplest way to cook them and brings out their incomparable savor more than any other method of cooking:

Truffes sous la Cendre

Clean and season the truffles and soak them in brandy for an hour. Enclose each in a strip of bacon fat and then in a triple covering of white parchment paper. Wrap these in green leaves, if possible, and then surround them with live coals. Cook for about 30 minutes, then remove the outer layers of paper and serve in the first paper envelope, accompanied by fresh butter.

Sometimes the recipe calls for a pastry crust under the paper, which hermetically seals in the flavor. In either case the truffle becomes an aromatic jewel that ranks with the great delicacies of the world.

But, you are protesting, why talk so much about something that is unobtainable — which a fresh truffle certainly is — unless our inquiring American pigs can nose out some black nuggets at the base of our own oak trees? And about such exotic recipes? Can't some epic be achieved with canned truffles?

An epic *can* be achieved, and here is the recipe, from the spirited pen of Edmond Haraucourt, who for years presided over the destinies of the Musée de Cluny.

Grillade aux Truffes

Choose a large, thick beef steak, lean and tender. Buy it preferably the night before; blanket it with quarters of truffles (fresh or canned), so that they may spend the night together. Then, the next day, spread a thin coating of butter on one side of the steak. Pepper it, but do not use salt. Put it on a grill and broil it over a vigorous fire made with twigs and clippings from grape vines, which, in this case, are far more satisfactory than charcoal.

As soon as a crust forms on the underside of the steak, place on the upper side (which has not been buttered) the quarters of truffles and liberal lumps of butter. Then slow down the fire. The butter melts, becomes charged with the essence of the heated truffles, and penetrates into the meat.

Your culinary tact will tell you at what point to remove the truffles and to turn your steak, taking care to stir up your fire of fagots and vines. Replace the truffles on the steak thus turned over and allow it to cook according to your tastes. Then salt it and serve.

39

And Edmond Haraucourt concludes: "You may decorate your plate with the quarters of truffles, but it won't do any good to eat them; their soul is in the steak, with that of the vine."

Somehow it is consoling to learn that a truffle has a soul. We made it our symbol of departed splendors, of a standard of civilized living that would never return. But if it has a soul, it should be imperishable. And, despite the turmoil in the world, the pigs are still sniffing at the roots of the oak trees in Périgord.

HE UNEASY CALM THAT REIGNED IN THE BECKS' French household in the month of June 1939 was shattered abruptly one fine Monday morning early in that month when this portly *père de famille* went to his desk at the Paris office. There was a letter from the New York headquarters — two precise and matter-of-fact paragraphs dictated by the general manager — which blew our domestic picture to fragments. With the perspective a distant observer often enjoys, my firm had seen the writing on the wall, while its European agents were so close to the impending danger that they were merely troubled and befogged. The firm had decided to pull out of Europe, wherever possible, without delay. My orders were clear: to close the Paris office within a month and to make steamship reservations immediately. And then the sentence: "Your new post, Mr. Beck, will be with the Boston office."

A shocked, hollow pall settled upon our little family of expatriates when I brought the news home that evening. In a few hours our pattern of living had undergone a violent change. Gone was the too-good-to-last picture of a reposeful, civilized, well-nourished existence in a sleepy French town. Since my orders virtually meant rushing back with a wife, two children, and four toothbrushes, it was clear that our old stone house at the edge of town would have to be abandoned to an uncertain fate, together with all its furnishings, its two inexcusably luxurious American bathrooms, its books and prints and pictures. The prospect grew darker by the minute as we discussed it. What would happen to little Phinney's triumphant vegetable garden? And Alfred, the pet duck; would he end up again a prize in a shooting gallery? And would somebody eat Marius and Olive, our rotund pet rabbits? What fate awaited our venerable Hotchkiss car?

But blackest of all was the thought of parting with Clémentine, our pink-cheeked treasure in the kitchen. Clémentine, who had initiated

41

us into the higher art of French cooking, who had been nursemaid, wine-counselor, and *Cordon Bleu* all in one—Clémentine, who could make the best *sauce béarnaise* and the most delectable *gratin d'écrevisses* in all the Oise, was utterly irreplaceable. As the Beck family sat pensively at the garden table, absentmindedly munching fat strawberries, her loss loomed larger and larger. After all, we might rent the house to a responsible tenant. We might sell the car, with all its wheezes, and arrange with the neighbors for a fine home for Alfred and Marius and Olive. But it was heartbreaking to give up Clémentine. Never again would we find anyone with her innate courtesy, her good cheer, and her willingness to work like a trooper. It was with a heavy heart that *madame* went to the kitchen and told Clémentine the news. The Beck family was going back to *l'Amérique*. Strangely enough, Clémentine did not seem perturbed. Instead a strange light came into her eyes, which *madame* did not quite understand.

The next day brought a brighter mood to the Beck family, stimulated no doubt by the sight of large colored deck plans of the S. S. *Champlain*. As we got down on our hands and knees on the floor and began to study the cabin space, the lounges and dining salons and bars of the handsome French liner, the old anticipatory thrill began to seize us once again. The wanderlust in our bones began to stir. Our long-dormant yearning for things American—football games, fat newspapers, silk stockings, good cigarettes, toothpaste, dill pickles, oil heaters, and other creature comforts, the scamper of a squirrel on autumn leaves, gasoline at seventeen cents a gallon instead of three francs a quart—all these quiescent longings flared up into pleasant anticipation. After all, it was about time for us to go back to the United States. Daughter Diane was thirteen and impatient to return to the liberties she had briefly known in the land of open backyards, movie matinées, and saddle shoes. Little Phinney, born in Paris, did not yet know this freedom. Like the goose who knows no other way of eating except having corn rammed down its throat, the youngster was quite reconciled to living behind high stone walls and wearing a girlish *tablier* to school daily. A little American public schooling ought to be good for him about this time of his life, we thought. All in all, the prospect was rather exciting—until we thought again of Clémentine, and of a future without her.

It was at this point that little Phinney, having more imagination than the rest of us, went into the kitchen where Clémentine was pounding out some *quenelles de brochet* in the stone mortar.

"*Dites, Clémentine,*" began the little fellow, "why don't you come to America with us?" It was a spontaneous question, quite as forthright and unexpected as Clémentine's reply, which was, in substance, "I'd like nothing better."

When Phinney dashed in with news of this brief but vital conversation, a whole new world loomed up before our giddy eyes. America with Clémentine! Ah, that would be something else again! We had assumed that Clémentine, like most French people with an immovable love of their own *patrie*, would be unwilling to travel to foreign lands. Come to think of it, she was un–French in several little ways. She was something of a spendthrift and refused to count her *sous*. She apparently needed few friends, refused to gossip, and had only scorn for bicycle races.

Madame Beck made a great effort to walk, not run, to the kitchen, where the startling news was confirmed. Clémentine admitted that she had always been eager to see *l'Amérique*, the land of the *gratte-ciels*, of *Hollyvood* and the *coo-boys*. Her one ardent passion had been the movies. (We had never thought of that.) Garee Coopaire and Robaire Taylorre were her male gods, although she had to admit that Eddie Nellsonne (we never *could* get her to say Nelson Eddy) sang much better and was almost as *beau*.

Furthermore Clémentine, for all her comeliness and cheerful spirits, was entirely resigned to the spinsterhood that seemed to be imposed upon her by the lack of a dowry. She had no family entanglements and no terror (indeed, no concept) of a foreign language. When our beaming emissary returned from the kitchen, it became clear that the Beck family had been offered an incredible stroke of good fortune. We had an accomplished French cook who was eager to sample life in a little New England town. The perfection of the picture was not marred by a visit to the American consulate in Paris, where it was learned that Clémentine might enter the United States under the French quota, provided that she could furnish the necessary *dossier* of documents, and that I, as her prospective employer, could guarantee she would not become a public charge. Clémentine, accustomed to red tape as an integral part of French life, found the list of required documents, certificates, and official stamps to be child's play. And as I produced evidence to convince the vice-consul that Clémentine would find good employment in America and would never have to go to the poorhouse, I couldn't help but think of the number of covetous friends back in Boston who would love to relieve me of the pleasant responsibility of a French *Cordon Bleu!*

A busy interlude of three weeks lay ahead of us before the *Champlain* was due to sail — three weeks to pack, to pay the bills, and to say *au revoir* to many French friends. Early in this period we transferred the duck and the two rabbits to the hospitable hutch of our neighbor, Monsieur Dupont. Then we rented our house to a dashing, red-coated colonel attached to the local garrison of Sudanese soldiers. (Subsequent events in September made his tenure a brief one, but his languorous *maîtresse* lingered on after the beginning of the so-called phony war and finally departed after the Christmas holidays. Unhappily, she neglected to turn off the water when she left, and during the coldest January in years, the pipes froze all over the house. With the February thaw came the deluge. When our vigilant Monsieur Dupont perceived a sizable rivulet of water flowing out from under our front door, he dashed to the water department and had the meter shut off. But not before the entire house was flooded and the wine cellar transformed into a chilly swimming pool.)

Packing was a problem. We made a "must" list first of all. One of the first items was the library of French cookbooks that we had collected with zeal over a period of years. It contained everything from a rare edition of Brillat-Savarin and a gargantuan *Ali-Bab* to mere pamphlets from remote Burgundian print shops. *Tante Marie* and other old stand-bys were there, of course, together with more flighty essays by Paul Reboux, Paul Poiret, Prosper Montagné, Edouard de Pomiane, and a dozen other gifted voluptuaries. The books might consume a whole valuable wooden case, but all the Beck family agreed that they were vital to Clémentine's happiness in America.

The question of kitchen utensils was no less vital. Clémentine's gleaming copper *batterie de cuisine* could never be left behind, nor could the squad of earthen casseroles that had given us so many beautiful *ragoûts*

and *daubes*. Nor her quintet of sauce whisks, nor the ten gleaming tempered steel kitchen knives of all sizes, nor the pepper mills, the pastry molds, the skewers, pastry brushes, mortar and pestle, wine baskets. And the scales! Ah yes, the scales with the metric weight. They were important, for most French recipes begin by specifying 250 grams of something or other. Above all there were the salad baskets, those simple and invaluable institutions that just don't exist in otherwise enlightened America. And so another wooden crate was filled and well padded with excelsior.

What else would we be unable to find in a little town outside of

Boston? (It is apparent, I trust, that the Beck family resolutely refuses to live in a big city.) Daughter Diane was the first to think of it—*foie gras* and truffles. Unforgivable luxuries they are, but so very reasonable when ordered by mail in France from the estimable Monsieur Delsaut, *restaurateur et marchand de comestibles* in a small town in Périgord. So we dispatched a fat order without a moment's delay. One-pound and two-pound cans of whole *foies gras truffés*, whole boned chicken stuffed with *foie gras*, galantine of turkey with the same rich accompaniment, and then a large flutter of smaller cans of whole truffles in Madeira. There might be a little tussle with the Customs officers when we arrived in New York, but such precious cargo was worth it. And every one of our old friends would prefer a pound of *foie gras* as a coming-home present to a bottle of Chanel No. 5 or a Charvet cravat.

The gastronomic instinct asserted itself, even in the chaos of packing. Incredulous friends dropped in to say goodbye to the precipitant Becks and usually stayed for dinner. This gave us a chance to give a farewell salute to some of the French dishes we feared we would never, never find in America. First of all, the market was filled with big, beautiful English sole, the most adaptable of fish. Clémentine gave us *filets de sole Dieppoise, Bercy, Mornay, Orly, Marguery,* and *Régence,* until we drank up all our Chablis and began to yearn for red meat. *Morilles à la crème* was another specialty that we couldn't hope to shop for in Faneuil Hall Market. These exquisite aristocrats of the mushroom family (despite their plebeian warts) seem to belong to France alone. Their peculiar flavor is utterly unlike anything we have ever tasted.

Wild strawberries were at their peak in the adjacent forests at this particular moment, and we bought baskets of them promiscuously from the picturesque old denizens of the woods who picked them in the early dawn and hawked them from door to door. Clémentine's *tarte aux fraises des bois* was one of the classics of her repertoire, and we enjoyed them almost daily during those last two weeks. Her trick, first of all, was to make beautiful, rich, tender (but not too short) pastry shells. I've watched her do it often, but my attempts to imitate her have been woeful, and I just don't feel qualified to pass on the secret. Five minutes before we were ready for dessert, Clémentine would fill the cooled pastry shells with the uncooked wild strawberries. Over them she poured a moderately thick raspberry syrup. Into a hot oven she popped them, and when they came out two or three minutes later they defied description. The strawberries had become partially cooked. The pastry was hot and crisp and the whole thing was permeated with a mysterious perfume, which could be traced to the raspberry syrup. Accompanied by a cool Vouvray, usually a Château Moncontour, these wild strawberry tarts brought an indescribable sense of well-being to our little family and to its guests sitting outdoors

45

46

LA MAISON BECK

in the long June twilight. In fact, they usually called for another bottle of Château Moncontour from the *cave*.

The days raced on, and the final preparations grew so intense that we forgot all about food. Our crates and trunks were shipped by train, but we decided to take the aging Hotchkiss to Le Havre with as many suitcases as it would hold. (The Hotchkiss is a French automobile, and its name is pronounced Utch-keess.) Two days before sailing time, we were ready to go. The Utch-keess rumbled out through the old gateway of our house for the last time, loaded to the fenders with its baggage and five passengers. We closed the gate, shook hands with Madame Barbique, the husky *femme de ménage* who was to clean up after our departure, and took one last, lingering look at the old L-shaped house on the edge of town, the place we had fondly considered our permanent home. The *maison* Beck, lying low at the turn of the road, wasn't impressive. Its severe stone wall and the tiny windows facing the street gave scant suspicion of the warm and hospitable sunken courtyard that lay inside. We gazed longingly at those steep tile roofs pierced by ample dormers, at the old stone-and-brick barn that served as garage and guest house, at the row of slender, French-poodle poplars aligned along the stone wall, and we all gulped. The last look at the *maison* Beck made the whole family misty-eyed. The car jolted down the esplanade and over cobbled streets that in a year would be filled with German soldiers. We drove slowly past the post office and the Hôtel du Nord, which next year would be mere rubble, and finally out onto the country road leading toward the west. There we stopped for one more sentimental instant and looked back at the spires of our little town, a midsummer silhouette framed in a clump of roadside trees — one last affectionate look at the place that had furnished the Beck family with its first taste of civilized living. There were lumps in four throats, I think, but Clémentine, squeezed in the back seat, was anything but tearful. Her black eyes sparkled with anticipation and adventure. Le Havre, a transatlantic crossing, New York, *les gratte-ciels et les palais du cinéma* lay ahead.

And so the Utch-keess rattled on, toward Normandy and the good S. S. *Champlain*, which, in a few months, would lie at the bottom of the ocean.

47

48

MIDSUMMER SILHOUETTE, SENLIS

A WEEK AT THE END OF JUNE CAN BE SPENT IN many idyllic ways. One of them is to cross the Atlantic on a nice, comfortable French boat, one whose deck steward is attentive, whose chef is a supreme artist, and whose captain gives regal cocktail parties. The S. S. *Champlain* provided the Beck family with just such an interlude in that early summer of 1939 — a week when we could relax and forget the hurried departure from our French home, a week during which we could catch our breath before the excitement of settling down again in some undetermined town near Boston. The Becks relaxed mightily, slept late, reveled in an abundant cuisine, and tried to ease their collective conscience for such *gourmandise* by playing half-heartedly at shuffleboard and deck tennis. Little Phinney had enough energy to ride the electric horse, but the rest of us just dawdled. But, if four members of our party were frankly droopy, the fifth was the exact opposite. For this was the first crossing for Clémentine. Her eyes shone with excitement from the moment we arrived in Le Havre. She was pacing the decks, taking everything in, long before the boat left its pier. Within a few hours she was on excellent terms with several comfortable and dowdy French families. We didn't have to worry about Clémentine. She was a *débrouillarde*, and completely at home. For the *Champlain* was still France.

The voyage was calm and uneventful, and apparently on schedule. But for some reason best known to the captain, the ship arrived in New York harbor just as dusk was falling. This was inconvenient, but it gave us a breathless glimpse of the Manhattan skyscrapers at twilight, a thousand lights twinkling from their dim, spiny silhouettes. The sight brought forth Clémentine's most eloquent adjectives. *"Ah! Ça, alors! C'est formidable!"* She repeated this phrase a dozen times. *Incroyable, fantastique, immense, bizarre*—Clémentine trotted them all out in her awe and excitement.

49

MANHATTAN TWILIGHT

She was less impressed with the weary formalities with the Customs officials, but as we stood on the solid concrete of the pier I noticed that she didn't miss a thing. The *Champlain* was France afloat, but *this* was *l'Amérique*. She took a startled look at the scurrying Western Union boys and at the policemen in shirt sleeves, a sartorial liberty that no French *gendarme* is ever permitted save in the privacy of his own bedroom. She observed that many of the men in the waiting crowd wore strange seersucker suits and that the women's hats were even more comical than those she had seen in Paris. And everybody, it seemed, chewed gum. She blinked a bit, too, at the sudden appearance of small, tough green paper money instead of the iridescent pictorial tableaux on the French bank notes she had known all her life.

It is my good fortune to have a warm-hearted boss, one who looks after his European agents and incidentally owns a station wagon. The problem of landing five people in New York on a summer evening was simplified enormously by this ample and providential conveyance, which was waiting at the pier in the charge of a smiling black chauffeur. Little Phinney and Clémentine were enraptured by his enormous pink-and-white smile as he loaded the eighteen bags in the back of the station wagon. They giggled together and Clémentine whispered that he reminded her of that "*drôle de nègre dans le cinéma.*" Perhaps she meant Stepin Fetchit. We packed ourselves cozily into the "*drôle de camion,*" as she called the station wagon, and began the trip to the country home of my company president, just over the Connecticut line. In a few minutes we were lost in the roar of a hundred cars in one cluster on the elevated highway — all going at the same speed, the same intensity, in the same direction, with the same colorless expression on each driver's face. Clémentine seemed a little appalled. "*Il y en a, des voitures,*" she murmured weakly, and joined Phinney in gazing at the lofty lights and silhouettes of Riverside Drive. She was duly impressed by the George Washington Bridge, but seemed more intrigued by the toll gates, where we left a dime every so often. "*Ça n'existe pas en France,*" she remarked. It was the first hint that possibly *l'Amérique* might have some drawbacks after all. We rolled swiftly over the cement parkway. Little Phinney slept heavily. Clémentine observed sleepily that such *autostrades* would be wonderful in Burgundy, and then dozed herself, thoroughly and happily exhausted by her first few hours on American soil.

The next morning Clémentine awoke to greet a new world — and really new. She had slept in a room with a bath, in the servant's wing of a fairly imposing Connecticut country house. Sunlight filtered in the window through neatly starched curtains. Oval rag rugs were on the polished pine floor. A Maxfield Parrish fantasy with shadow-splashed jugs

and reclining maidens hung on the wall. There was a small radio on a table beside her chintz-covered boudoir chair. She found pale green pine-scented soap in the bathroom. The towels, the plastic goblet, and, most miraculous of all, the *papier hygiénique* all were tinted the same green color. Perhaps Clémentine thought of some of the gloomy top-floor cubicles, lighted by a small pane of glass in the ceiling, that she had occupied when she had served as cook in Paris apartments. Perhaps she had forgotten Paris completely. I can't say, but I can report her reactions upon being confronted with the mystery of the modern American kitchen.

My host had installed a dream kitchen in his house — four walls of sleek efficiency, which are the delight of the industrial designer, but which proved to be perplexing to the good Clémentine, whose first sight of a kitchen had been in her grandmother's ancient stone house in Beaune.

The first glimpse of this kitchen left her wide-eyed and bewildered, but thoroughly enchanted. Here was an immaculate worktable that seemed to run all around the edge of the room, dipping now and then to become a sink or a corrugated drain for dishes, then suddenly changing into a stove with strange red-hot spirals, then pausing to allow space for a gigantic, streamlined, wind-resisting refrigerator, then continuing as a worktable. It seemed to be covered with a rough, pinkish Irish linen, until Clémentine touched it and found that it wasn't what it looked like at all, but some smooth, spotless, inexplicable plastic. Underneath were strange doors with modernistic chromium handles, under which was an indented space to allow for the cook's toes. Overhead were more doors, just far enough back so that the cook couldn't bump her head on them. There was a wide, cheerful window over the sink, framed by dainty pink curtains and by six pots of pink geraniums on six little projecting shelves. But what impressed Clémentine most of all was the tiny desk in one corner, complete with desk lamp, pad, pencil, and a library of cookbooks. She was radiant with admiration. After this, the laundry chute and the garbage disposal trap door were anticlimactic. Yet she seemed perplexed. Except for a whistling tea kettle, which she loved, there wasn't a pot, a pan, a knife in sight. I explained this to Araminta, the duchess of this cuisine and a personage of notable poise. She obliged by opening all the mysterious doors and revealing a battery of dishes and kitchen paraphernalia that reassured us at once. But we missed our copper kettles and earthen casseroles, without which we feel no kitchen can be complete.

This one day in Connecticut, a stopover before the repatriated Beck family pushed on to Boston, was of course a memorable adventure. Everything seemed strange and new to us — the size of the Sunday-morning paper, the abundance of automobiles, the existence of popcorn, squirrels, mosquitoes, gin, and chocolate fudge cake wrapped in cellophane. Yet with all these new and fascinating distractions, we were conscious of a fact of far greater significance — *this* was Clémentine's first day in contact with *la cuisine américaine!* This day in gastronomic history is worth recording.

During her entire lifetime Clémentine's breakfast had consisted of a bowl of *café au lait*, made with hot milk and very strong black coffee, and perhaps a *croissant* or *brioche* from the neighborhood *boulangerie*. (Or just a crust of toasted French bread.) She knew that some Americans, the Becks for example, added fruit to this fundamental fare, but she was totally unprepared for the surprise of a Yankee breakfast. The whole Beck family longed to peek into the kitchen that morning and to watch Clémentine's expression as the panorama of that American Sunday breakfast unfolded before her. It began with a large glass of orange juice that had been squeezed by a versatile mechanical mixer. Then came a bowl of those crispy, crackly, crunchy, de-e-e-e-licious flakes to which certain baseball players attribute most of their prowess. (And owe much of their income.) Then the great American classic, ham and eggs, accompanied by blueberry muffins and cinnamon rolls. And with this — coffee. But not the coffee that Clémentine had known all her life, made from the nice black bean roasted until it resembled a succulent shoe button. This was American coffee — delicate of aroma, yes, but tasting to the European palate like a pale and watery thing. Unadaptable Americans who visit Europe howl first of all about the bad coffee. Clémentine, bless her heart, had a look of infinite *tristesse* in her eyes when we mentioned the subject, but she uttered not a word of disapproval.

The soul of democracy, Clémentine was quick to make friends with Araminta. Young Phinney reported with wonder that they were conversing fluently, one in Burgundian French, the other in Alabama English, and getting along famously, with the supplementary use of sign language. Clémentine watched the Sunday dinner being prepared, and the succession of strange dishes that passed before her eyes must have seemed quite as exotic as Araminta's luxuriant Southern drawl. First we were served honeydew melon with a slice of lime. Then Araminta's admitted masterpiece, Southern fried chicken, with peas and carrots. Clémentine was impressed with the succulence of the chicken, but asked us afterward with a worried look if all Americans boiled their vegetables in water and then threw the water away (together with most of the taste). We looked worried too, and admitted that most of them did, along with their English cousins. Alligator pear salad was next on the menu, followed by peach cobbler, two dishes as completely foreign to the little Burgundian as couscous and chow mein. Another startling fact may have dawned upon her — that the customary glass of wine, which she had always enjoyed with her meals in France, was replaced by a glass of ice water in America.

Breakfast and dinner held their surprises, but Clémentine did not become genuinely goggle-eyed until suppertime, when our host invited her to join in that noted American institution, the Sunday evening barbecue. With something approaching stupefaction she watched him wheel out a portable grill, complete with a glittering array of accessories, and then start a charcoal fire. The whole picture may have become slightly blurred after that. There were cocktails, which Clémentine refused with a frightened smile. Then a platter of steaks and double-thick lamb chops appeared, bordered with bacon and ready to be grilled. A triumphant shout from both Diane and Phinney announced the one gastronomic treat they had been yearning for — hot dogs! A tray of cold cans appeared, and Diane took delight in informing the bewildered Clémentine that they contained beer. And finally, great ears of yellow corn were bared (the kind that never grows in France), and were prepared for the grill. It was too much to expect any newly arrived Burgundian to take in her stride. Clémentine blushed and retired into a confused silence. But a moment later little Phinney was tugging at her elbow. "*Venez*, Clémentine! *Vous allez voir! Les chiens chauds!*" He tugged more, until she came close to the grill, where a fine specimen of the great American hot dog awaited each of them, "with both," as they say in the trade. Then the two retired to a little table and began their feast. Phinney's eyes shone with delight as he clutched his roll in one hand and his soft drink in the other. Clémentine's reserve suddenly melted. She poured her beer out of the can into a paper cup and began to consume her *"chien chaud avec moutarde et peekaleelee."* A broad smile crossed her face. The Americanization of Clémentine had begun.

THE BECK FAMILY'S FIRST AND ONLY WEEK ON Beacon Hill was a confusing interlude, given over to group acclimatization to the American scene and, more important, house hunting. But the heart of Boston furnishes an easy transition for the bewildered European, and the Becks, fresh from France, felt very much at home there. Not that Louisburg Square resembled the Place Jeanne d'Arc in our little French town, but somehow the atmosphere seemed the same, calm and unharried. And Charles Street, filled with antique shops, book stores, little hole-in-the-wall restaurants, and soul-satisfying fruit stores, might almost have been the Rue St. Hilaire in Senlis, except that it was incessantly choked with automobiles. Young Phinney Beck, aged ten, and Clémentine, aged forty, became immediately attached to the swan boats in the Public Gar-

56

den. They graduated rapidly to a rowboat and spent most of those early July days paddling idly about the pond, chattering in French, and counting the number of stories on the Ritz and other *gratte-ciels* of the neighborhood. That left the rest of us free to look for a place to live.

Our first adventurous move was to acquire a secondhand car of undreamed-of splendor, at a price we considered a fantastic bargain. It was heavy, luxurious, powerful, and to our inexperienced eyes, a thing of aristocratic beauty. It took us weeks to realize that it was a dead ringer for those ominous, slinking cars that belong to ex-bootleggers and cut-rate funeral directors. It was shiny black, with plenty of gleaming chrome, and it had immense cylinders instead of those little pistons the diameter of a demi-tasse we had known in France. True, it burned twice as much fuel as our chuffing little Hotchkiss, but then gas was less than half as expensive in America, which evened things up. Clémentine was immensely impressed, and so were we all, as the three elder Becks glided heavily out of Boston on the first sortie in search of a house.

There are many unspoiled towns within a commuting radius of Boston, towns free from any taint of suburbanism and as Yankee in flavor as Wiscasset or Peterborough or St. Johnsbury. The Beck family explored many of them in this week of scouting. We listened to the hymns of praise chanted by their real estate men. We walked enraptured down their elm-arched streets, admiring the spatter of sunlight and shadow on their white clapboard houses, the serenity of their shaded town squares, the shimmering whiteness of their Colonial church spires. Many things seemed strange. Ladies shopping in shorts and high school boys with their shirt-tails hanging out made us blink a little. Peasant handerchiefs on the heads of gay young ladies in sports roadsters seemed peculiar, too. Three out of four children seemed to be licking an ice cream cone or a lollipop. We noticed a good many studious newspaper readers on the street corners, intently scanning reports on world affairs in a newspaper called the *Racing Form*. Most of the conversations we overheard had something to do with My Laddie paying thirteen dollars in the fourth race. The effrontery of the American telephone pole, offering a gratuitous disfigurement to almost every street, came as a distinct aesthetic shock to us.

But these jarring notes were soon forgotten in the excitement of looking at old New England houses. We saw all types, from pitch-roofed cottages to three-story mansions in the best whaling-captain tradition. Finally, on a rocky hillside overlooking the harbor of Marblehead, the old seaport north of Boston, we found the Almost Perfect Solution. It was a gambrel-roofed house with two stories, built in the early years of the eighteenth century. Its clapboards were weathered a silvery, salt-spray grey. Its shutters were a faded green. But its window boxes rejoiced in a fresh riot of contrasting color, and several squads of seven-foot holly-hocks stood sentinel around the gate. Pictorially it was irresistible. Functionally it was almost as good. Most of the rooms clustered about one huge central chimney, which contained no fewer than five fireplaces on the two combined floors. The rooms retained their old paneling, wide floorboards, and corner cupboards, and their ceilings were low enough to cause apprehension to any six-footer. Most of the fireplaces had kept their

58

SUMMER STREET, MARBLEHEAD

Dutch tiles, and the original stair rail with its turned balusters was still in place. Yet by some subtle means central heat had been introduced, and radiators lurked behind half-visible grills. Two bathrooms had been squeezed in upstairs.

To the gastronomically minded Becks, however, a house stands or falls on its kitchen. And this kitchen was a poetic combination of the practical and the picturesque. Its ancient brick fireplace was ostensibly the same as in 1715, although the flue had been blocked up against winter weather. But it had early andirons and was surrounded by an exhibit of kitchen ironware that would do credit to a museum. There were skillets, ladles, trammels, tongs, griddles, skewers, pots, and toasters and a dozen other utensils once indispensable to the pioneer housewife. This feature of the old kitchen had been preserved for sentimental reasons. The corner cupboards were as useful as ever. Otherwise the room had been drastically modernized. Its sleek white stove, refrigerator, sink, worktable, and cup-boards were as spotless and efficient as anything you would find in a Park Avenue penthouse. Here indeed was a shrine for a *Cordon Bleu* like our Clémentine. Like her, it was modern, yet steeped in tradition. We didn't look any farther. Within a week we had moved into the old gambrel-roofed house on the hill, and Clémentine found herself installed in the setting where she would produce her greatest culinary triumphs. Sur-rounded by her own copper kettles and earthen casseroles, with a five-foot shelf of French cookbooks against the wall, she was smiling and eager, ready to attempt the Great Experiment and to prove that *la cuisine française* can thrive in a New England village.

Clémentine's first test, however, came not in her proven field of cooking but in her initial collision with the English language, of which she knew not a word except "okay." She came to grips with this vexing matter by assuming that if she spoke French very slowly and smiled, somehow the other person would understand. The blank look on the bewildered faces of visitors who pushed our doorbell proved that this assumption was very faulty. As a baffling barrier to the door-to-door sales-men she was priceless, but as a transmitter of messages she was cryptic and indecipherable. *"Monsieur Flouenne a téléphoné," "Madame Joesnoé est venue dire bonjour"* they would read, but to this day we don't know who Mr. "Flouenne" or Mrs. "Joesnoé" was. Clémentine distinctly was not the bilingual type. Yet when the telephone rang insistently in our absence, she was confronted with a problem that *had* to be solved. She was thus forced into learning a sentence in English, and she did it her own individual French way. On a piece of cardboard by the telephone she inscribed one phonetic message for use in all emergencies: "Madame Beck is aôutt. Shi weill retournne att sevenne au'cloque." And it worked beautifully.

Clémentine feared at first that the telephone was going to supplant the market basket in our household. This seemed to be a strange land, where *madame* went to the telephone and recited a monologue of her wants, whereupon a jaunty young man with a pencil over his ear would appear about an hour later, loaded with endless paper bags, and the morning shopping was done. She learned a lot from the delivery boys. One of them, maliciously and with a straight face, taught her to say "okydoke" instead of "okay." He made her understand that it was more dignified and suited to her. Their treachery was somehow subverted, for we noted with satisfaction that quite soon the delivery boys were saying "*bonjour*" as they left their packages.

To make Clémentine feel a little more at home, we subscribed to a small French-Canadian newspaper published in a neighboring city. But this paper perplexed her almost as much as the Boston *Globe*. When we read some of the headlines we understood why. One of them ran:

BEAU SUCCÈS DU WEENIE
ROAST DES DAMES MOOSE

What were Weenie Roasts and Dames Moose, she wanted to know, and rightly. Another was:

STEVE (CRUSHER) CASEY
A ÉCRASÉ BIBBER MCCOY
AVEC CARESSE DE L'OURS
À L'ARÈNE DE RUE HANCOCK

This one on the noble art of free-for-all wrestling stopped us completely. We advised Clémentine to skip the sporting page.

At the end of a month Clémentine had proven quite conclusively that languages would never be her forte. She confided triumphantly to Madame Beck that she now understood the phrase that all these Americans use when they leave the front door — "That phrase 'sank you,' that means *'au revoir'* — I've learned *that* much!"

In one way, this small American town was all that Clémentine expected. The faintly Moorish movie palace had pictures every night and not just on Saturday night alone, as had been the custom in our French town. The radio could produce music of some sort at any time of the day, even before breakfast, and not merely during those rare hours when a band concert was taking place in Evian-les-Bains. She found the American *coiffeurs* to be almost as adept as the French ones, after she had learned to ask for a finger wave (written in her phonetic notebook as "fine guerre ouéve"). The five-and-ten-cent stores, the fire department, and the soda fountains were a source of wonder. But what impressed her most about the American way of life, to judge by her conversation those first few days, was the waste — and the generosity. The wastefulness of American packaging shocked us all at first. Fully half the weight of our purchases seemed to go into the trash barrel. The economical Clémentine began to save paper bags, until the pile became overwhelming. The quantity of good bottles and jars and cartons that we had to throw away scandalized us. Another thing impressed her mightily — the amount of work done for her by the merchant. Bread and bacon were sliced, fillets were removed from fish, heads were pulled off of shrimps, olives were pitted before they reached the kitchen table. And there was no need to boil the milk as she had always done in France as soon as it was ladled out by an itinerant milkman. We decided not to bewilder her further by showing her the miracle of frozen foods.

But the open-handed American way struck her more forcibly than anything else, I think. Our house seemed to be bombarded with miniature cans of soup, with samples of soap, toothpaste, and cornflakes. There were baseball caps for little Phinney, sponsored by a flour mill, a thermometer from the oil man, and a three-minute hourglass from the gas company. The climax was reached one morning when the doorbell rang and Mrs. Beck was confronted by a gushing lady, exuding sweetness and good will, who explained in a rich contralto voice that she was the North Shore Hostess. At her elbow was a bright-eyed messenger boy carrying a large basket of assorted groceries. She did not reveal the purpose of her visit at first, and my wife, unaccustomed to super-salesmanship with a smirk, tried hard to say she didn't want any. But the contralto gurgled on, finally explaining that she was bringing this basket purely as a gift of welcome from the merchants of the North Shore. One by one she pulled the

61

offerings from the basket and deposited them on the dining room table. A neat little speech accompanied each article — the coconut cake in cellophane, the box of aspirin from the drugstore, the honorary guest card from the gasoline station. The munificence of the North Shore merchants didn't stop there, of course. A huge bunch of hot-house grapes made us the loyal customers of Mr. Popopulous, fruit dealer. What else could we do, after such a Lucullan gift? A leg of lamb left us obligated to Mr. Wilcox, the butcher. There was a smoked fillet from the fish store, a can of fly spray from the hardware man, and a package of macaroni from the grocer. The candy store wished us well with a dozen lollipops tied with a green ribbon, the garage offered to fix a flat free of charge, and the insurance company wanted to make an inventory of our furniture "without any obligation." The only thing I looked for and didn't find was a pint of bourbon from the package store.

The splendor of it all overcame Clémentine.

"*C'est formidable, quand même!*" she exclaimed when we brought the free plunder into the kitchen. It was the only time she had used that awestruck phrase since her first glimpse of the Manhattan skyline.

America was truly the land of marvels. This was indeed the new, the more abundant way of life.

HE ADVENTURE OF ADJUSTING THE EXPATRIATE
Beck family to an entirely new life in a small New England "hill town"
by the sea produced many engaging episodes. One of them, an occasion
that little Phinney Beck and I anticipated with the greatest zest, was
Clémentine's baptism into the mysteries of an American grocery store.
My son and I carefully prepared the way for this big moment in the life
of our French cook. We paid a formal call upon Mr. Eustis Calkins, a
tall, thin-faced man with a shy smile, who is the town's outstanding
grocer. Mr. Calkins runs an honest, prosperous, old-fashioned rural store,
inherited from his father. "Plain and Fancy Groceries—Fresh Vegetables
and Fruit—Meats and Kitchen Ware" reads the letterhead on his grocery
slips. The walls, shelves, and country-store bins are given a new coat of
white paint every year. Mr. Calkins prides himself on having the best old
Coon cheese and the best cider in the county. One senses quality in
everything on his shelves, but it isn't showy. Customers go into the icebox
to pick out their own meat, a pleasant little formality on hot summer
days. Two unsmiling, lynx-eyed ladies preside in the cashier's coop. It is
a real New England store in the best tradition. I explained to the sympathetic proprietor that we appreciated his good-will gift of a package of
macaroni, and that we would like to introduce our French cook to the
secrets of his store, warning him that she didn't speak a word of English.
His face lighted up at this, and he confided that he had been a doughboy
in the Yankee Division and perhaps hadn't forgotten all his soldier French.
We felt sure that we had paved the way for Clémentine.

She was visibly excited the next morning, dressed in her best city
clothes, her cheeks bearing a fine Burgundian flush, as the three of us
stepped down the elm-vaulted street. But Phinney and I felt the weight
of our responsibility. We were giving her a first glimpse of marketing in
America—the same Clémentine who shopped at Les Halles in Paris and
who knew well the bounteous markets in Beaune and Dijon. Would she

63

64

NEW ENGLAND HILL TOWN (MARBLEHEAD)

suffer from stage fright and lose confidence in her ability to achieve *la cuisine française* in this land of doughnuts, chowder, fried clams, and blueberry pie? Would she sniff at the straightforward and unadorned wares of this Yankee grocer?

We should have known better. Clémentine, full of the excitement of a strange land, seemed to like everything. She shook hands with Monsieur Calkins and chattered gaily when he dusted off his faded French. Clémentine's cooking is loyal and simple, flattering the taste before it flatters the eyes. Eustis Calkins reflected the same quality in his store, and Clémentine seemed to sense it. The colorful splendor of his vegetables attracted her first of all. There were many things here that she had never seen before — parsnips, for example, and lima beans, summer squash, cranberries, alligator pears. Never had she seen such large eggplant, such opulent black cherries, or such prodigal quantities of grapefruit, known to her by the poetic name of *pamplemousse*. In France she had known Brussels sprouts as the most ordinary of vegetables. But here in Eustis Calkins's stand they were packed like precious things in small wooden boxes. Endive, grown in Belgium, had always been cheap in our French town. Here it was presented as a luxury for the "summer people" at an outrageous price. And for the first time in her life Clémentine gazed upon a basket of blueberries. She tasted one with interest and asked for the name, which proved too much for her untutored ear. She promptly thought up the term *les petits machins bleus*, which remains the official name for them in the Beck household.

Curiously, the flexible French language has no common word for "berry" or for "nut." You regale yourself in France on *les fraises, les framboises,* or *les groseilles*, but there is no general term. As we speculated on the nature of *les petits machins bleus*, I recalled Clémentine's marvelous wild strawberry tarts in France, and with a gleam in my eye, bought a box of large cultivated blueberries. Her blueberry tart, which later was to win phenomenal acclaim at the church food fair, was the result. But more of this later.

When we told Clémentine that we could buy all the flour we wanted, in large white sacks, she was astonished. It isn't that way in France, especially at this grim moment. There the grocer sells it to you in pound packages. Homemade bread is unheard of. Why, that would put the *boulanger* out of business. It just isn't done. The plot of that memorable film *The Baker's Wife* would have been impossible if the townspeople had been accustomed to making their own bread. Sliced American bread in cellophane puzzled Clémentine. Those even white slices might be fine for *croques monsieur* (sandwiches of ham and cheese sautéed in butter and covered with a cream sauce), but they didn't have enough substance for her idea of good table bread. Nothing to get your teeth into — no crisp crust to carry that fragment of Camembert.

We inspected Mr. Calkins's shiny electric four-grind coffee mill and told Clémentine that she would have no further use for the antique little grinder she had been using laboriously for so many years. We explained to her the workings of a charge account. She could just point to what she wanted. No cash would be needed; no market pocketbook had to be kept ready for delivery boys. They would just leave a lot of little buff-colored slips, which Monsieur Beck would pay with another little slip at the beginning of the month. It all seemed surprisingly simple. Clémentine was suitably impressed.

The grocery department was the most bewildering, I think. She looked with uncomprehending eyes upon rows of breakfast food boxes with short and snappy titles, upon the growling refrigerator for frozen foods, upon such strange articles as baking powder and sandwich spreads. Cookies in cellophane were a novelty that delighted her, but why cans of baby food, dog food, cat food? What was peanut butter? Why did they sell paper towels? What were those big *cornichons* in the five-gallon jar?

Mr. Calkins had been very patient in showing us about the store. The moment had come to show appreciation by placing our first order. I asked Clémentine for the slip of paper on which she had written down her immediate needs — and began to translate. The next few moments were awkward for us all. Here is what Clémentine had decided she needed most:

1 bottle Madeira
1 bottle Kirsch
Coarse salt
Greek olives
Leeks
Shallots
Whole vanilla beans
Chervil, tarragon, thyme, basil — and parsley
Black and white peppercorns
Small new potatoes
Lettuce
Eggs

Mr. Calkins shook his head in a perplexed negative as I read off the items one by one. It was his turn to ask questions. What was Kirsch? Why Greek olives? Wouldn't onion do as well as shallots? We were visibly relieved when the end of the list disclosed some familiar staples. We added some crook-necked squash to the list, ceremoniously shook hands with the now befuddled Mr. Calkins, and our long-anticipated visit was over. The three of us were a little subdued on the way home. Perhaps New England would turn out to be barren soil for Clémentine's *cuisine française* after all.

But again we should have known better. Clémentine returned to her sunny kitchen full of confidence, eager to get her hands back in the mixing bowl. I found her Madeira, shallots, leeks, and all the rest in Boston. The old familiar fragrance of French cooking began to seep past the kitchen door. After a month of upheaval we were ready to resume our gastronomic existence—just where we had left off in France. Going over the menu notebook where those early days are recorded, I find one particular day's fare that expresses the structure of French family meals very well. It happened to fall on a Friday. Here are the menus, written in Madame Beck's fine hand. They are balanced, temperate, and as French as *pot-au-feu*—and they are composed of basic materials that anyone can buy in America.

DÉJEUNER

Hors-d'oeuvre — Salade de Tomates

Oeufs Durs Mayonnaise

Maquereaux aux Olives

Pommes Vapeur

Salade de Laitue

Fruits Rafraîchis

Vin blanc

DÎNER

Soupe aux Poireaux et Pommes de Terre

Omelette aux Fines Herbes

Courgettes au Four

Fromage — Vin Rouge

Tarte aux Petits Machins Bleus — Vouvray

Café

Detailed comment on such simple cooking is hardly needed, but Mrs. Beck's and Clémentine's notes on the recipes have multiplied and they have specifics to offer . . .

Salade de Tomates

Small tomatoes, chilled, not peeled, sliced thin with a very sharp knife, sprinkled with chopped parsley, and seasoned with oil, wine vinegar, salt, and pepper. All of France serves tomatoes this way. And the Becks belong to the French school of thought that believes lettuce and tomatoes to be unfortunate companions in a salad and that raw tomatoes are best when they are allowed to do a solo.

Maquereaux aux Olives

This simple recipe comes from the eminent Dr. Edouard de Pomiane, and it transforms the humble mackerel into something aromatic and delicious.

Have small fresh mackerel cleaned, allowing 1 per person. Stuff each fish with a half dozen pitted green olives. Grease a shallow baking dish, preferably of earthenware, with olive oil. Repose the fish side by side in the dish, sprinkle them with a little more oil, and salt and pepper them, using freshly ground pepper. Surround the fish with a generous quantity of pitted black or so-called Greek olives. Bake the mackerel in a 350° oven for 20 to 30 minutes, depending on their size, basting frequently. Present in the baking dish, with each fish decorated with peeled slices of lemon. Serve with steamed new potatoes.

Note: Bulk olives should be used, of the Greek or Italian type. The conventional bottled or canned olives don't work nearly as well. Clémentine would allow the black olives to remain unpitted, but not the green ones inside the fish.

Courgettes au Four

This is the recipe Clémentine used for the crook-necked yellow squash in Mr. Calkins's store. She had long used it for *courgettes*, the cucumber-shaped yellow summer squash no different from ours, and for zucchini.

Split the squash in two lengthwise and allow a half or a whole squash per person, depending on their size. Parboil them for 5 minutes, more or less, depending on size; do not allow them to become soft.

Drain them, arrange them, skin side down, in a shallow baking dish, and sprinkle them with finely chopped shallots (or onions, but shallots are better), salt (only a little), freshly ground pepper, and then fine bread crumbs. Dot with a small amount of butter and place a strip of bacon on each. Bake in a 350° oven for 20 minutes, or until the squash is tender and the bacon is browned. Add a *small* amount of water to the dish if necessary.

Try this if you would endow this Yankee vegetable with a little Gallic glamour—and note that Clémentine much preferred our good breakfast bacon for this dish to the heavier salt pork called bacon in France.

Tarte aux Petits Machins Bleus

This is the mighty successor to the wild strawberry tart of Senlis days. Mrs. Beck assures me that a 9-inch round pie pan is the most practical, but Clémentine frames her tart shells in pans about 7 inches square, serving four people each, without seconds. Miraculously, the shells are unmolded and they are about ¾ inch deep. She has her own secret for making pastry, flaky or *brisée*, and you probably have yours. The baked pastry shells are completely cool before they are filled, only moments before reheating and serving.

With a patience that brings its own artistic reward, Clémentine fills the shells with neat rows of large raw blueberries. She has ready a fresh raspberry syrup, for which can be substituted raspberry jelly whisked with a bit of water. Allowing 5 minutes to serving time, she pours the syrup over the blueberries, pops the whole thing into a hot oven, and brings it to the table hot and indescribably fragrant.

A clean little Vouvray or Anjou is all that is needed to complete the utter sublimation of the American blueberry.

LÉMENTINE HAD A LOT OF ADJUSTING TO DO before she became reconciled to the way food is purveyed in an old, yet modern, Yankee seaport town. She was still perplexed by the myriad gaudy packages with peppy names in the grocery store. She was more puzzled by Mr. Wilcox, the butcher, who never had any veal and who refused bluntly to cut up his sides of beef the way they do in France. Why did the *pâtisserie* sell pots of baked beans on Saturday night, she wanted to know. The corner drugstore, nine tenths of whose space was given over to a magazine stand, a soda fountain, and cigars, cosmetics, and pin ball machines, left her totally bewildered. If you could see the funereal little *pharmacie* back in our French town, with two large snakes pickled in alcohol as the only window decoration, you would understand why Clémentine was dismayed, if dazzled. Once, on her Thursday off, the exploring Clémentine wandered into Jerry's Diner, which happens to be the headquarters of all the high school hep cats. To the accompaniment of "The Jumpin' Jive" on the juke box and the raucous shouts of the exuberant "alligators," she had her evening meal and came home a shaken woman. It takes a little time for a full-fledged Burgundian to become adjusted to the tempo of Tommy Dorsey.

But *one* local institution in Marblehead was pitched precisely to Clémentine's old-world viewpoint — the fish store of Mr. Job Stacy. Repeated coats of white paint, inside and out, could not disguise the antiquity of Stacy's Fish Shop, installed in a low frame building that resembled a pure Cape Cod cottage. Back in the 1870s, Job's grandfather had cut a many-paned shop window in the street façade of the house and established the business. Job and his brothers (who do most of the fishing) inherited it as a matter of course. Job takes charge of the shop, and his brothers, who are distinctly less personable and given to Saturday night bacchanals, preside at the picturesque old fishermen's shanty at the water's edge, where the nets, lobster pots, and Newburyport rum are stored.

There is no hint of pretension in Stacy's Fish Shop. The window contains the same exhibition of giant sea shells, coral curiosities, mounted lobsters, and stuffed fish that has been there for years. Once you are inside you will observe a Spartan exhibit of cod liver oil flanked by a few wooden boxes of salted cod fillets and a lonely squad of catsup bottles. Clean sawdust is on the floor. Before you is a small white marble counter, covered with chopped ice that all but conceals a few freshly caught haddock and cod. That is all you see as you enter Mr. Stacy's shop, except a blackboard. It isn't impressive.

But there is one hint that indisputable treasures are concealed in icy bins in the back room. It is on that blackboard, upon which Job lavishes a fine Spencerian flourish. When the Beck family studied this handsome document for the first time, a ray of pure rapture burst through the clouds. We began to realize our enormous good fortune in choosing this New England seaport as our home. For Job Stacy lists upon his blackboard an almost utopian stock of freshly caught fish. He has haddock, mackerel, and young cod at excursion rates. And there are handsome butterfish, rock bass, perch, and bluefish. He has fillets of cusk, plaice, and flounder, besides smoked fillets and finnan haddie of unimpeachable integrity. His bins hide an ample supply of halibut, swordfish, and salmon. He has clams — soft-shelled ones for steaming, cherrystones for appetizers, and for your chowder ponderous quahaugs. He has oysters — bluepoints, Cotuits, and Narragansetts. His lobsters are so alive they are athletic, but he has lobster meat if you prefer it. In season you can find tender young soft-shelled crabs, or you can have shrimps or crab meat at any time. He has not only the large sea scallops, but those rarities of the American *gourmandise*, small Cape scallops as well.

It was natural that Clémentine should share our enthusiasm, once we introduced her to Mr. Stacy and his well-stocked back room. Here was a shop that reminded her of France and of the amiable Monsieur Chollet, who used to sell us *merlan*, turbot, and sole. Clémentine began to pay almost daily visits to Mr. Stacy's shop, chattering affably in French, a language that he obviously did not understand, until she finally thawed out his Yankee reserve very perceptibly. Meanwhile the Becks saw the beginning of a dream come true. Our table became beautified with the freshest of Atlantic fish, cooked as a French *Cordon Bleu* would do it.

Here I would like to share our good fortune with you by tearing a few leaves from Clémentine's notebook. There is nothing brilliantly original about any of these recipes. They merely follow the old French fundamentals. But to judge by the comments of our dinner guests, they have opened up a new vista to at least a few New England hostesses. And

73

FISHERMAN'S SHANTY, MARBLEHEAD

since they can be achieved rather easily in an American home, we hope that they merit your sympathetic consideration.

Clémentine's approach to preparing New England fish was refreshing and direct. It never occurred to her to fry fish in deep fat. Fried scallops, fried oysters, fried clams, fried "fillet of sole"—the inevitable vocabulary of the restaurant cook in these parts—did not become a part of her culinary jargon, and we were certainly just as glad. Clémentine took the simplest and most obvious French path, which was to bake this clean saltwater fish in white wine with mushrooms. The unassuming haddock and baby cod take on surprising distinction when prepared in this rudimentary manner:

Haddock au Vin Blanc

Place haddock fillets in a shallow buttered baking dish. Add at your discretion thinly sliced mushrooms and thin slices of small white onions, though chopped shallots are best. Season with a little salt, pepper from the pepper mill, a bay leaf, and a sprig of thyme. Sprinkle with fine bread crumbs and dot well with butter. Pour a generous glass of dry white wine into the baking dish and bake the fish in a moderate (350°) oven until just firm, basting now and then—it should not take more than 20 minutes. Serve with steamed potatoes and a trickle of lemon juice.

The French cook *dorade*, pike, sole, flounder, and many other fish in this way. An utterly simple recipe, it lends itself to many of our own fish, from fresh and salt waters, and it has the potential power to improve conjugal harmony in American households by at least three percent, especially if the fish is served with a worthy dry white wine.

Scallops are a favorite standby in New England, where I'll wager that not one in fifty escapes being fried in deep fat. A few are doubtless broiled on skewers and served with a *maître d'hôtel* butter. Those are the fifty-to-one odds. Yet Madame Prunier lists fifteen other ways to cook them. Clémentine was impressed when Mr. Stacy delivered a pound of scallops all cleaned and removed from their shells. But she missed the flat shells, which are essential to her method of cooking them. We rescued a dozen or more shells from the Stacy shack by the sea, and Clémentine proceeded with her old familiar *coquilles Saint-Jacques au gratin*, the classic French way of preparing scallops. A few American cookbooks cite variations of this dish. André Simon and Jeanne Owen both give fine versions, but most books ignore the basic recipe.

FISHINGPORT SUNSET

Coquilles Saint-Jacques au Gratin

To serve four: Slice ¾ pint of sea scallops. (If you have tiny bay scallops, these are left whole.) Sauté the pieces gently for 3 minutes in 2 tablespoons of hot butter, with a little pepper and 1 chopped shallot. Add 2 tablespoons of fine bread crumbs and ¾ cup of dry white wine and simmer the scallops for 8 to 10 minutes, or until the sauce is slightly reduced and thickened.

Add 1 tablespoon of finely chopped parsley, and salt if necessary, and fill four scallop shells with the mixture. Sprinkle the *coquilles* with more fine bread crumbs and with grated Parmesan and dot them with butter. They may now be set aside and reheated and browned lightly under the broiler just before serving.

The same recipe can be applied to any firm white fish and is excellent for dressing up leftovers. Small individual baking dishes can be substituted for the shells, of course, and small onions can replace the shallots. Clémentine carries the same idea a little further in a recipe that she has adapted from an obscure French cookbook. So much of her own creative ability is shown in this dish that we have always referred to it as "Clémentine's Flounder." It is something of a showpiece, yet its ingredients are so simple that it can be achieved by any good cook with access to a fish store and it works handsomely to improve frozen fillets. Here it is, and we feel certain you are going to like it once you try it:

Clémentine's Flounder

For six people: Select 12 flounder fillets of even size. Salt and pepper them lightly, dip in milk, then in flour, and brown lightly on both sides in butter. Place, scarcely overlapping, in a long shallow baking dish.

Dice 6 sea scallops and place in a casserole with butter the size of an egg; a half pound of mushrooms, minced; a few pinches of chopped fresh herbs (parsley, tarragon, chives, chervil); a clove of garlic, a shallot, and a medium-size onion, all minced; and salt and pepper. Cook on a brisk fire for 5 minutes, then slowly, stirring often, for 10 or 15 minutes, by which time the liquid from the mushrooms has evaporated. Cover the fillets with this savory mixture.

If you have saved the bones of your fish, boil them, strain the liquid, and use it as a base for 2 cups of the fairly thick béchamel sauce (see page 214) that is next on the program. Mix 1 ounce of grated Swiss cheese, 1 ounce of grated Parmesan cheese, and 1 cup of heavy cream with the sauce. Pour this on top of your dish. Add a few dabs of butter, sprinkle lightly with grated cheese, and brown briefly in a 400° oven. Serve in the baking dish.

If there were space for only two of Clémentine's master fish recipes, the Beck family would be unanimous in choosing this one and Lobster Delmonico for the honor. The latter dish was Clémentine's triumph for the winter. We had the temerity to serve it to a few native sons and daughters of this old seaport, where there are only two ways to cook lobster. You either boil 'em or you broil 'em, that's all there is to it. But this seraphic dish won our friends over to *la cuisine française* completely, and we think it will enrapture the readers of this book as well. It is adapted from the recipe of Monsieur Baccou, formerly chef of the Restaurant Marguery in Paris. The counterpoint of its two sauces, one with the rich savor of old Port wine, the other an absolutely delicious cream sauce, is superb with the fragrant lobster meat and dry rice. It's extravagant, and perhaps you had better postpone it for the Duration. But *some* day try:

Lobster Delmonico

For eight persons: 4 lobsters weighing 1½ to 2 pounds each; a pint and a half of thick fresh cream; the yolks of 6 eggs; a half pint of good Port wine; butter.

Cooking of the lobsters: Prepare a *court-bouillon* consisting of a bottle of dry white wine, the same quantity of water, salt, pepper in crushed grains, minced carrots and onions, parsley, thyme, and a bay leaf. Allow this to simmer for 30 minutes in a large kettle. Plunge the live lobsters into the *court-bouillon*, which should now be boiling vigorously, cover, and steam for 12 minutes after the liquid returns to a boil.

Remove the lobsters and allow to cool. Detach the tails, remove the shells, and cut the meat into thick slices. Also remove the large pieces of meat from the claws. Melt butter the size of an egg in a *plat à sauter*, in which you align your pieces of lobster meat. Salt lightly, heat, and add the half pint of Port wine. Allow to cook down gently. Light the Port with a match, if it is still strong enough in alcohol, and allow it to burn out. Then keep hot until time to serve.

The sauce: In the top of a double boiler, make a *liaison* with the fresh cream and the 6 lightly beaten yolks of egg, adding salt and a spot of cayenne. Allow to thicken, stirring often, over

77

very gently simmering water. Stir in slowly 8 pats of sweet butter and add the lobster roe, if there was any. Serve very hot in a sauceboat. (The *plat à sauter*, by the way, in which the lobster is reposing, is Clémentine's large tin-lined oval copper skillet, which comes to the dining room for the serving of the dish.)

We have always considered these two dishes to be Clémentine's masterpieces of fish cookery, but her biggest victory with seafood came about entirely by accident. On Sunday afternoons, she was in the habit of taking long bicycle rides to satisfy her curiosity about this strange new land. She returned from one such expedition to a promontory of the

Marblehead shore nearly scarlet with excitement and called elatedly to my wife, *"Madame! J'ai trouvé des moules! Des quantités de moules!"* It wasn't the first time that Clémentine had appeared with such news. We all remembered well the snails she had discovered in our French garden and rushed into the kitchen. Now, wrapped up in somebody's Sunday newspaper, here were large clusters of small, purplish black mussels. Clémentine had pedaled far that day, to a rocky point jutting out into the Atlantic. Seated on the rocks and watching the waves break at low tide, she suddenly saw something to thrill her thrifty Burgundian soul — great patches of perfectly good mussels, the very same kind of mussels they serve at Prunier's in Paris. Clémentine could conceive of only one course of conduct — to gather handfuls of these toothsome mollusks at once, wondering in the meantime why they were being ignored by all the other

Sunday trippers. When the Beck family sat down to soup plates heaped full of *moules à la marinière* the next day, we wondered, too.

And, my good New England neighbors, especially you in the state of Maine, something ought to be *done* about this! Quantities of these delicate and absolutely delicious mussels cling to the rocks on your jagged shore! Some of them are within the range of oil refineries, glue factories, creosote mills, and disposal plants and are entirely inedible. But others cling to clean rocks in bountiful patches, washed only by pure sea water. Your ancestors knew that mussels, when properly scrubbed and steamed, were a dish any gourmet would cherish. There is a fine old Yankee recipe for mussels dating back to 1763. Why do you fishermen of Maine·scorn them now, or use them for bait, rather than exploit them for the multitude of voluptuaries who would welcome them in the markets? Listen to this simple bourgeois French recipe for mussels, gentlemen, and try it some cold winter evening. Perhaps then you will send more of your long-overlooked treasure to the big city vendors.

Moules à la Marinière

(A PEASANT VERSION)

Brush and scrape the mussel shells and wash in several waters, scraping away all the "beard" with a knife. (Maybe this laborious procedure is the reason mussels aren't popular.) To serve two or three, place 2 quarts of mussels in a pan, add 4 or 5 sections of garlic, chopped fine, a good fistful of minced parsley, a little freshly ground pepper, and 2 ounces of butter. Salt is *not* needed. Cover the pan, place over a brisk fire, and cook for 5 or 6 minutes, shaking the pan 2 or 3 times. Remove the lid. The mussels are open, ready to be served with the sauce in soup plates.

We await your reaction, gentlemen, with genuine eagerness.

WITHIN A FEW WEEKS AFTER OUR COOK HAD been transplanted so quickly from France to New England, she had adapted herself with good humor and a lively interest to almost all of our strange American ways. She was flexible enough to accept (with a giggle) the idea of pushing a double-decker baby carriage at the serve-yourself super-market. She welcomed the convenience of our new mechanical mixer, paper towels, and the sneeze-proof miraculous soap flakes about which persuasive young announcers talked so chummily every morning on the radio. She even went bowling at the Y.M.C.A. with little Phinney on Ladies' Day. On a few subjects she remained inflexible in her opposition. Chewing gum, pineapple with ham, jelly with meats, flour-thickened gravy — for these there was no excuse.

But on the whole Clémentine got along so famously with the merchants of our little town, despite linguistic loggerheads, that we, the Becks, feared that her piquant French temperament had softened and become *all* sweetness and light. Her tranquility was becoming alarmingly un-Gallic, and we were genuinely relieved to see her return from shopping one morning, bristling with indignation. With fine French eloquence she told us that she had come to grips with Mr. Cletus R. Wilcox, the town butcher, over the matter of an *entrecôte*. She had pointed out to the butcher exactly the cut of meat she desired and exactly how thick she wanted it to be, and he, the supercilious wretch, had absolutely refused to cut it for her. Her black eyes flashed with vexation. Why had the stupid man tried to force a heavy T-bone or a sirloin upon her when she had explained (very slowly and with emphasis — in French) that Madame Beck wanted thin *entrecôtes minute*, served with *sauce béarnaise* and *pommes soufflées*, a classic dish that *any* butcher ought to know about. Why, when she had gone through an elaborate pantomime and almost cut the slices herself, had the stubborn brute stood there, arms crossed, shaking his head? Would

Madame Beck please go down to the butcher shop and tell him how to cup up a side of beef, explain what an *entrecôte* is, and what is meant by the *culotte, jarret, noix, aloyau, faux-filet, gîte à la noix, bavette,* and *plates-côtes*? And would she ask him why he didn't have any veal?

Thus, in bold relief, an elemental fact was thrust upon us: the technique of dismembering a side of beef differs radically in France and in America. And Cletus R. Wilcox was not one to change his lifetime habits for any mere family of returned expatriates with a jabbering French cook. You either take what Cletus offers you, or you go somewhere else. A rather ponderous man, whose white apron has an impressive overhang, Mr. Wilcox is a political pillar in the town and a tireless enthusiast for country square dances. In addition he is something of an artist, a fact he demonstrates weekly on his spacious plate glass windows. High above the reach of meddlesome children he uses chalky poster paints to depict ornamental calves' heads, fleecy sheep, prize bulls, boars, and geese. His resplendent Thanksgiving turkey is an annual masterpiece, calling for much overtime and exposure on a stepladder. Beneath his works of art is a price list of the week's specials. For twenty years Cletus has lettered this list with infinite patience, knowing that it is certain to be defaced by the fingers of some mischievous gamin into phrases that are Rabelaisian, if not rustically obscene. The ingenuity shown by the sidewalk wits in altering such fine terms as Fancy Brisket, Face of the Rump, Tender Broilers, and Lamb's Fores is endless and inspiring.

From the very beginning there was a lack of deep understanding between Mr. Wilcox and Clémentine. He was instinctively hostile to "furriers" (which term included the Becks) and responded to our sprightly comments with a cold aloofness. Though she had scant respect for Mr. Wilcox as a tradesman, Clémentine felt no reproach for the quality of his meat and poultry. In fact, the massive sides of beef that came to his icebox from Chicago elicited her rapt admiration. But there was a hopeless clash of ideologies on how this precious article should be parceled. We tried to tell her about chuck roasts, porterhouse, and top of the round, and even told her the little legend about the beef-loving Henry VIII and his christening of "Sir Loin." But *biftek*, *rumsteak*, and *rosbif* were the only terms she seemed to master. And when she spoke of having *rosbif de mouton* for Sunday dinner, we realized that her grasp on this word would always be a faltering one.

We still feel the impact of that first battle between Clémentine and Mr. Wilcox, and our relations with him continue to be cool. We get our fowl and lamb from him and the beef for Clémentine's *ragoûts* and *daubes*. But we humor her about the other cuts of beef and get them at the Faneuil Hall Market in Boston, where a burly surgeon named Mike will give us any cut we desire. *Entrecôte minute* still appears triumphant on the Beck family table, accompanied by a rich, tarragon-fragrant *sauce béarnaise*.

Market day in France had been a picturesque affair for the Becks. Our village square, dominated by the Gothic church and an ancient half-timbered house, sparkling with canvas-topped shelters and resounding with the cacophony of dozens of shouting salesmen, was a scene of colorful animation. We were enchanted to find that historic Faneuil Hall and Quincy Market could be every bit as lively and pictorial. Clémentine's feud with Mr. Wilcox gave us an opportunity to explore Boston's famed market and to uncover riches that could never be found in a small town. We have steered clear of the dangerous subject of who has the better technique, the Latin or the Anglo-Saxon butcher, but we do know that a large American market can furnish even an Escoffier with everything he needs.

Being a staunch Burgundian, Clémentine is naturally adept at preparing the classic *boeuf bourguignon*, one of the noblest standbys of *la cuisine française*. The French housewife's genius in making a commonplace stew into something exotic and supremely flavorful is demonstrated in this aromatic dish. If you could wander over the hillsides of Nuits-Saint-Georges or Vosne-Romanée on an autumn evening, as in the peaceful days, and could peer into the kitchen of the wine grower's house, this is the dish that most likely would be simmering on the stove—a peasant dish, if you will, but fit for any patrician palate. At the risk of repeating a well-known recipe, we would like to give you a Burgundian's own version of it, straight from her most-used notebook:

MARKET DAY IN LILLEBONNE

84

FANEUIL HALL MARKET

Boeuf Bourguignon

For four people: In an iron *cocotte* or heavy casserole, bubbling with 2 tablespoons of hot butter, brown 2 pounds of good lean stewing beef cut into 1½-inch cubes, a few pieces at a time, until the meat is "closed." Remove the pieces to a bowl as they are browned. Stir a tablespoon of flour into the juices in the *cocotte* and simmer, stirring, to make a *roux brun*. Add salt and pepper and 1½ cups of a good red wine.

Brown apart in a skillet 2 coarsely chopped onions in 1 tablespoon of butter. Return the beef and its juices to the *cocotte* and add 1 carrot, another onion, 1 clove of garlic, and 2 shallots, all finely sliced, and a *bouquet garni*, a piece of cracked veal knuckle, and the browned onions. Add then ½ cup of Madeira and enough water to bring the liquid just to the level of the meat.

Put the lid on this poetic ensemble and allow it to simmer very gently, covered, for 2½ hours or more, until the meat is tender and the sauce is a rich, dark brown. One half hour before the dish is done, add a liqueur glass of brandy and ¼ pound of raw mushroom caps. Finish the cooking with the lid on the *cocotte*, unless you judge the sauce not to be reduced enough.

Steamed new potatoes are the best companion piece, and so is a vigorous red wine, such as a Corton, Pommard, or California pinot noir. A cold winter's night can be brightened in many ways, but rarely in a more earthy and satisfying manner than this.

Most of the beef recipes in Clémentine's notebook are rather conventional and bring no startling new contribution to cooking lore. She has one specialty, however, that stands forth from the rest. It is full of surprises. It is supremely delectable, and it can serve as a *pièce de résistance* for a cold supper for guests with absolute majesty. Some readers may be disturbed over the vagueness of this recipe for *boeuf farci*, the casual mention of a "pinch" of this and a "little" of that. Whenever I press Clémentine to be more specific she assures me that I'm asking the impossible and that something *has* to be left to the intuition and good taste of the cook. So take your intuition in one hand and a fine earthen casserole in the other and embark upon:

Boeuf Farci

Cut about 4 pounds of lean beef (face of the rump) into slices less than half an inch thick. Rub each side of the slices with freshly ground pepper. Cover one side of your first slice with thinly sliced truffles and thin slices of lean salt pork and then with a layer of the following mixture, finely chopped:

    1 clove of garlic
    2 shallots
    3 medium-size onions
    a handful of parsley
    a few chives
    a pinch of cinnamon
    a pinch of ginger
    a dash of nutmeg
    2 ground cloves
    salt and pepper

Now place another slice of beef over the first one, add salt pork, truffles, and the seasoned mixture as before, and repeat until all the slices are in a neat block. Then tie together carefully with string.

Place a good piece of butter and a small layer of chopped salt pork in the bottom of your casserole. Put the block of beef on this, together with a calf's foot (or a fresh pig's foot) and a veal bone. Pour over this the following sauce, previously prepared:

A piece of butter the size of a tangerine, melted without browning and blended with a spoonful of flour. To this add:

    3 wine glasses of water
    1½ glasses of dry white wine
    1 tablespoon of brandy
    ½ lump sugar
    a few pinches of spices (those used before)
    ½ teaspoon curry powder
    a little thyme
    1 bay leaf
    2 celery leaves
    1 large tomato, cut into pieces
    1 branch parsley
    2 whole carrots
    1 small whole white turnip
    1 chopped onion

Cook this sauce, tightly covered, over a slow fire for 1 hour before pouring over the meat.

Cover the casserole tightly, and cook over a very slow fire for 4 hours.

When done, slice your carrots and turnips and place these in a deep *charcutier*'s mold for *pâtés*. Place the meat in the dish so that the strips of beef run horizontally and remove the string. Strain the sauce through a fine sieve and add one envelope of gelatine that has been soaked in a little water. Stir over low heat to dissolve completely and pour the sauce over the meat, which should be covered by it. Let cool and place in the refrigerator. Unmold onto a platter the next day and serve cold.

If your labors are not repaid a hundredfold as you slice through these layers of aromatic beef, Clémentine will be surprised and *désolée*. Truffles, of course, are just about unobtainable at present, and Clémentine substitutes thin slices of mushroom.

Madam, perhaps *you* are the martyred wife of a reminiscing veteran of the World War who has been talking for the last twenty-two years about the wonderful omelettes he used to get in that little restaurant in Blois, or about the magnificent beef dish that was served to him and his brother officers by the Comtesse de Chose in her château near Dijon. If so, place before him Clémentine's *boeuf farci*, resplendent in its aromatic aspic, and if he has any sense of fair play he'll never mention the Comtesse again!

ROOSTING ON ITS ROCKY HILLSIDE, OUR RAM-
bling little gambrel-roofed house, first American abode of the expatriate
Beck family, proved to be a heart-warming choice in many ways. It was
compact, picturesque, and functional. Its arteries were in good condition,
and its mechanical appliances all worked at the touch of a button. True,
we bumped a lot of heads before learning the technique of living in low-
ceilinged rooms. The cold air had a disconcerting way of filtering up
between the ancient floorboards. And though a heated two-car garage had
been built in one of the wings, there was nothing that vaguely resembled
a wine cellar. We recalled the beautiful Romanesque *cave* in our French
house, and the fact that our much-loved Utch-keess had to freeze its bones
in the barn, and decided that there must be something fundamental in the
comparison. You pamper your car in America, your wine in France.

Physically the gambrel-roofed house was a successful experiment.
Socially, to our surprise, our hurried repatriation was far from a failure.
Being obvious "furriners," we were ready to accept temporary ostracism
in this New England town until we could prove our salt. To our en-
chantment, the period of quarantine was brief. Some of the entrenched
First Families of the town came to call, often inviting us to dinner. It was
instinctive New England hospitality, we felt, that opened these thresholds
to us. And yet we wondered if there *could* be another reason. We noticed
that our hosts were invariably sleek and well fed and that they talked a
good deal about food. Almost without fail they brought up the subject
of our Clémentine, the Burgundian *Cordon Bleu*. Quite soon, one evening,
a plump hostess, after her third glass of sherry, had let the cat out of the
bag. The Marblehead grapevine had circulated the news that those newly
arrived Becks had a French cook, a fabulously skilled French cook from
Burgundy. The story had improved as it was bandied about: Clémentine
had been awarded diplomas with bright red seals; she had been the chef
in a famous restaurant in Lyon; she had won blue ribbons in cooking

88

HOUSE ON THE HILLSIDE

competitions judged by famous French gourmets and had been kissed on both cheeks by the Minister of Agriculture.

It became abundantly clear to us that, if our newfound friends were politely solicitous about the Becks, they burned with curiosity about the culinary treasure in our kitchen. Clémentine, without knowing it, would be the steppingstone to our Social Success. We allowed their curiosity to build up to the itching point—even considered planting false rumors to the effect that Clémentine had once cooked for the Duc de Vendôme—and then invited six strategic guests for dinner, six guests who would be sure to broadcast extensively the next day. We knew that we would be judged by one of Brillat-Savarin's most famous maxims: "Tell me what you eat, and I will tell you what you are." Our acceptance into the charmed circle of those invited to Mrs. Amory Forbes Whipple's Cotillion appeared to hinge on Clémentine and her deft touch with the sauce whisk. We had read plenty of fiction about life north of Boston, but nothing as strange as this.

With such signal recognition at stake, it was natural that we worked out the menu with more than usual care. Clémentine's eyes sparkled with anticipation when we went into her sunny kitchen and announced that we were having *invités*. She seemed pleased and relieved. The secluded home life of the Becks had troubled her a little, I think. From the kitchen library we brought forth our favorite cookbooks: Montagné, *Ali-Bab*, André Simon, Richardin, Escoffier. Out came the oilcloth-covered notebooks in whose neatly penned pages reposed most of Clémentine's culinary secrets. Madame Beck sat down at the kitchen table, pencil in hand, and we all joined in the grave conference on the composition of this, our first formal dinner in America.

". . . with the oysters, would Madame want the conventional French sauce made with wine vinegar and chopped shallots? Wouldn't Monsieur Beck's Chablis be offended by the vinegar? Perhaps a trickle of lemon juice would be better. . . ."

". . . we might have a classic *soupe aux poireaux*, but a *petite marmite* would be lighter . . ."

". . . *moules marinières* would be a little mussy for Mrs. Whipple. And Mr. Ames doesn't like lobster—or, rather, lobster doesn't like Mr. Ames. We might give them fish, but Mr. Shrewsbury has been eating fish daily since childhood. Perhaps Cape scallops *en brochette* with a good *maître d'hôtel* butter would turn the trick."

Not until the discussion reached the *pièce de résistance* did our views take tangents. Madame was partial to a *gigot*. I veered toward a *filet de boeuf*. Clémentine thought she could captivate everyone with her *rôti de veau*, with mushrooms, truffles, baby onions, and green olives, provided she could get the veal. We were approaching a stalemate.

In case of divergent views, menu makers the world over have turned to chicken as the perfect compromise. So did we. For the next few minutes we pored over Clémentine's notebooks, containing a score of classic chicken recipes we had known in France. They made reminiscent reading. Old friends were there—*poulet chasseur, poulet normand, coq au vin, poulet en casserole à la paysanne,* and especially that humble and utterly delectable standby, *poule au riz.* Just a barnyard fowl fricassee, if you wish, but with what a difference! We decided that it would not be dressy enough for our formal splurge, but I cannot refrain from giving you Clémentine's version:

Poule au Riz

For six people: Put a whole trussed fowl weighing 5 or more pounds in a deep kettle with salt, pepper, parsley, 1 bay leaf, a pinch of thyme, 2 cloves of garlic, 1 stalk of celery, and 1 quartered onion. Add 2½ quarts of water (or half chicken stock and half water), or enough almost to cover the bird. Let it simmer gently, with the lid of the kettle askew, until it is tender. This may take 2 hours.

Wash 1½ cups of rice and cook it in 3 cups of stock from the chicken pot; add a little more stock if the liquid is absorbed before the rice is tender.

In the top of a double boiler, beat together 3 egg yolks and 2 teaspoons of lemon juice. Add gradually 2 cups of the chicken stock, strained, stirring constantly with a whisk. Continue cooking the sauce, over simmering water, stirring often, until it is smooth and lightly thickened; taste for seasoning.

Carve the chicken. Put the cooked rice on a hot platter, arrange the pieces of chicken over it, and sprinkle with minced parsley. The sauce (which brings unusual distinction to Clémentine's recipe) should be presented separately.

91

The plebeian *poule au riz* had to be ruled out, so the conference continued. "Shouldn't we serve a simple roast chicken, beautifully browned and basted? Why not stuff it with fresh tarragon and serve it with a plain salad?"

"Good idea, but where can we find those branches of fresh tarragon? How about a bird stuffed with our *farce Cassini*? Ah, that *farce Cassini*! Remember how we captivated Monsieur Gébaud, the chubby French industrialist, with a chicken filled with that divine mixture? And how his sales resistance melted after the third helping and the third glass of Corton?"

Clémentine rustled through her *carnets* and brought forth the formula for this appetizing stuffing. It has sublimated more than one bird for us, and we hope that it does the same for you. *Le voici:*

Poulet Farci Cassini

First requisite, a large, tender roasting chicken to serve six. Second requisite, its stuffing, composed as follows:

One half pound of mushrooms. Chop the stems and the tops, unpeeled, and brown them gently in butter in a small casserole.

One third pound of bacon, cut into small squares. Brown it lightly in butter and add the bacon bits to the casserole.

Dice the chicken's liver, brown lightly in the bacon fat, add ½ pound of cooked ham, well chopped, and add the following to the casserole:

Two cups of bread crumbs, salt, pepper, a little nutmeg, and a pinch of sage. First mix well with a wooden spoon and then add to the casserole. Now mix all the ingredients together.

Fill the cavity of the chicken with this savory mixture, sew it up, truss the chicken, and roast it in a moderately hot oven for about 20 minutes per pound, or until well browned and tender. Baste it often.

If a duck is stuffed with the above mixture, add a small glass of Port and a liqueur glass of brandy.

Poulet farci Cassini seemed like our dish until we recalled that the doughty Major Whipple had a great weakness for rich sauces. Thus, by process of elimination, our choice came down to *poulet Cintra*, a seraphic dish credited to one of the most celebrated restaurateurs in Lyon, Louis Bouvier. On Monsieur Bouvier's shoulders, and on Clémentine's, rested the ultimate success of our dinner. The decision was made. A leaf of lettuce, a fragment of cheese to go with that treasured bottle of Musigny 1934, and a light fruit dessert would follow, of course, but we all agreed that *poulet Cintra* would make the meal. Clémentine beamed and bristled with assurance. She had prepared the dish often in Paris.

"Just get me some tender chickens, Madame, *c'est tout*," she said.

The following evening we knew that Clémentine's confidence was more than justified. Never had she risen to the occasion more nobly. Everything clicked. Her *petite marmite* was inexpressibly fragrant. Her scallops were both juicy and brown. And her *poulet Cintra* turned out to be a masterstroke. Our guests stayed until midnight, bathed in the blissful aura of good food and wine and openly covetous of Clémentine, who had to come to the pantry door for a rousing ovation. All our guests begged for the *poulet Cintra* recipe. Major Whipple began to speak soldier French in spite of his wife's warning glances. Mrs. Shrewsbury shed her dignity and developed a case of the giggles. We ended up by singing French nursery rhymes. *"Frère Jacques"* was rendered sonorously in a rich roundelay. Then we did *"Sur le pont d'Avignon"* with elaborate bows and curtsies. Finally we sang *"Savez-vous planter les choux,"* and when Mrs. Whipple solemnly planted cabbages in the rug with her nose, I felt that our future was assured. The evening was an undoubted triumph. Ah yes, the Becks made the Cotillion. The following Friday night my good wife waltzed serenely with Major Whipple and, as the evening waxed warmer, I shagged ceremoniously with Mrs. Shrewsbury.

The menu for that memorable dinner has been carefully preserved. It marks a milestone of some sort in the Becks' culinary pilgrimage, so perhaps I may be excused for inscribing it here:

Les Huîtres au Naturel
Petite Marmite
Coquilles Saint-Jacques en Brochette
Poulet Cintra
Petits Pois à la Française
Salade de Laitue
Fromage
Fruits Rafraîchis
Café
Chablis Vaudésir 1929
Château Pape-Clément 1928
Musigny 1934
Champagne Krug 1926
Grande Fine Champagne de Luze 1898

Those wines are not easy to find now, but aside from that, the dinner can be achieved easily here at home. And as for *poulet Cintra*, here is the recipe. I hope it brings you as much pleasure and adventure as it brought to the Becks.

Poulet Cintra

Unit recipe for four: Cut a tender chicken into 8 pieces. Brown the pieces on all sides in hot butter, along with a whole shallot and a whole clove of garlic, both peeled. Add a half cup of light

Cintra port, or some port of comparable quality, a half cup of dry white wine, a liqueur glass of Cognac, and a liqueur glass of good cherry brandy. When this boils, light with a match and shake the pan until the flame dies. Allow the sauce to simmer down gently to about half, by which time the chicken should be cooked. Remove the pieces of chicken and arrange them graciously on a serving platter.

Finish your sauce with a good cupful of heavy cream and 2 egg yolks whisked together. Cook until it thickens, stirring briskly and taking care not to boil. Strain, pour over the chicken, and serve immediately.

Note: Mrs. Beck has made these observations: The method of cooking proves to be a *sauté* and the chicken, from the beginning of browning to its removal to the platter, will cook perhaps 30 to 35 minutes. The pieces are turned once or twice. The pieces of white meat are best removed 5 to 7 minutes before the others. These are things Clémentine's *carnets* do not always tell us!

ITH THE PASSING MONTHS CLÉMENTINE BE-
came thoroughly initiated into the mysteries of this thing known as the
American way of life. The initiation was supervised by various members
of the Beck family, each of whom squeezed the maximum of enjoyment
out of each revelation. Showing America to the wide-eyed Clémentine
became a favorite pastime. Little Phinney, now eleven, enjoyed it the
most and achieved the greatest triumph when he took Clémentine to
Revere Beach on a summer Sunday afternoon. He persuaded her to ride
in the front seat of the roller coaster. He manipulated a mysterious machine
until, by some strange magic, it produced a pencil with CLEMENTINE BOU-
CHARD stamped on it in gold. He lured her into a gaudy place called the
Temple of Terror and into an automatic photo booth where they took
their own tintypes. With a certain sadistic joy he prevailed upon the
reluctant Clémentine to try that sorry saltwater specialty known as a "chop
suey sandwich." But that was all. When he proposed pink popcorn balls
she would have none of them.

Diane, in turn, took her to Boston and introduced her to the big
city department store, the perpetual adventure of Filene's Basement, and
the quaint business of a drugstore fountain lunch. Mrs. Beck saw that
Clémentine was welcomed into the congregation of St. Joseph's Chapel,
the first time, incidentally, that she had ever been in a wooden church.
Such things don't exist in France. For my part, I introduced her to the
routine of the local savings bank, where she learned to her astonishment
that she could open an account with only a dollar and without a *carnet de
naissance, certificat de domicile,* or anything to prove that her father had
done his military service.

We parceled out these revelations sparingly, for there weren't too
many of them, and the day was sure to come when Clémentine would
lose that astonished look and would accept all this as a matter of course.
We still held in reserve such typical American exhibitions as ice hockey

and the rodeo, but the spectacle that, early on, whetted our anticipation above all others was the Self-service Push-your-own-double-decker-baby-carriage Super-Market. This unique facet in the jewel of American living was as unknown to the Beck children as to Clémentine. To obtain the maximum effect, the whole family would have to take part in the pilgrimage. Our enthusiasm must seem puerile to some readers, to whom such a market is a commonplace, but in the eyes of the Becks a supermarket meant mystery and high adventure. We have gone to market *en famille* with Clémentine many times, but never so exultantly as on this chosen Saturday afternoon when we parked in the market's private lot, received a ticket from the attendant, and looked up to see it in all its chromium and apricot splendor — the SUPER-MARKET!

There could be no more decisive break with the Old World than this. My mind shot back to one of the unassuming *épiceries* in Senlis, a low stone building next to the café at the crossroads. Everything had been serene and atmospheric at this corner — until May 1940. Monsieur Lebec, the proprietor, could give you the very best wine vinegar or dried prunes or tapioca if you asked for them. But he didn't have fresh vegetables (those were sold by the *marchand de légumes*), nor sausage (you found that in the *charcuterie*), nor bread (you go *chez le boulanger* for that), nor eggs, cheese, and butter (they are in the shop of the *marchand de beurre*), nor cakes and candies (the *pâtisserie* has them). If you were to ask Monsieur Lebec for paper towels, soap flakes, or clothesline he would stare at you in blank amazement and tell you to go to the *marchand de couleurs*. We had always taken this shop-to-shop marketing for granted. Yet here before us was a store where such odd requests could be satisfied in an instant and where you could obtain a gallon of pickled limes, a box of bird gravel, or a hundred clothespins without even asking for them — just by picking them up and putting them in your perambulator. Yes indeed, this would be an eye-opener for Clémentine and for the excited little Phinney, jabbering French at her side!

The door of the supermarket was mysteriously opened for us by the electric eye, a contrivance that fascinated Phinney. He passed back and forth through the obedient doors, radiant in his discovery. Clémentine was impressed, but puzzled. Inside, the vast hall was tinted in pale pastel shades and bathed in pink fluorescent light. The mellifluous voice of Bing Crosby filled the air, accompanied by the hiss of a phonograph needle. He was singing softly of love in bloom. Clémentine liked that. We passed through the turnstiles and took possession of our double-decker baby carriages, a novelty that sent Diane and the little Burgundian into a spasm of giggles. Phinney took up the idea of being an ambulant shopper with gusto and abandon. A wild glint shone in his eyes. Here was a new game.

Everything looked strange and wonderful to him. Imagine helping yourself to five pounds of marshmallows!

Diane, the purist, appeared to be half hilarious, half appalled at the sight of honeycomb tripe in jars, fudge ripple ice cream in cartons, and shaggy coconut cakes in cellophane. Repeatedly she launched prep-school-girl noises of disgust — groans, squeals, and grunts. Clémentine's attitude was that of a half-puzzled, half-amused visitor to the zoo. She was obviously enjoying this glimpse of a strange new land, but what she saw either mystified or troubled her.

It is hard to recall who asked the most questions. What was Bab-O, little Phinney wanted to know? And Karo, Thrivo, Crisco, Bosco, Brillo, Marvo, Rinso, Flako? Why did they all end in "o"? The gallon jugs were too much for Diane. Who would want a gallon of mayonnaise or dill pickles or olives, or mustard, peanut butter, catsup, or piccalilli? Clémentine's questions were thoughtful. Would *madame* tell her why there was so much grape juice for sale, but no red wine? *Madame* tried to explain, and incidentally pointed out the battery of other juices in cans — from apples, prunes, tomatoes, oranges, carrots, pineapple. Yes, there was even clam juice, even *jus de choucroute*. Clémentine gulped, and smiled bravely. When we came to the flour department her mood became radiant. Ah, to be able to buy flour in big, colorful, twenty-four-pound sacks! And to buy cake flour, poetically named after swans or snow or thistledown! A package of Softaswansheen pastry flour became the first item in her perambulator. But she paused perplexed at the next counter. Here were the "mixes."

"Just add water and mix, ladies. No fuss, no bother, no wasted time. Just mix — and pop our ready gingerbread in the oven. Your husband and kiddies will love it!"

The voice belonged to an immaculate, rather cold young woman with flawless make-up and eyebrows that enthralled Diane. In front of her was a small electric oven, which she obligingly opened, presenting each of us with a miniature minute-mix muffin topped off with apple butter. We munched appreciatively while she pointed out the ramifications of the mix marvel, which is such a boon to the hurried housewife and which makes hubby so happy. "Just add water and mix — and you have corn muffins, pancakes, waffles, fruit cake, biscuits at will. No fuss or bother! Or pie! Just try our ready-mix piecrust. Fill it with delicious instant lemon pie filling, which comes in this little box . . ." But the Becks had slunk out of hearing, a faint nausea written on their features.

The Andrews Sisters were doing a job on the Hut-Sut song as we tripped past the jiffy-jell and junket department and into the canned meat sector, where Phinney was translating labels for our mystified *cuisinière*.

"*Tiens, Clémentine!* Lamb stew. *Ça veut dire ragoût de mouton en boîte. C'est drôle. Regardez les pieds de cochon! Et ça, alors? Mais, c'est du chien dedans!"*

They had paused before a pyramid of cans, each labeled with a handsome collie's head. For a few fleeting moments, until we cleared the matter up, both of them thought, aghast, that they were looking at canned dog. Clémentine had been used to the customary canned peas and sardines in France, but she was unprepared for the diversity of the canner's subtle art in America. The cascades of tinned beans, soups, vegetables, and fruits that towered above her were alarming. Why, *madame*, would they want to put potato salad in cans, or French fried onions, or walnut meats? *Madame* didn't have the answer, but she assured Clémentine that Americans didn't really live out of cans entirely. They also live out of cellophane — witness a broad area of cellophane-covered cakes and cookies, witness the fresh spinach encased in this transparent wrapper, or the "veg-mix" of raw carrots, peas, and beans. These impressed her, but she was more fascinated by the many-colored dried beans, peas, and lentils that came thus protected.

The suave voice of the store announcer began to emerge from the loudspeakers. "Hurry, boys and girls, this is your very last chance to get Bob Strongheart's own spy detector! Only one box top from crisp, delicious Smirkyoats and ten cents and this great secret weapon is yours. Step to the back of the store, boys and girls, and meet Bob Strongheart's own secret agent!" Little Phinney's eyes opened wide. He pried a dime out of my pocket and was off at a gallop. Diane disappeared, too — in the direction of the candy counter, where we found her gazing curiously at strange confections she had never known in France — jelly beans, gum drops, peanut brittle. I searched for the cheese stand, and Mrs. Beck aimed for the coffee grinders. Clémentine was suddenly left very much alone. It was some time before we found her again. She was hemmed in by gaudy-labeled powdered soaps on one side and by breakfast foods on the other, and she appeared dazed. Chipso and Oxydol and Super-Suds shouted to her on the left, offering her free clothespins and wash rags. Krumbles, Crackles, and Krispies screeched at her on the right, promising her secret decoder badges and comics. Clémentine was befuddled. She gazed uncomprehendingly at cans of floor wax, fly spray, and liquid fertilizer. There was a homesick look in her eyes. My wife decided that it was time to go home.

As our perambulators were pushed through the shuttle and the cash registers began to sputter, I couldn't help contrasting the selections made by Phinney and Clémentine. The young man's basket expressed his prodigal mood perfectly. He had fifteen inches of fig bars in cellophane, a quart of strawberry pop, a jar of pickles, and, of course, a triumphant

box of Smirkyoats, complete with spy detector. And what did Clémentine emerge with? Precisely the same articles she would have brought home from the Rue St. Hilaire. Her basket held flour, milk, butter, Parmesan cheese, sliced ham, lettuce, peppercorns, and a package of dried green peas. The impact of Super-Market upon the little Burgundian cook had been a resounding one (she still had that dazed look), but it was not enough to alter her charted culinary course. One look at that basket and I knew that the Becks were still going to enjoy French food at home.

A true *Cordon Bleu* is only temporarily stunned by the vision of ready-mixes and Strawberry Fluff. Clémentine proved this conclusively when we had driven back to the gambrel-roofed house on the hillside and unloaded the groceries on her kitchen table. She was surrounded once again by her familiar sauce whisks and peppermills and copper casseroles. She began to sing "*Sous les ponts de Paris,*" and we could hear her whipping up a batter that didn't sound ready-mixed. That meant she would be making *crêpes*, Softaswansheen *crêpes*. Our anticipation mounted, for Clémentine can do exotic things with French pancakes. For dinner that night the Becks feasted on *crêpes Parysis*, one of the most unctuous and succulent dishes we have ever encountered. From super-American Super-Market, Clémentine had extracted one of the Frenchest dishes imaginable. Respected reader, we entreat you to do likewise. Here, in a very few words, is the recipe:

Crêpes Parysis

On very thin unsweetened French pancakes spread a thin slice of cooked ham. Sprinkle with grated Parmesan cheese and cover

99

with a *béchamel* sauce. Roll up the pancakes, place in a shallow baking dish, dot with butter, and place in the oven. Serve very hot. Allow 2 or 3 *crêpes* per person and follow with a green salad.

Upon reflection, it is obvious these instructions are not entirely adequate. The making of *crêpes* and *béchamel* will be found on page 214. The rolled *crêpes*, freshly made and their sauce hot, go into the oven (at about 350°) immediately, once dotted with butter, for 6 to 8 minutes. If prepared ahead, before baking a last-minute covering *au gratin* of a little more *béchamel* and Parmesan is advised. They will be bubbling and ready in about 15 minutes.

ETAILS OF THE EARLY GASTRONOMIC ADVEN-
tures of the Beck family in America might have become dim and half
forgotten in this chronicler's mind, were it not for a few infallible re-
minders on the kitchen bookshelf. From the day we moved into this
removed Massachusetts town, Clémentine has kept an invaluable set of
books. Not mere soulless ledgers, but a daily menu book, an ever-thickening
volume of recipes, and an account of the ingredients, that is a model of
exactitude, if not of English phraseology. Upon our arrival we bought
her a quartet of looseleaf notebooks from Mr. Woolworth's *Cinq et Dix*,
an institution the thrifty Clémentine admires greatly. These supplemented
the *carnets* that she had brought over from France. Fortunately for us,
Clémentine's zeal, both as a cook and a scribe, is unflagging. The story of
our new gustatory life in America has swollen to nine notebooks, all
penned in the neat handwriting Clémentine learned at the convent in
Beaune. But the *pièce de résistance* of her library, beyond any doubt, is her
French scrapbook, a bulky, half-filled tome containing an utterly fascinating hodgepodge of culinary data. Most of it comes from French books
and magazines, but the more recent pages glitter with color from the
advertising pages of American women's journals. Clémentine is a push-
over for toothsome color photographs of cakes and fancy salads.

It was my rare privilege to thumb through this library, including
the hilarious scrapbook, at will. More than once I have felt like a crass
interloper, especially in those pages where Clémentine becomes absent-
minded and uses the menu book as a diary, or as a phonetic spelling book.
(Her struggle to master the pronunciation of Quaker Oats, spoken in
France as *Quackairre Wats*, is an example. In the menu book she has penciled
it: *Coü ai kèrre Ootz*.) These accumulated data, dull in some spots but in
others rich in reminiscences of our first winter in New England, sparkle
with a few highlights I cannot resist sharing with you. Clémentine's scrap-

102

SUMMER SHADOWS, MARBLEHEAD

book contains an exultant recipe for plum cake, for instance, that is too savory to remain in hiding. She blushed when she saw me translating it.

"*Mais, Monsieur,*" she protested, "that isn't a serious recipe! It is written by a person who ignores *la cuisine,* but I found it so *drôle* that I had to cut it out." I assured her that many another kitchen executive will find it droll. It is, as the expression goes, "very French." Little Phinney has no truck with that kind of literary criticism. He just thinks it's a howl.

THE DISTRACTED CUISINIER
(A One-Act Recipe)

On the kitchen table are visible: a large mixing bowl, some egg shells, a partially spilled package of flour, a bottle of red wine, and a glass, a salt cellar, a peppermill, some onions and mushrooms. As the curtain rises, Bastide, the bibulous butler, is standing before the kitchen table and seems to be immersed in the preparation of a batter. Beside him is an open cookbook, which he consults frequently.

MONSIEUR PIC (the master of the house, entering the kitchen): *Eh bien,* Bastide — what have you been doing here, puttering around the kitchen for an hour or more?

BASTIDE (joyously): Ah, Monsieur Pic, I was about to prepare a little surprise for you. You see, I'm making a *caque* . . .

MONSIEUR PIC (surprised): A *caque?* What can that be, a *caque?*

BASTIDE (in an explanatory tone): *Eh bien!* It's a kind of English *gâteau* with *plumes.* A cake with feathers! Oh, these English!

MONSIEUR PIC: An English *gâteau* with feathers?

BASTIDE: Look for yourself, Monsieur Pic: it's written in the cookbook . . .

MONSIEUR PIC (reading): Ah good! A cake . . . a plum cake. One does not say *caque,* Bastide; one says a cake. (Bastide absentmindedly turns a page in his cookbook.)

BASTIDE: When it's written *caque* you are supposed to say *quèque!* Ah, these English!

MONSIEUR PIC: But I didn't realize that you had a talent as a cook, my good Bastide.

BASTIDE (very proudly): Monsieur Pic, you should know that in my family we have been cooks from father to son since the Middle Ages!

MONSIEUR PIC: *Et alors,* this plum cake, how is it advancing?

BASTIDE (urgently): Just taste the beginning of this batter, Monsieur Pic.

103

Only ten minutes have I had my hands in it, and taste it already! Taste it, taste . . .

MONSIEUR PIC: No, no . . . I thank you, Bastide, not now. What is it composed of, your batter?

BASTIDE (counting on his fingers): *Eh bien!* I have in there one hundred and seventy-five grams of powdered sugar, one hundred and seventy-five grams of lukewarm butter, one hundred and seventy-five grams of lemon juice, four entire eggs, three hundred grams of flour, one hundred and seventy-five grams of Corinthe raisins, a little orange peel, and a pair of cufflinks . . .

MONSIEUR PIC: And a pair of cufflinks?

BASTIDE: That is to say, they weren't mentioned in the cookbook; but they fell in and I haven't been able to recover them.

MONSIEUR PIC: *C'est charmant!*

BASTIDE: And if you will permit me, I am going to continue with my cake, Monsieur Pic. Let's see . . . (reading) at the end of ten minutes add a good glass of red wine. There, that's an excellent idea —a good glass of red wine. (He pours the wine into his mixing bowl.) *Voilà!* What if I put in two?

MONSIEUR PIC: *Mais non!* When it's written one glass of red wine, you must put one, not two. (During this time the convivial Bastide fills a second glass of red wine.)

BASTIDE: *Eh bien*, I'll drink the second one myself. (He downs it.) It comes down to the same thing. And now what do they say? (reading) Add now a quarter of a pound of salt pork cut in squares . . . (laughing) Salt pork in a *gâteau! Ah, ces Anglais!* (He puts salt pork in his mixing bowl.)

MONSIEUR PIC: It is curious, this recipe—a plum cake with salt pork. Perhaps that wouldn't be so bad.

BASTIDE: Wait, wait, that isn't all. (He reads.) Add a little salt, some pepper, and a dozen little onions. (He adds all this to the mixing bowl.)

MONSIEUR PIC: But this isn't a cake, it's a complete meal!

BASTIDE: Wait, wait . . . (reading) Add now a quarter of a pound of mushrooms . . .

MONSIEUR PIC: A quarter of a pound of mushrooms!

BASTIDE (putting in the mushrooms): I'm adding them. A quarter of a pound of mushrooms . . . Ah, these English! And a glass of rabbit's blood . . .

MONSIEUR PIC (with surprise): A glass of rabbit's blood! But your recipe is completely crazy!

BASTIDE: But, Monsieur Pic, it's written in the book! Look for your-self . . . (Bastide looks very closely at the book. He perceives that he has turned two pages at once.)

BASTIDE: Oh! *Catastrophe!* I have turned two pages of the book at the same time! On one side of the page I began with the recipe for a plum cake and on the other side I have continued with the recipe for a *gibelotte* of rabbit!

CURTAIN

Clémentine's book of menus contains no character as theatrical as Bastide, but its pages recall many of the epicurean high spots of those snowy months. For example there was the dinner given in honor of that classic personage, the fat bachelor desperately trying to get thin. We invited him and that nice college girl (who was also worrying about her figure) to a dinner contrived expressly for their sad predicament and assured them they could eat just as much as they wanted without gaining an ounce. With almost pathetic eagerness the half-famished pair followed our advice and polished off the dinner with joy and abandon, down to the last drop of black coffee. I'm not sure that we were fair to make them such a promise, especially since they came back for seconds, but at least we made an attempt in the right direction. Here is the menu. Aside from the wines, were we deceitful hosts?

> *Amontillado Sherry*
> Consommé Madrilène
> Grilled Entrecôte of Beef
> Epinards en Branches
> *Richebourg 1934*
> Imported White Asparagus — Sauce Vinaigrette
> Fruits Rafraîchis
> Café Noir

105

This menu serves as a reminder that the least fattening food is far from the least expensive. *La gourmandise* carries certain penalties, including the high cost of getting thin. By contrast, it is consoling to observe that many of the most nourishing dishes are the cheapest. Rice, potatoes, spaghetti, dried peas, beans, lentils — all of these foods, blacklisted for the martyrs on a diet, can be prepared cheaply and deliciously. The man with the lower income can nourish his family well for less, proving that there is justice in the gastronomic law.

Another page in the menu book recalls the visit of our fastidious acquaintance Monsieur de Coudray, a true *fine fourchette* whose wool business brought him to Boston once a year. In the tradition of the authentic traveling gourmet, he was interested first of all in tasting the *spécialités du pays*. Clémentine understood this point of view perfectly and spent days with Madame Beck in planning the following menu of American dishes that are either unknown or exceedingly rare in Europe. Monsieur de Coudray was visibly impressed, especially with the soft-shelled crabs. When he toasted Clémentine as our *cuisinière internationale* at the end of the dinner, she was rapturous. Here is the menu, proving that the Americanization of Clémentine had made impressive strides:

Littleneck Clams
Soft-Shelled Crabs Meunière
Lake Elvira
Baked Smithfield Ham
Southern Batterbread
Fresh Lima Beans au Beurre
Zinfandel
Grapefruit and Alligator Pear Salad
Apple Pan Dowdy
Vermont Cheese
Coffee

Menus are useful, but the rarest nuggets in Clémentine's notebooks are without question her recipes, though they are not always explicit! Thumbing through them, I recently spent a reminiscent half hour reading about her various ham dishes. Repeated mention of *jambon* recalls vividly a major gastronomic adventure for us all. For the first time we enjoyed the luxury, banal to Americans but almost unattainable to Europeans, of cooking a whole ham entirely for ourselves. Many things had impressed Clémentine in this American town, but nothing quite so much as the prodigal quantity of hams hanging in Mr. Wilcox's butcher shop. The idea that we could buy such a treasure, and at a reasonable price, flabbergasted and fascinated us all. Americans might be deprived of truffles and fresh *foie gras au naturel*, but this made up for it!

In France ham was a precious thing from Prague or Westphalia, to be bought in thin slices at fat prices. The Archbishop of York received scant reverence from Frenchmen compared to the *jambon d'York*. Ham was a jewel of the *charcutier*'s art, to be served in the ritualistic setting of puréed spinach and *sauce madère*. One slice per guest, perhaps two, was allotted to accompany a good *cervelas* sausage on sauerkraut to make *choucroute garni*. Above all, it was a luxury, to be used sparingly and with the greatest possible effect. The idea of possessing a *whole* ham was unthinkable. Clémentine had seen plenty of shimmering glazed hams in the

shops of Paris, surrounded by glittering squares of aspic and bejeweled with truffles, but these were virtually museum pieces. She told us that in her girlhood she heard that *Madame la Comtesse*, who lived in the château in her native town, used to serve whole *jambon de Bayonne* cooked in Chablis for her grandest dinners, but Clémentine had never actually seen this miracle.

You can appreciate, therefore, the awe with which Clémentine viewed our first magnificent ham when little Phinney proudly placed it on the kitchen table. He and I had sought it out in Faneuil Hall Market, and it was a good one. She was mightily impressed. But, for the first time, her confidence seemed to be shaken. How to cook this treasure? Her neatly penned *carnets* held no such secrets. Phinney didn't help matters much when, with a fiendish look in his eye, he unearthed a superb two-page color advertisement showing a baked ham with fried pineapple and a side dish of sweet potato crowned with toasted marshmallows. Here was the place for Mrs. Beck to step in, and she did so with sureness and authority. Ignoring Escoffier and *Ali-Bab*, she turned to a trusted American cookbook, found a famous and familiar recipe for baked ham, and took complete charge, with Clémentine an impressed onlooker. The resultant masterpiece, served for Sunday dinner with a buttered purée of fresh spinach and a good Meursault, left the Beck family enraptured and proud of American cooking. It was Mrs. Beck's day, and Clémentine joined in the applause. Her day would come later.

Clémentine's acquaintanceship with a whole baked ham may have been meager, but her artistry blossomed in full when it came to making symphonic dishes with the ham that remained. Her *carnets* had plenty of ideas for this. She gave us ham soufflés and omelettes, of course, usually adding a few pimientos and a spot of cayenne to give them more character. In France, I recall, she often added sautéed *morilles* and sprinkled the dome of an omelette or soufflé with finely chopped truffles. She gave us a gorgeous, flaky *pâté en croûte*, filled with morsels of ham the size of hazelnuts, mixed with mushrooms, aromatic sausage meat, a smattering of truffle and pistachio, and a flavoring of old Madeira. She rolled up the ham in French pancakes, used it as a carpet for a handsome chicken dish, made it into a sublimated ham sandwich, and finally, when there wasn't much left to slice, she ground it up very fine and made a French classic, *mousse de jambon*. And the ham bone, needless to say, was used in making pea soup.

Of course, there are innumerable dishes made from cooked ham. Clémentine's recipes may or may not add to the documentation you have on the subject. But because they are purely French, and simple, and extremely palatable, they are worth recording. Here are four of them, which the Becks urge you to try. The first is really a chicken dish, but ham plays its part:

Poulet du Cloître

(OR THE CLOISTERED BIRD)

Cut a young chicken to serve four into 8 pieces and brown them in butter in a casserole. When the pieces are golden, add salt, pepper, and a few pinches of allspice. Cover tightly and braise over a very slow fire for 45 minutes, or until tender. Now add a half pint of cream and a half pound of mushrooms, which have been previously trimmed, sliced, and sautéed in butter. Stir gently and allow to cook 15 minutes longer.

Warm some thin slices of cooked ham in butter, then add 2 tablespoons of Madeira (it can be sherry). Remove the ham and pour the remaining liquid into the casserole. Beat up 2 egg yolks in a bowl with some of the sauce from the casserole.

Place the slices of ham on your serving platter, and then place the pieces of chicken on these. In the casserole, finish the thickening of your sauce with the egg yolks, stirring continuously, and pour over the chicken. Serve immediately, very hot.

Croque Monsieur

This is the sublimated ham sandwich:

Trim the crusts from thin slices of white bread. Mix grated Swiss cheese with just enough heavy cream to make a paste and spread a generous layer of it on each piece of bread. Put the slices together into sandwiches, with a thin slice of ham in between. Dip the sandwiches in beaten egg and sauté them in hot butter until they are crisp and golden on each side.

In advance, have ready a cream sauce made with 1 tablespoon of butter, melted and blended with 1 teaspoon of flour, 1 cup of cream, stirred in gradually, 2 tablespoons of grated Swiss cheese, and salt and pepper. Blend the cream sauce well, let it thicken slightly, and serve it over the *croque monsieur*. This is enough sauce for 4 sandwiches.

Jambon à la Crème

Mrs. Beck devised this very pleasant means of using leftover ham:

For four people: Heat four ¼-inch-thick slices of cooked ham in ¼ cup of white wine and 1 tablespoon of butter (or melted ham fat) until the wine has almost evaporated. In a separate skillet, sauté 8 good-size mushrooms, sliced, in 1 tablespoon of butter for 5 minutes.

Measure out 1 cup of cream. Blend ½ teaspoon of potato starch with 1 tablespoon of the cream until smooth. Stir in the rest of the cream, 1 teaspoon of tomato paste, 2 teaspoons of port, a few drops of brandy, pepper, and salt sparingly to taste. Add this sauce to the mushrooms, heat, and simmer together for about 2 minutes. Put the ham on a hot platter or individual plates, spoon the rose-colored sauce over it, and serve with rice.

Mousse de Jambon

Finally, when your slices of ham grow so small that they approach the scrap stage, here is Clémentine's way of rescuing them:

To serve six or more: Put enough cooked ham through the finest blade of a meat grinder to make 3½ cups. Grind the ham several times if necessary, to give it a very fine, smooth consistency.

(To grind in a food processor, if you are using pieces of ham larger than mere scraps, cut them into approximately even ½-inch dice.)

Dissolve 1 envelope of gelatin in ¼ cup of chicken stock. Heat another 1¼ cups of stock in a saucepan and stir the gelatin mixture into it. Beat 2 egg yolks lightly in a bowl and gradually stir in the warm stock. Return the mixture to the saucepan, reheat it, stirring constantly, until it just begins to thicken, then set it aside to cool.

Whip ½ cup of cream and beat 2 egg whites stiff. Mix together the ground ham, the thickened chicken stock, and the whipped cream. Stir in ¼ cup of port and then fold in the beaten egg whites. Pour the mousse into a mold and chill it for at least 3 hours. Turn it out onto a platter just before serving and decorate it with watercress and thinly sliced, unpeeled cucumber.

Needless to say, the Becks have never enjoyed a ham and its aftermaths quite so much as this one.

F CLÉMENTINE HAD PROVEN THAT A NEW England town could supply the fundamentals for a transplanted *cuisine française*, she also realized that there were gastronomic gaps to be filled before her genius could return to its full radiance. The local Yankee tradesmen were more than cooperative, once their reserve had been melted by her Burgundian smile, but she would often come back from a shopping tour almost empty handed, perplexity and frustration written on her Gallic features. Why didn't the grocer carry chicory, or at least coffee roasted to a respectable black? Why was it so hard to find leeks, the touchstone of her best soups? Why didn't Mr. Wilcox have an occasional rabbit, goose, pheasant, or guinea hen in season? Clémentine accepted Madame Beck's explanation of these essential shortages with sympathy, but no amount of elucidation could clear up the most baffling mystery of all— why was there no veal? Weeks would go by and the nearest approach to veal in her kitchen would be the picture of the calf's head on the pantry box of gelatin. Why would an intelligent butcher carry a counterful of corned beef and salt pork and not one single little *côtelette de veau*? What good is a *boeuf à la mode* without a calf's foot? Doesn't a steer have its period of adolescence in America?

Clémentine's questions came thick and fast, and Mrs. Beck did not have all the answers. She tried, a little weakly, to explain that our stock breeders have concentrated on beef, pork, and lamb, but that if they really put their minds to it they could produce milk-fed veal as tender and delicious as the best in Europe. Veal was not as rare in other parts of this country as it was in Mr. Wilcox's sawdust-sprinkled sanctum, we assured her, and promised to try to solve the problem. Cletus Wilcox grew frigid when we asked him point-blank about it, adopting an indifference toward veal and toward us that was Olympian in its hauteur, and remarked that he stocked veal only when his cherished customer, Mrs. Amory Whipple, in the big white house up on the square, wanted sweetbreads or a leg of

SKYSCRAPERS OF MENTON

veal. "The rest of my customers are beef eaters, and I'm proud of it," announced Mr. Wilcox, belligerently, and that was that.

But veal was too important to the gastronomic existence of the Becks to be abandoned without a struggle. We thought longingly of the delicate, juicy little *rôti de veau*, surrounded by onions, peas, mushrooms, and green olives, that Clémentine used to prepare in an iron *cocotte* in her French kitchen. We remembered her suave and colorful *veau Marengo* and the *foie de veau poêlé à la bourgeoise*, which used to enchant our guests, and the longing for tender young veal grew deeper and more gnawing. (We conveniently overlooked the maddening regularity with which bland, beige veal had been served to us in the Pension Bellevue and the Albergo Santa Caterina a few years back. What would a European *pension* do without *noix de veau?*) We haven't yet been able to understand veal's lack of popularity in America. Whatever the reason, our national well-being has not been improved by making veal play second fiddle. To a French housewife, veal is a jewel of many facets. Her faithful *Tante Marie* cookbook lists dozens of ramifications: *escalopes, fricandeau, blanquette, fricassée, côtes, paupiettes,* and so forth. Then there are the spare parts, the sweetbreads, liver, kidneys, tripe, brains, and tongue — all urgently recommended by both gourmets and the thrifty housewives. Together they offer a full orchestra to a skillful cook for the performance of symphonies of veal!

Veal makes us think back to the winter long ago that we all spent in a rococo villa in Menton, on the Riviera. During those peaceful days in that frontier town, Clémentine did her shopping in a crescent-shaped string of food stores facing the old fishing port. Towering up behind these aromatic shops were the shabby skyscrapers of the ancient town, decked with banners of multicolored laundry, as picturesque a heap of Latin masonry as you could hope to find in all Europe. Somewhere in that crescent of shops was the *boucherie* of Monsieur Martignetti, and we'll never forget it. Here were displayed the most memorable calves' heads we had ever seen. The doorway of the shop was always flanked by two of them, somnolent, superbly sculptural, pale bluish-white in color. These sentinels gave the place a certain funereal air, which, frankly, disturbed the Becks a little, except for little Phinney, who was awestruck and intensely inquisitive about this amazing phenomenon. Nor will we soon forget the first time Clémentine brought a whole, white calf's head home and proudly displayed it to us in the kitchen. Even she had a little trouble converting us to *tête de veau à la vinaigrette*, but little Phinney was a rabid, whole-hearted disciple from the start. Mrs. Beck and I went about it rather gingerly, but soon came to relish the jiggly parts and the ears, which Burgundians can prepare in numerous ingenious ways. We never

113

could quite get around to eating the eye. Diane screeched with anguish and looked the other way whenever the dish appeared. She was thirteen before she was finally, but then totally, won over.

But, like many an acquired taste, *tête de veau* became the dish we longed for most intensely once we were settled in this veal-less New England town. It was the lure of *tête de veau* that sent us reconnoitering in the neighboring city, intent on finding a Yankee equivalent of Monsieur Martignetti's *quai*-side butcher shop in Menton. Our search ended in a blaze of glory when we discovered Mr. Ettore d'Angostino and his Latin

food shop near the textile mill. The gastronomic gap in our New England resources was filled, once and for all, when we became his favored customers.

For all its Colonial wooden architecture, the d'Angostino shop is the essence of Latin Europe, once you are inside the door. First of all, it has the characteristic smell, that pungent and indescribable mélange of olives, pickles, cheese, herbs, garlic, and sausage. Fat clusters of smoked provolone cheese, straight from Wisconsin, dangle from the ceiling, along with dried peppers, long, lean hams, and well-laced Chicago salami, done up in red, white, and green paper. The shelves bulge with gallon tins of oil, varying in price depending upon whether it was pressed from olives, peanuts, corn, or cottonseed. There are tubs of olives, both green and black, to tempt the filching fingers of the neighborhood kids; there are ample jars of green tomatoes in brine, mixed pickles, and anchovies, and sunbursts of silvery salted herring in wooden tubs. But there are American touches, too. Spaghetti, and all its farinaceous cousins, are packed in rose-bedecked cardboard boxes with little cellophane windows. Herbs, spices, and dried mushrooms are parceled out in cellophane envelopes glued to a sheet of cardboard. The black-roasted coffee comes in sealed cans, the *mortadella* is "skinless," and the artichoke hearts repose in glass bottles. A picture of Private First Class Joe d'Angostino, U.S. Army, is prominently displayed on the cash register, along with a carefully penned sign: "We don't talk about the war and we're 100% for the U.S.A." Papa d'Angostino is a torrid baseball fan and was in a state of suspended ecstasy for almost two months during Joe DiMaggio's record batting streak. There is no question about the Americanism of the d'Angostinos. To prove it conclusively, Mama, who must weigh about two hundred and forty, is now taking a first-aid course.

The Becks warmed up to the d'Angostinos at once. Clémentine was a little more reserved. All her life she had been accustomed to referring to her country's Latin neighbors as *"ces jouers de mandoline,"* but the Americanized d'Angostinos won her over once she saw their American icebox, which was clean, odorless, and a veritable bazaar of veal. There on a hook was our long-sought *tête de veau*, as impassive and sculptural as ever. There on the thick wooden table were small veal roasts cut the European way, cutlets of magnificent thickness, and *escalopes* that had been paddled to almost transparent thinness. A Franco-Italian *rapprochement* was inevitable.

Veal is once again an institution in the Beck household, and while we don't dare spring it on our New England friends, *tête de veau à la vinaigrette* frequently trembles on our plates in all its delicately poised splendor.

Which of the boundless veal recipes in Clémentine's notebooks shall we choose as her *chef d'oeuvre*? After the customary family conference, with Clémentine's complete approval, the Becks have selected a cherished favorite, the extraordinary baked whole calf's liver. The recipe originates with the celebrated Prosper Montagné, gourmet, writer, and restaurateur of rare charm and accomplishment. In unison we entreat you to try:

Foie de Veau Poêlé à la Bourgeoise

Note that when the liver is almost done, in 45 minutes, you need to have ready a *garniture bourgeoise* (see page 203) of carrots and onions.

The whole liver should be from a young calf; the recipe specifies that it should weigh 3 pounds. This is rather small and may not be easy to find. Then, ideally, what you want is a

3-pound center-cut piece from a larger, but not too large, liver cut on the bias so that your piece approximates an oval, not a chopped-off, shape for even cooking.

Three pounds will serve at least eight. Best, however, is to serve fewer and to plan for plenty left over, for liver thus cooked is so delicious cold that it will remind you of a *terrine* of real *foie gras*.

Cut 4 ounces of salt pork into long thin strips and moisten them with a little brandy. Roll the strips in a mixture of minced parsley, freshly ground pepper, and a pinch each of powdered cinnamon and clove. With a larding needle, run the seasoned salt pork through a small whole calf's liver (about 3 pounds). In a covered bowl just big enough to hold it, marinate the liver for 4 hours in 3 tablespoons of olive oil, the juice of ½ lemon, salt, pepper, and a little more cinnamon and clove.

Melt 2 tablespoons of butter in a heavy casserole, add the liver, the marinade left in the bowl, 1 onion and 1 carrot, both cut into small pieces, and a *bouquet garni*. Bake the liver, covered, in a 350° oven for 45 minutes, basting it often with the juices that accumulate in the casserole. Then add a *garniture bourgeoise* and bake it for another 15 minutes. Remove the liver to a hot platter and surround it with the *garniture*.

Add ½ cup of dry white wine to the juices in the casserole, simmer this sauce for 5 minutes, and strain it into a small saucepan. In a small bowl, mix a spoonful of the sauce with 1 beaten egg yolk, slowly stir the egg mixture into the sauce, reheat it, stirring constantly, until it just begins to thicken, and pour it over the liver.

When you carve the liver, make the slices thin, spoon sauce over each serving, and finish each plate with portions of carrots and onions from the *garniture*.

I F, UPON RETURNING FROM FRANCE, THE BECK family had been repatriated to New York City instead of a little Yankee town, this chapter of our gastronomic adventures would be very uneventful. For it deals with cheese and the initial shock we suffered, along with our Burgundian Clémentine, when we first encountered the cheese department of Mr. Eustis Calkins's grocery store. A well-stocked Lexington Avenue emporium would have dazzled us to such an extent that we would have forgotten all about the splendors of the cheese we had left behind us. But the meagerness and mystery of Mr. Calkins's rural cheese counter filled us with perplexity and with nostalgia for the good old days, when a noble slice of Brie had been a commonplace on our French table. Weeks went by before we discovered that a genuine treasury of American cheese awaited us.

The estimable Mr. Calkins was strangely shortsighted on the matter of cheese. He apparently believed that only one type really counted, this being good "store" cheese. He discreetly kept a few such excellent, well-aged Coon cheeses in his icebox for favored customers, but the only articles visible to newcomers, such as the Becks, were the processed cheeses in cardboard boxes, the "spreads" in giddy glass jars, and a few lonely baby "Holland" cheeses, which, when we tasted them, were rubbery and cow-y to a disheartening degree. His stock did contain a respectable Limburger, which went well with beer, crackers, and caraway seed, and a few novelties such as grated "Parmesan" in shaker cans and smoked hickory cheese, which tasted like smoked hickory, all right, but precious little like cheese. The worthy hickory, we decided, was a great leveler, making turkey, oysters, cheese, and salmon all taste exactly alike, and like h—ickory.

Having brushed up on the libel laws, I will skip adroitly any translation of Clémentine's remarks when she first sampled Mr. Calkins's heatproof, handle-proof, time-proof products, especially those sown with

117

chopped pimiento, pineapple, sage, olives, nuts, and processed chives. Her open-faced horror at these gave us a few moments of pure ecstasy. She admitted privately to Mrs. Beck that she knew cheese was sometimes made from strange things, such as the milk from camels, reindeer, buffalo, and even llamas, but why drag in the vegetable kingdom? The French purist versus the restless American innovator! A great gulf separated them.

The Becks fell into the easy and unpardonable error of judging American cheese by what we found in this one rural store, without even tasting the Coon cheese in Mr. Calkins's icebox. We began to recall dreamily the noble, gargantuan pancakes of Brie, the cartwheels of Gruyère, and the silvery mounds of Roquefort that Madame Legendre used to display in her cloistered corner of the *marché* St. Pierre in Senlis. We remembered, with a sigh, the fabulous combination of *coeur à la crème*, *fraises des bois*, and *crème d'Ysigny* — the most voluptuously rich evidence of the talent of Normandy cows ever put before us. We meditated upon the soundness of the old saying "I prefer cheese without dinner to a dinner without cheese." Most of all, we retained the memory of the occasional flawless Camemberts that had found their way into our *salle à manger*.

A really perfect Camembert has always been a rare jewel, even in the peaceful days, and one that few gourmets are lucky enough to find. The Becks were fortunate in France, for we had a friend and business associate who knew how to pick them. Monsieur de Bessières, the head of our Brussels office, never failed to stop at the famous cheese shop on the rue d'Amsterdam in Paris to select a Camembert for us before he came to spend the night in our guest room. Many a cheese was removed from its wooden box for a knowing poke of his thumb before he made a final choice. This gallant gentleman had brought roses to Mrs. Beck on the occasion of his first visit, but a weekend in contact with Clémentine's cuisine had shown him that a Camembert would be considered a far more fragrant flower in the Beck household. And besides, he knew that a bottle of my treasured Grands Echezeaux 1929 would be waiting to accompany it. And how the Belgians love Burgundy! Ah, the good Papa de Bessières! Where is he now? We'll never forget the roguish and only slightly apprehensive look in his eye when he told our dinner guests, including a wide-eyed maiden from Vermont, how a seasoned gourmet avoids conversation at a dinner party in order to pay undivided attention to the food. It is a simple and conventional formula, he explained, and one guaranteed to silence the chatty ladies on either side of the diner, as well as the sweet talkative creature across the way from him. You simply address the lady on your right: "Are you married, Madame?"

"*Oui, monsieur,*" she replies. "For more than five years . . ."

"Do you have any children?"

119

OLD FARMYARD IN THE BRIE COUNTRY

"Yes."

"Ah! And by whom?"

It's brutal, but he is reasonably sure of no further conversation on the right. To his fair neighbor on the left he begins the same way: "Are you married, Madame?"

"*Oui, monsieur.*"

"Do you have any children?"

"No, not yet. . . ."

"Allow me to congratulate you . . . I admire your *savoir-faire.*"

This excommunicates him as a complete boor from the lady on the left, but there remains the inquiring spinster across the table, who will perhaps plague him with banalities. To her he says: "Are you married, Madame?"

"*Non, monsieur.*"

"Ah! And . . . do you have any children?"

From that point on, he has achieved complete tranquillity to enjoy his dinner. At what price is an interesting question . . .

Clémentine liked to prepare Papa de Bessière's Camemberts with consummate care. Along with most Burgundians, she believed that any good Camembert is better without its *croûte*. Painstakingly she would slice and scrape until every trace of the crust was removed. Then she would butter the outside of the cheese very lightly and powder it generously with finely chopped roasted almonds. The result, combined with that robust and seductive Grands Echezeaux from the *domaine* of Romanée-Conti, was little short of fabulous.

Nothing could have been better from the standpoint of sheer *gourmandise*, but our son Phinney much prefers a picturesque adaptation of the same theme, which we call "Clémentine's Oriental Garden." This is one of the whimsies of the irrepressible Paul Reboux. It isn't gastronomic, but it's fun. If you want to make your children into cheese lovers, try this:

Take a Camembert, Brie, or Bel Paese, or some other creamy cheese, and remove its crust. Mix with a little cream cheese and, when you have achieved a good thick paste, arrange it on a plate in a circle or rectangle about three quarters of an inch deep. Make this plateau slightly hilly in spots. Then, with bread crumbs, trace out the design of a formal garden. Plant little groves of trees with sprigs of parsley. Make elms of small celery branches and rocks with half walnut shells. Place a small mirror in the middle to represent a pond and bridge it with a graceful arc of grapefruit rind. Make some red flowers with the skins of radishes and borders of paprika and grated lemon peel. Your lawn can be made of finely chopped chives and watercress. There is no limit to the ingenuity you can show, and it is all edible and harmonious except, of course, the mirror and the walnut shells. If you decide to make this playful dish, remember that it should be concocted at the very last minute before serving and that all the ingredients of the landscape should be thoroughly chilled.

We are ashamed to admit that weeks went by before the fog began to lift and the bright realization dawned upon us that there *is* noble cheese in America, and plenty of it. The first day that our shopping radius lengthened to Faneuil Hall in Boston, we found plenty of evidence that the cheesemakers of America have not been asleep, even if the Becks have. We came home laden with undreamed-of treasures from Wisconsin, a fragrant and subtle cheese from Vermont, and a distinguished slice of Port-du-Salut made by the Trappist monks in Canada. A fine Gallic mist clouded the emotional Clémentine's eyes when we proudly opened our bundles on her kitchen table. Before long we realized that we had overlooked a very good domestic Gruyère, a well-balanced pineapple-shaped cheese from Connecticut, and an excellent "Parmesan" from South America. Bel Paese, we found, was now made in the United States. So was the worthy standby, crème de Gruyère. Among the stalactites hanging from the ceiling of Mr. d'Angostino's Latin grocery, we found superb smoked Wisconsin provolone. And finally, to cap the climax, we were voted into the select circle of customers who knew about Mr. Calkins's superlative Coon cheese. The splendor of it all overwhelmed us.

The result was that Clémentine's cuisine took an immediate upsurge. We began to revel in soufflés, omelettes, and *fondues* perfumed with kirsch. *Fromage de Coon* became a current household expression. Clémentine used this good American product with scintillating success in the countless French recipes that end with the words *gratiner au four et servir très chaud*. We thought of the music-hall verse . . .

Versez sur ma mémoire chère
Quelques larmes de Chambertin
Et sur ma tombe solitaire
Plantez des soles — au gratin . . .

and felt very thankful.

From Clémentine's notebook I have translated a recipe that has brightened our apéritif hour many times. We think, Americanized as we have become, that it's scrumptious. She calls it, more plainly:

Baguettes de Fromage de Coon

Cut well-aged Coon cheese into rectangular sticks about 1½
inches long and ⅜ inch square. (Square or triangular shapes are
good also, if you prefer.) Let the cheese sticks stand in
lukewarm milk for 10 minutes. Then roll them in flour, dip in
beaten egg, and roll in fine bread crumbs. Cook quickly in deep
oil that is hot enough to brown a cube of bread in 30 seconds.
Serve immediately, just as your apéritifs are being poured.

Try this simple recipe, we beg you, and forgive us for being so
hasty and naïve in our appraisal of American cheese!

ALTHOUGH SHE HAD GROWN FOND OF HER NEW England setting, complete with tile bathrooms, mechanical mixer, and a chance to see three different cinemas per week, Clémentine had her moments of nostalgia and intense homesickness. We observed that a faraway look came into her eyes, particularly in the autumn, and it was not difficult to understand. October, the bacchic month, is by far the most exciting time of the year in her native Burgundy, an enchanted moment when the lush hillsides are tinted a burnished gold and when everyone, from school children to nonagenarians, turns to the stimulating business of picking the grapes quickly and sending them to the *pressoirs*. From early childhood Clémentine had joined in the *vendange*, picking the fat bunches of grapes and piling long flat baskets of them into the two-wheeled carts that creaked and jostled on the way to the wine presses.

The *vendange* was a moment of gaiety and triumph, not to mention relief at escaping the curse of a rainy summer and the terrible threat of last-minute hailstorms, and it ended in a bacchanalian fête in the village square. To the *vignerons*, who clinked glasses of their own red Burgundy in the Café du Commerce, it meant that their prosperity was secure for another year. To the younger generation it meant music, dancing, and a feast prepared by the best cooks in the village. Barrels of Yankee apples and high school football rallies were no substitutes for the October *vendange* to Clémentine.

Her native village near Beaune, in the heart of the most famous thirty-mile strip of vineyards in the world, intrigued the Becks enormously. We made it a frequent subject of conversation and learned much about it. Although less famed than its neighboring towns of Pommard, Volnay, and Meursault, its entire existence centered about the pinot grapevine. The mayor of the *commune* was a ruddy gentleman who lived in a château, and who had the immense distinction of owning parcels of Corton, Montrachet, and Clos de Vougeot. Clémentine's face was radiant with pride when she told us that *Monsieur le Maire* was her godfather. Three generations of her family had cared for the vines, and her father had been a *maître de chaix*, supervisor of the cellars of one of the fine growths of the Côte de Beaune.

To Clémentine wine had always been a noble thing. From early childhood she had been taught to respect it. She showed us an old maxim that had come from her primer in the little convent school in her native town. *"Le Raisin a toujours été consacré à Dieu. Raisins blancs et noirs servent à faire le bon vin qui est nécessaire sur les Autels; il réjouit le coeur de l'homme, sert de lait aux vieillards, de nectar aux repas, fait le bon sang, lorsqu'il est pris à propos. Mais il gâte tout quand on en prend trop."*

When we first asked about her childhood home, Clémentine brought forth a faded photograph of the *maison* Bouchard, a picturesque structure built in a round tower, which once had been a part of the medieval town fortifications. The façade had been squared off to resemble any bourgeois stone dwelling, but beyond this point the house developed a plump circular bulge that personified well-fed Burgundy itself. Clémentine eagerly pointed out the features of the house to us. On the ground floor was a wide passageway reserved for her father's carts and casks. Next to this was a narrow hallway, then the *salle à manger*, and then a one-story wing containing the most important room in any Burgundian household, the kitchen.

It was here that *Grand-mère* Bouchard presided. Clémentine didn't hesitate to call her the best cook in Burgundy. Tears welled in her eyes when she described the ancestral *cuisine* and its talented, vigorous old overseer. A towering stone fireplace dominated the room, and across its massive lintel was hung the most beautiful collection of copper casseroles that Clémentine had ever seen. Sunlight poured in the front windows, brightening patches of red tile floor, but the rear of the room was always dim. The patina of generations of cooking smells, smokes, and vapors clung to the walls and the beamed ceiling. In the semiobscurity at the rear of the kitchen was a massive iron cookstove whose slow fire was never allowed to go out. Here the incomparable chemistry of *Grand-mère* Bouchard's cooking took place. Twice weekly the nostrils of the Bouchard family would welcome the divine scent of grandmother's *boeuf en daube*. It was a complex aroma, compounding the bouquet of aristocratic Volnay with the fragrance of thyme, rosemary, and bay leaf and the solid incense of good massive beef. "Chanel has never made a perfume as exquisite," said Clémentine. *Grand-mère* Bouchard took the luxury of fine cooking wine as a matter of course. She could poach her trout in Chablis without feeling extravagant, and her *boeuf bourguignon* could luxuriate in a Pommard, fabulous as that now seems. Clémentine grew very earnest in discussing her grandmother's art. "It was cooking without pretension, *vous*

CLÉMENTINE'S CHILDHOOD HOME

comprenez, madame, but it was nourishing, delectable, and, above all, *soig-née, tellement soignée!*" How much that word *soignée* means!

A few of *Grand-mère* Bouchard's ancient recipes, handed down to her from earlier generations, have found their way into Clémentine's notebooks. Although we can't aspire to cook with Chablis or Pommard, she has prepared many of these classic Burgundian dishes in our American kitchen with shining success, using good California wine. The range of wine recipes in her *carnets* is tremendous, varying from one that timidly specifies a teaspoonful of *xérès* (sherry) to the swashbuckling and su-premely extravagant recipe of Jean de Bonnefon that begins: "Plunge a langouste, a fat and very lively langouste, into two quarts of extra-dry Champagne, which have been heated to the boiling point. . . ."

The Beck family huddle has finally broken up after the selection of three of Clémentine's favorites, which should be new to some expo-nents of wine cookery. The first is:

Poulet Sauté "Bouchard"

(CHICKEN GRAND-MÈRE BOUCHARD)

Cut a handsome, tender chicken to serve four into 8 pieces and season with salt and pepper. In a casserole place a piece of butter the size of an egg. Heat over a brisk fire. When the butter ceases to sing and takes on a fine nutty color, toss in the pieces of chicken. Turn the pieces as they begin to brown, and then place the casserole, covered, in a moderate (350°) oven. Baste the chicken frequently with the butter.

When it is nearly cooked, in about 30 minutes, toss in a few mushrooms. Then, a bit later, remove from the oven and place over low heat on the top of the stove. Add a sherry glass of brandy, which you burn off. Add a wine glass of Madeira and a cup of sweet cream or *crème fraîche*. Allow to simmer for a few moments, remove from the fire, stir in another spoonful of butter, and serve.

The following dish was prepared with a good pinot noir from California:

Rognon de Boeuf au Vin Rouge

Remove the fat, membranes, and hard center core from a beef kidney (which will serve two or three). Rinse the kidney well and cut it into slices about ¾ inch thick.

Melt 2 tablespoons of butter in a saucepan. Brown in this 2 onions, chopped fine. Moisten with 1 cup of red wine. Add salt and pepper and boil vigorously until the volume is reduced by half. Add ¼ pound of mushrooms cut into slices and allow to boil for 2 more minutes.

In an iron skillet place a good spoonful of butter and cook the slices of beef kidney in it for 5 minutes on each side. Do not overcook. Sprinkle with a teaspoon of flour, turn the slices, and pour the wine and mushroom sauce over them. Allow the sauce to come to a boil, add a small glass of brandy, and boil for 3 more minutes. Pour into a hot serving dish and serve with steamed potatoes.

A perennial favorite with the Beck family, easy to do and easier to applaud, has always been:

Bananes Flambées

For six people: Peel 6 ripe bananas and remove the strings. Arrange the bananas close together in a shallow buttered baking dish. Add 2 tablespoons of water to the dish and sprinkle the bananas with lemon juice, dot them with butter, and dust each one with a teaspoon of sugar. Bake them in a 400° oven, basting once or twice and adding a little water if necessary. In 20 minutes, the bananas should be soft and beginning to glaze.

Warm 2 tablespoons of kirsch, brandy, or apple brandy and pour it over the bananas just before bringing the dish, very hot, to the table. Light the liqueur with a match, shake the dish gently until the flame dies, and serve. Cold whipped cream on top is very good.

Clémentine's most fascinating recipe in the bacchant domain, however, is not a dish but a bottle. She taught us the trick when she first came to cook for us in France. In our garden she observed espaliered pear trees, clinging like giant seven-pronged candlesticks to the masonry of the south wall.

"Ah, Monsieur," she exclaimed, "you have a fine installation there for imprisoned fruit, as one does it in Normandy." Imprisoned fruit was a perplexing term, and Clémentine explained further. The trick, she said, consists of getting a very large and perfect specimen of fruit inside a very large bottle and then preserving the fruit in brandy, Calvados, or Armagnac. Many an enterprising French restaurateur has used this contrivance to *épater les clients*, and no Normandy *auberge* with checkered tablecloths can afford to be without one. Neither could the eager Becks, once we learned the secret.

And the secret is simple. You merely force the fruit to *grow* in the bottle. Clémentine knew how, for her father used to do it, to soften the fiery impact of Burgundian *vieux marc*. The flavor of fresh fruit rounded off its savagery, he claimed. Clémentine taught the Becks, and it is with enthusiasm that we pass her father's method on to you, especially to those of you who have a place in the country and a few fruit trees.

Look over your tree carefully in the springtime, when the blossoms are gone and the fruit is just beginning to form. Choose a few choice specimens, each at the end of a branch, and insert the branch gently into the neck of a large bottle, until the fruit is well inside. The next job is to support the bottle so that it stays in place in the tree. This may be done with ropes, if the tree is large enough, or it may be necessary to build up wooden supports to hold it. Our dainty little candlestick fruit trees were criss-crossed with scaffolding during the process. It certainly doesn't beautify your fruit tree for a season, but the result is worth the temporary blemish. Once your pear or apple or peach is comfortably installed inside the bottle and allowed to breathe through the neck, which must always be kept open, it begins to prosper in a spectacular fashion, or else to languish and shrivel up. Both the intensified sunshine that comes into the bottle and the forced heat inside stimulate the fruit to prodigious growth.

It begins to outgrow its brothers on the outside, and finally dwarfs them. A perfectly gargantuan piece of fruit is the result when it is ripe and ready to be disengaged from the stem. Rinse the bottle carefully and fill immediately with good brandy, Armagnac, or apple brandy, and allow to stand for a few weeks. Your fruit becomes beautifully preserved, taking on a deep golden color and lending mystery and flavor to the liquid within. It will stay preserved for years, too, if the level of the brandy is kept high enough to keep the fruit submerged.

Chances of success in this praiseworthy venture seem to be about one in five, but if four of your attempts fail, the fifth will be a miracle, and you can serve your guests sumptuous fruity liqueurs from a bottle of imprisoned fruit for the next decade. A double magnum, a jeroboam, or one of those chestnut-shaped Armagnac bottles is perfect for the purpose, but even an American gallon jug will do for this noble experiment.

B Y THE TIME THE REPATRIATED BECKS HAD BEEN in America for a year we had many things for which to be thankful. We were safely settled in a hospitable New England seaport. We had friends. The schools were good. The comforts of living were almost too good. We still found life exciting. Thanks to the genius of our *Cordon Bleu*, we had proven that gastronomy could be as much of an adventure in America as it had been in France. The little towns of Senlis and Marblehead were not totally different after all.

There was little temptation to celebrate this first anniversary, however, for it fell in the early days of June 1940, when our well-loved France, bruised and bewildered, lay on the brink of disaster. For the Becks, and for all Americans who knew France well enough to love her, it was a somber and fearful moment. It left us with throbbing temples and with forlorn, desperate hopes, first in Reynaud, then in Weygand, and finally in Pétain. The news stunned and upset Clémentine, while raising her Gallic ire at the iron-heeled *boches* and the betrayers of her country. The impact of the headlines announcing the Fall of France was, briefly, too much for her. She asked us to excuse her and hurried to a favorite park bench facing the Atlantic, where she brooded most of the day. When she finally reappeared in the kitchen she was red eyed and silent, but we could hear her muttering things about pigs and camels under her breath, a reassuring sign that her spirit was far from broken.

We didn't pay much attention to gastronomy during those tragic days. Clémentine found herself opening cans of corned beef hash perfunctorily and without protest. Her thoughts were far away, in Beaune, where her family awaited the thirsty invaders. Considering her aged parents, and the fact that her brother was stationed in the Maginot Line, Clémentine's worries were so much more vital than those of the Becks that we were almost ashamed to be concerned over the fate of our old farmhouse in the Oise. But when the newspapers mentioned our little

131

COURTYARD OF THE CHAMBERLAIN HOUSE, SENLIS, 1931

town repeatedly during those fateful days, we couldn't help but think of the steep-roofed house at the edge of the town where we had spent so many tranquil years. We thought of our collections of books and prints and pewter and of the old furniture we had acquired after haunting antique shops and the *marché aux puces*. We thought of our Chagall watercolor and our old Spanish parchments and felt a momentary sadness — but not for long. Possessions seemed trivial indeed at such a time. We thought of the old courtyard of our farmhouse, paved with grass-grown cobblestones, and wondered if German army wagons were already using it as a parking place. At the far end of the courtyard was the barn, dominated by an octagonal *pigeonnier*, where we had kept the Hotchkiss touring car. Who had it now? Had some French acquaintance been wise enough to appropriate it and to hurry southward in it ahead of the exodus from Paris? We hoped so. Crouching close to the barn were the rabbit hutches and the private apartments of Alfred, the duck, and Gringoire, the great grey goose. What chance had *they* of surviving a Nazi invasion?

We waited long, uncertain weeks before the first letters trickled in from France. When they came, a pale ray of sunshine brightened our household. Clémentine's family was safe, if indignant. Her brother, together with two million other brothers, fathers, and sons of French families, had been taken prisoner. As for the *maison* Beck, a letter from our *notaire* disclosed that it was undamaged, save for a slight peppering by shell fragments. The courtyard, however, had not fared so well. The notary hinted that Monsieur Beck might be a little distressed to observe the condition of the *pigeonnier*, which had suffered a direct hit. In one paragraph he then sketched some of the more tragic damage done to the town. The church had been hit, and the commercial hotel by the station had been destroyed for the third time in seventy years. A part of the shopping street, embracing the *pâtisserie*, the *mercerie* of Mademoiselle Drouin, and the *quincaillerie* of studious little Monsieur Escaffre, had been made a shambles. A high-explosive bomb had dropped squarely in the Place du 14 juillet, leveling its quiet fountain and all the buildings facing it. "The restaurant of your friend Monsieur Gébaud was obliterated, and he is now in the hospital," the letter continued. "It was necessary to amputate his right arm."

With a jolt this casual sentence brought the war very near to the Becks. For Léon Gébaud had been a true friend, one of the few Frenchmen I could *tutoyer* with entire ease. We were invariably his customers on Clémentine's Thursday night off and always had an apéritif with him in the kitchen while he helped the chef put the finishing touches on the *plat du jour*. To dine Chez Léon was to enjoy the best restaurant in the town and to come away with a renewed appreciation of the art of the innkeeper.

For twenty years Léon had presided over the destinies of this rural *café-restaurant*, and in that time he had established himself among the towns-people as a chef, a genial host, and a true philosopher. He was a handsome man, with clear blue eyes, a flowing blond moustache, and a rather wistful

smile. The formalities of being a restaurateur made him endure a high white collar, but he counteracted this discomfort by wearing black felt *pantoufles* for all occasions instead of shoes. He had a fine scorn for pol-iticians, for the *nouveaux riches*, and especially for the Germans, whom he considered thick-skulled automatons, devoid of any trace of humor or imagination. Léon was a *cycliste* in his youth, and when we knew him he still took his recreation by pedaling to the forest and gathering wildflowers.

His *café-restaurant* had thousands of counterparts all over France. The center of the largest room was given over to two antique billiard tables. The walls were lined with large areas of mirror, beneath which stretched red plush *banquettes*, worn rather threadbare in spots and handi-capped here and there by a broken spring. In front of the upholstered benches were rectangular marble-topped tables, scrubbed clean for the afternoon card players. At apéritif time Léon was certain of the patronage of many of the town's foremost citizens. Monsieur Fidelin, the bewhis-kered mayor, was sure to be there for his Picon *citron* and two rounds of *belote* before dinner. Monsieur Huguet, the *pharmacien*, never missed an afternoon game of backgammon with sprightly old Colonel Lavasseur. As the hour approached seven, the marble tops were covered with red and white tablecloths, and Léon's dinner menus, mimeographed in pale violet ink, appeared on each table, accompanied by sizable carafes of *vin rouge*. At the corner of the building was a smaller dining room with six tables, reserved for ladies whose sensibilities were offended by billiard players. During the long winter months Léon's hospitable café was the

133

134

CHEZ LÉON

pleasantest spot in the old town, largely because of the tact, politeness, and unfailing good cheer displayed by the *patron* himself. With the arrival of warm weather his regular guests—billiardists, *belote* players, and gourmets alike—shifted to tables in the garden at the rear of the café. The trees in this tranquil spot had been trained to form an almost rainproof shelter. Clean white pebbles covered the ground. Along one side of the garden a grass-grown alley ran almost down to the river, providing the perfect terrain for leisurely games of *boules*.

That is all there was to Chez Léon—except for the cooking and the conversation. There was no radio, no electric piano, juke box, or pinball machine. It was simplicity itself. A French child can play for hours with nothing but a hoop, and this typical café suggests that a French adult is hardly more exacting about his recreation. I submit that the *café-restaurant* is one of the most civilized of man's institutions and that a good café proprietor is a distinguished member of society, especially when he is also a superlative chef, as Léon was. His duties as a host did not allow him to do much of the cooking, but he trained his own chef, planned the menus, and went to Les Halles at daybreak five times a week to do his own marketing. His knowledge of *la cuisine* was, in our eyes, limitless. Once we had gained his friendship, Léon's kitchen and many of its secrets were open to us. Some of the choicest recipes in Clémentine's notebooks were contributed by this generous, kindly, civilized man, whose picturesque old *café-restaurant* is now a heap of rubble and who, if he is alive, is maimed for life.

We thought often of Léon during those calamitous days in the summer of 1940, and we continue to think of him, wondering whether he is carrying on with one arm, picturing the expression of quiet loathing with which he observes the Nazi occupation troops, trying to imagine the sulphurous adjectives he is applying to Pierre Laval. We think, too, of his love of good food. Léon, who was prodigally extravagant with butter and eggs, what somber light now shines in his eyes when he claims his ration of one egg per month! How long since he has made his fabulously rich *sauce béarnaise*, his *gratin de queues d'écrevisses*, his incomparable *volaille truffée demi-deuil*! Has he been able to hoard enough butter and white wine and to find a few slices of salmon to make his favorite dish, *le saumon poêlé au Vouvray*? In that martyred, humiliated, and plundered land the chance is remote indeed that any Frenchman can assemble such treasures at this moment. For this reason we used to feel guilty every time Clémentine prepared this dish for our New England table. But gradually Léon's favorite salmon has taken on added significance. Each time it appears we drink a toast in clear, white wine to a sensitive, civilized, and courageous friend, a true Frenchman who reviles the collaborationists, and who, along with the vast majority of his countrymen, looks to the Allies as France's one hope of liberation.

The recipe for Léon's salmon dish is extremely simple, but it is different, and it prevents the dryness one often encounters in broiled or sautéed salmon. The Becks and Clémentine join in the hope that you will try it during the hot summer months and that perhaps you also will feel inclined to drink a toast to Léon Gébaud and all the true, silent, suffering, but—never forget this—indomitable Frenchmen he typifies.

Le Saumon Poêlé au Vouvray

Sauté slices of fresh salmon in generous quantities of fresh butter until they are about half cooked and lightly browned. Add salt. Then add two or three glasses of dry Vouvray, or a good dry California white wine, according to the quantity of salmon. Boil over a brisk fire until the liquid is greatly reduced, but leaving enough for a rich and generous sauce. Pepper the fish lightly, add chopped parsley, and serve with steamed potatoes.

T HE SUMMER OF 1940 WAS A MOMENTOUS ONE for Clémentine. The Fall of France mystified and saddened her. The impact of the tragic news was shattering. The Beck family tried hard to take Clémentine's mind off her troubles, but solace came to her from an absolutely unexpected source, from a genial French-Canadian house painter and in the unprecedented form of—romance. This is how it started.

A new coat of paint had been decreed by the owner of our gambrel-roofed house, and one spring morning three painters began to install their trappings in the little courtyard facing the kitchen and the dining room. At first Clémentine watched them with indifference from her open kitchen window. Only little Phinney, idling at the breakfast table, paid much attention. Then strangely familiar scraps of conversation began to float through the screen. It sounded peculiarly like French. It *was* French—in spots. One of the painters was rinsing his brushes and saying, *"Mais, ce* Jimmie Foxx, *il a perdu son* punch. *Il faut un jeune pour* first base." His companion disagreed. *"Mais non!* Jimmie *fait du bon travail. Ce qu'il faut, c'est des* pitchers. *Sauf pour le pauvre vieux* Lefty Grove, *les* Red Sox *n'ont rien, absolument rien!"*

Little Phinney's face lighted up. He rushed into the kitchen and asked Clémentine if she had heard those magic words. She nodded excitedly, but remained primly in her kitchen when Phinney edged cautiously into the courtyard and began to make friends with these remarkable men who looked like any other Yankee house painters, but who carried on their baseball talk in French. Clémentine's natural reserve prevented her from speaking to the gentlemen, but no such restraint troubled them when noontime came around and they were thirsty for water. They piled into her kitchen, sniffed the fragrant *ragoût* on the back of the stove, and before the day was over were calling her *Mademoiselle* Bouchard. Clémentine seemed startled but pleased, a condition that became more accentuated as the days went by. One of the painters, a jocular, robust

Acadian whose first name was Armand, began to linger overtime in Clémentine's kitchen, to the slight displeasure of Madame Beck. When we
learned that he was a widower with two children, a ghastly premonition
swept over the whole family. Could it be possible that he would rob us
of our precious Clémentine by proposing marriage? And days later, when
he took Clémentine to the movies (the first time such a thing had happened
in all her forty-one years), we were in a torment of apprehension. But
Clémentine, prompted by an indiscreet question from little Phinney, reassured us. Her marrying days were long since past. But she began to
sing again in her kitchen.

The Becks were much relieved when Armand gathered up his
paints, brushes, and ladders and departed. We couldn't help liking him,
though we were chilled at the thought of what his courtship might mean
to us. He was unfailingly glib and cheerful. He wore a bespattered straw
hat instead of the conventional painter's cap and was given to incessant
whistling. Phinney thought he was wonderful. He spoke to us in breezy
English and when forced to speak French with Clémentine did so in a
shamefaced sotto-voce. She plainly tried to discourage him as his advances
continued, and our barometer of hope rose perceptibly. But Armand's
ardor was getting warmer with the weather, and he was undismayed. He
began to call her on the telephone, a liberty she considered scandalous in
its impropriety. She scolded him roundly for it, but apparently without
effect, for calls from the ebullient suitor continued. He used the mails,
too. Clémentine blushed becomingly when we brought her letters penned
in a strong masculine hand. We noticed that she reached for them eagerly
and began to sing in the kitchen shortly thereafter. The courtship of
Clémentine was really under way. Little Phinney brought the final report
that made us decide she might soon be lost to us. He went on a picnic
with Armand, Clémentine, and Armand's two earnest youngsters. Apparently they had a wonderful time, although the little Acadians had
distinct difficulty understanding Phinney's Parisian French. Phinney reported that Armand and Clémentine held hands and that "Gee, they
giggled a lot." Clémentine was not the kind to hold hands lightly. We
knew she had definitely slipped away from us and we were not surprised
when she asked very quietly to speak to us alone one August evening.
Blushing furiously, with the same lively sparkle in her eyes we remembered from her first glimpse of the New York skyline, she stammered
out the news and proudly showed us the diamond on her finger. She was
a very surprised spinster of forty-one, about to embark upon a new and
uncharted career. "At my age, Madame, one hesitates," she confessed,
"mais c'est un brave garçon, et tellement gai!"

The news caused a mighty stir in the Beck household. "Clémentine
va se marier!" Little Phinney galloped through the house, shouting with

excitement. We began to look upon Armand with new respect, both as a gourmet and as a provider for his children. There remained only one hope of keeping Clémentine—for me to follow in the footsteps of that resourceful gourmet and jurist, Dodin-Bouffant, who married his cook rather than lose her. Mrs. Beck did not view this expedient with favor, and Armand became definitely accepted by the Becks as the qualified heir to all the culinary joys Clémentine had made known to us. We already knew why Clémentine had not been a bride in her own native Burgundy. The secret was not a tragic love affair but merely the fact that she possessed no *dot*, no nest egg in the form of a dowry to tempt the ambitious young men of the village. Armand had never even mentioned the antiquated institution of a dowry, she told us in surprise. Chalk up another bright mark for *l'Amérique. This* was to be a *mariage d'amour!*

The sudden, blinding change of acquiring an undreamed-of husband, two stepchildren, and a little white cottage all at a single swoop would have flabbergasted almost anyone, but not the level-headed Clémentine. She gave us a punctual two weeks' notice and worked valiantly in her kitchen, polishing the copper casseroles, changing shelf paper, and sharpening steel knives so that everything would be left in flawless condition. More important, she turned over all her notebooks and *carnets* to the Becks, inviting us to copy anything we liked. Our immediate and determined concern was not to lose Clémentine's recipes, even if we were doomed to lose her. The going-over we gave her culinary papers was devastating. The whole family set to work. Diane and little Phinney made their own lists of dishes that had to be preserved at all costs (*céleri rémoulade, escargots, mousse au chocolat!*). Mr. and Mrs. Beck clicked away at the typewriter, in shifts, eight hours a day. Later, we would condense, translate, weed out the recipes, reword them, and codify them with American weights, measures, and temperatures. But during those last days we just copied indiscriminately. Some of the recipes were Clémentine's very own. Others were culled from French cookbooks (and were often mouth-watering models of imprecision). A great number the Becks had unearthed and Clémentine had perfected them.

The phenomenal good fortune of having our own *Cordon Bleu* in a Yankee village, we realized, was too good to last. The miracle of enjoying an impeccable French cuisine cooked for us by Clémentine in the very stronghold of chowder, fried clams, and blueberry pie had to end. But the Becks were lucky enough to salvage a wealth of workable recipes that proved that the cooking itself *is* possible on our shores — and, in time, Mrs. Beck would confirm this triumphantly by becoming an accomplished French cook herself.

Saying good-bye to Clémentine was not easy for the Becks. We had hoped to lessen the ordeal by a mere gay handshake at the wedding, but Clémentine, with her inborn French instinct for the fitting ceremony, herself set the stage for the formal farewell. At her invitation, we drove out the day before the wedding to admire Armand's little white house on the outskirts of the neighboring metropolis. She was radiant with pride as she showed it to us. Obviously it was a thing of far greater beauty in her eyes than her old stone house in Burgundy, and we felt a little sorry about this. But it was a neat, attractive cottage, with a sizable vegetable garden behind and a verdant patch of lawn bordering the street. She took us inside and showed us the stuffed furniture, which impressed Phinney mightily, the large radio, the upright piano, the two standing lamps. We admired the pale lavender bathroom and the garage, which sheltered a large, shimmering secondhand car. Burgundy had never been like this. We looked in the kitchen and saw the sunlight streaming through salmon-colored venetian blinds. A pressure cooker and a glittering percolator were on the stove. Clémentine will miss that beautiful copper *batterie de*

BEND IN THE ROAD

cuisine, I thought. Armand arrived after a well-timed interval, along with his two meek and silent youngsters. They looked dazed, but happy at the idea of a new *maman*. "It won't take Clémentine long to fatten up those spindly legs," Mrs. Beck whispered. "A few of her Burgundian specialties and there will be color in those cheeks, too."

Armand looked very handsome in his blue serge suit, very content and very confident. He invited us to be seated on the davenport, while Clémentine went to the kitchen, her *own* kitchen, and brought back some salted almonds and a very good bottle of sherry. She had known for years this was the Becks' favorite apéritif. There was an awkward silence while Armand pulled the cork and poured out the rich amber liquid. Clémentine passed the tray to each of us, precisely as she had done for almost ten years, then to Armand, and, finally, as we had never seen her do before, she took a glass for herself. Then she stood beside *le beau* Armand, timidly placed her hand on his arm, and smiled. It was the happiest, most touching smile that had ever embellished her fine Burgundian countenance. We drank a toast to the happiness of Armand and his augmented family. We drank to Canada, to *l'Amérique*, and to *la belle France*, while Phinney and the little Acadians gaped. It was a tense moment, with tears welling up in Clémentine's eyes and a strange huskiness evident in the thickening words of Mrs. Beck. This had turned out to be a ceremony in which the reluctant Becks formally relinquished all claims to their cherished *cuisinière* and friend, and it wasn't easy. Even the debonair Phinney grew misty eyed. We clinked glasses once more, gulped a little, and shook hands with the lucky, lucky Armand and his spindly (but not for long!) children. Then, before the deluge, we dashed for our car.

 RECIPES

Extracts from Clémentine's Notebooks

The one hundred fifty or so recipes we have selected for this supplement to the story of Clémentine are all family favorites with the Becks and have been tested repeatedly. Many of them, we hope, will appeal to you. All of them are fundamentally French in their approach, and many are classic bourgeois recipes that have been foundation stones in French households for generations. Others show the creative touch of a modern innovator. They come from famous chefs and unknown grandmothers, from noted restaurateurs and gifted amateurs, from classic cookbooks and obscure Burgundian pamphlets.

It has been said many times that it is less difficult to discover a new star than to create an entirely new dish. Neither Clémentine nor the Becks make the slightest claim to the latter distinction. We have merely sought out and adapted these dishes to American measures and conditions. Our sources frequently go so far back into the folklore of French cooking that the recipes are anonymous. In other cases we are able to give due credit and thanks to a contemporary French source.

This book appears at a time when the conservation of food is a vital matter throughout the world and when extravagance has no possible excuse. Some of these recipes ignore this fact in a most glaring manner, and we hasten to point out that they are for reading purposes only. Our *boeuf farci*, for example, is definitely a dish to be postponed for the Duration, and for some time after that, but it makes good mouth-watering reading. While this and a few other recipes are inexcusable on moral and economic grounds, the great majority of these dishes are thrifty to prepare. They are adaptable to the American market basket, and they will provide a fresh approach, we fondly believe, to the planning of many an American family meal. Herbs and wine are used in a great many of them, and we would like to point out that neither of these ingredients need be costly. Our own American bulk wines, if chosen with discrimination, are excellent and inexpensive for cooking.

To retain some of the Gallic flavor of the recipes, we have tried to stay close to the original in making the translations, with the result that our English may sound strange and stilted in places. The accurate, well-integrated, foolproof American recipe with precise quantities, sequences, and temperatures is an admirable institution, but it rarely has a counterpart in France. The French recipe almost invariably presupposes an adequate knowledge of kitchen technique, a goodly number of earthenware casseroles with or without handles and tight-fitting covers, and a fair amount of creative ability and intuitive good sense on the part of the reader. These translations presuppose the same thing. You may be exasperated at the mention of "a little thyme," "a trickle of lemon juice," or "a few onions," and protest that it isn't specific. But Clémentine will counter with "How big is an onion?" and it is admittedly difficult to answer her. Discretion is a vital ingredient of a good French recipe.

PHINEAS BECK

Marblehead, 1942

Mrs. Beck's Extracts from Clémentine's Library

As Mr. Beck pointed out in the last chapter of the story of Clémentine, Mrs. Beck would become the family cook, and a fine one. The days of employing a cook at all, let alone a Clémentine, would soon be over.

When the selection was made of recipes from Clémentine's notebooks to be included in the first edition of *Clémentine in the Kitchen*, Mr. Beck took the lead with his favorites, leaning a bit heavily toward nostalgia and dishes of a certain grandeur. The effect was eloquent and the recipes did assuredly belong in a home cook's repertoire. But Mrs. Beck thought (and, later, so did Diane and little Phinney) that they gave a better picture of what Clémentine served when guests came to dinner than of what most distinguished her—how she cooked for the Becks every day in her unalterable French way.

In the years that followed, Mrs. Beck re-created in her kitchen the style of home cooking that Clémentine had taught her, using the old notebook recipes and the library of cookbooks (which expanded alarmingly as time went by). Alas, it was indeed evident that the assumptions of French authors and Clémentine's natural skills made it seem unnecessary to any of them to record their recipes with precision. This did not faze Mrs. Beck while she was doing the cooking, but, to communicate in print, the "admirable institution" of an accurate, well-integrated written recipe began to seem more desirable than Mr. Beck had assumed.

The one hundred and fifty recipes that follow were chosen by Diane from the vast number that Mrs. Beck tested and wrote down over the years. There are classic dishes, regional specialties, and much that is useful for special occasions. But many are plain and old-fashioned, simple and not at all extraordinary. These are the dishes that identify the Clémentine family style the Beck children grew up with, forty and more years ago. It is a style so French, so civilized, so knowing in its use of ingredients that it cannot become impractical or ever go out of date—though it does periodically go out of fashion because cooking has become subject to so many ever-changing "trends." Clémentine would find this instability perplexing. Is not a *poulet cocotte* always a *poulet cocotte*? Why, now, should it be newly fashionable as a dish of French "bistro" cooking?

It is amazing to remember that a *céleri rémoulade*, a *sole meunière*, a *pot-au-feu*, an *aïoli*, that same *poulet cocotte*, a fish poached with mushrooms in white wine were exotic to the Americans who loved Clémentine's story and read her recipes in the early 1940s. Once the war was over, for fully twenty-five years French cooking was the pilot cuisine for Americans who became interested in cooking well. It had been so long before, and it will remain so, because the French fundamentals are the basics of Western cooking.

But as to what can possibly be considered exotic, everything has changed. American cooks are now the most cosmopolitan in the world — there is not a corner of the entire geography of the earth they have not explored in cookbooks and often in practice in their kitchens. They can no longer be easily amazed — if that were a worthy objective, which it is not. But, to wish to please — ah! that is another matter. The simplicities, and complexities, of Clémentine's *cuisine bourgeoise* aimed above all to please. They still do, and they risk being forgotten. One looks at a list of *hors-d'oeuvre variés* and it seems as arcane today as it seemed novel in 1940. But offer them at your table now, and they are as fresh and pleasing as they were when Mr. and Mrs. Beck first encountered them in neighborhood restaurants on the Left Bank in the early twenties. In her collection, Diane has done the opposite of what Mr. Beck did in 1942 and has brought into it as much as possible that has more simplicity than it does glamour. Her choices are nostalgia of another kind.

Without doubt, something has been lost in the language that now renders recipes from Clémentine's notebooks and Mrs. Beck's additions to them. Mrs. Beck and Diane together had to devise a more specific way to write a consecutive recipe with the necessary details. Mr. Beck removed himself from this process of modernization; it was not at all close to his heart. He preferred a recipe written with resonance and uninterrupted by statistics. Consider this gentle jewel, quoted unchanged from his text in the original *Clémentine*:

Crème Bréalaise

Clémentine advises gathering 2 pounds of peas for this soup when they are very young and the peas "twice the size of the head of a pin" in the shell. Cook them, in salted water barely to cover, with their pods, cutting off the tips; add 1 cut-up head of green lettuce and a handful of chervil. When this is cooked but still bright green, drain off, saving the liquid, and mash and strain through a fine sieve. Pour over this purée, and its liquid, 1 cup of chicken bouillon. Cook together for a few minutes, reducing the liquid if necessary. Strain through a cheesecloth and thicken with 3 beaten egg yolks and 1 cup of thick cream mixed together. This soup should have a velvety consistency and a beautiful green color.

We hope you will make this lavish little soup and will forgive the rigidity of wording in the recipes that follow. Mr. Beck never intended them to sound as they now do. Nor, however, did he get out there in the kitchen and do the cooking, so as to experience the value of explicit instructions. What he did do was inspire us all — Clémentine, Mrs. Beck, Diane, and little Phinney (today the all-time expert on *foie de veau à la bourgeoise*).

The Becks hope the recipes will work for your purposes and that you will find poetry in the dishes themselves that may be lacking in the words. The book was made, at first, and is again now, for a reason you may already have observed, for love — of family, France, food, and the incomparable Clémentine.

DIANE BECK

New York, 1987

HORS-D'OEUVRE FOR APÉRITIFS

Amandes Grillées
TOASTED ALMONDS
Blanched almonds, butter, olive oil, coarse salt

These are the almonds that Clémentine served to accompany sherry.

To "toast" about 2 cups of blanched almonds, heat together in a skillet 4 tablespoons of butter and 3 tablespoons of olive oil. When the fat is hot but not brown, add just enough almonds to cover the bottom of the pan. Keep the heat moderate, stir the nuts several times, and, when they are pale gold on all sides, with a slotted spoon remove them to brown paper to drain; sprinkle them at once with coarse salt. Continue adding almonds to the skillet a few at a time until all are toasted.

Champignons Farcis   page 218.

Délicieuses au Fromage
FRIED CHEESE PUFFS
Swiss cheese, egg whites, bread crumbs

This is a delectable hot hors-d'oeuvre. Make a paste of 2 lightly beaten egg whites mixed with ¼ pound of grated Swiss cheese. Form the paste into little balls no bigger than marbles, roll them in fine bread crumbs, and fry them in very hot, deep oil. The *délicieuses* will puff up and become light and delicious, just as their name implies. Serve them immediately, with French-fried parsley if you wish.

Baguettes de Fromage de Coon   page 122.

Pâté de Crevettes

FRESH SHRIMP PÂTÉ

Shrimp, lemon juice, pepper, paprika, olive oil

Shell and devein ½ pound of cooked shrimp and put them twice through the finest blade of a meat grinder. Add 3 tablespoons of lemon juice, plenty of freshly ground pepper, a generous dash of paprika, and a pinch of salt, and mix well. Then add gradually about ½ cup of olive oil, blending the shrimp to a creamy paste. Store the pâté in a covered jar in the refrigerator and serve it on unsalted crackers or circles of toast.

To make this in an electric blender, cut the shrimp into small dice and put them in the blender with the lemon juice but only ¼ cup of oil. Blend well, adding the remaining oil a little at a time as it is needed to make the mixture blend smoothly, and season afterwards.

Canapés de Homard

LOBSTER CANAPÉS

Lobster, mayonnaise, lemon, white pepper, bread, parsley

If Champagne is the apéritif of the day, these are worthy of the occasion.

Carefully remove the tail meat of small boiled lobsters and remove the coral, if any, and the green tomalley. Save the shells and the rest of the meat for some other purpose, such as a bisque (see page 169). With a very sharp knife cut the tail meat crosswise into neat, thin slices.

Season homemade mayonnaise to taste with plenty of lemon juice, white pepper, and the tomalley (about 3 parts mayonnaise to 1 part to-malley). Spread thin 1½-inch circles of firm white bread with the seasoned mayonnaise and top each canapé with a slice of lobster. Decorate with a tiny sprig of parsley and with a scrap of the scarlet coral or a caper. Serve the canapés as soon as possible, but meanwhile cover them with aluminum foil and keep them in a cool place.

Purée de Foies de Volailles

CHICKEN-LIVER FOIE GRAS

Chicken livers, chicken stock, butter, brandy, Madeira, truffle

Cut ½ pound of chicken livers in halves, cover them with chicken stock, and bring to a boil; simmer the livers for about 10 minutes. Drain them, purée them in an electric blender, then strain the purée through a very fine sieve and cool it.

Cream ¼ pound of unsalted butter and beat in the chicken-liver purée. Add a little pepper, a pinch of salt (this is not to be a highly seasoned pâté), a few drops of brandy, 1 tablespoon of Madeira, and 1 very finely minced truffle. Blend the mixture very thoroughly with a small wooden spatula and pack it into an earthen jar or small bowl. If it is to be kept for any length of time, pour a thin layer of melted butter or chicken fat over the surface. Chill well in the refrigerator and serve on homemade Melba toast with apéritifs; or serve with French bread to accompany a green salad.

HORS-D'OEUVRE

Clémentine's very traditional repertory for first-course hors-d'oeuvre begins with the most common, those dressed with vinaigrette, followed by a few special recipes, including pâtés. Only one, or two, might be served, with French bread and sweet butter. Or she would present a feast of four or six or even more — *hors-d'oeuvre variés* — for a special occasion. Ubiquitous also were hard sausage, radishes, the best sardines, with lemon, and *cornichons* with the pâtés.

Under the heading of Cold First Courses are some of the Becks' favorites, separate courses that Clémentine also called hors-d'oeuvre.

Vinaigrette
OIL AND VINEGAR DRESSING

The point of departure for all vinaigrettes, or French dressing, is 1 part wine vinegar to 3 parts olive oil, plus salt and freshly ground pepper. The formula, however, *always* varies to taste, depending on the strength of the vinegar and the needs of the dish, the salad greens, or the vegetables being dressed.

The following recipes are merely notes that propose how best to present each hors-d'oeuvre *à la vinaigrette*.

Salade de Tomates
TOMATOES VINAIGRETTE

The tomatoes, unpeeled, are sliced thin, the slices are arranged neatly overlapping in a serving dish, and the dressing is poured over them. Chopped parsley is always added, and very finely minced white onion is also customary.

Salade de Concombres
CUCUMBERS VINAIGRETTE

The cucumbers are always peeled. If they are to be marinated, they are split lengthwise and seeded before slicing thin. Salt them lightly and marinate them in a small amount of dressing for 2 hours or so. Drain off the accumulated liquid and add more vinaigrette to taste. Toss well, place in a serving dish, and sprinkle with finely chopped parsley or chives. (Chopped fresh dill is excellent with cucumbers, but Clémentine did not consider it the proper herb to use.)

If the cucumbers are preferred still crisp, they are peeled and sliced shortly before serving (seeded or not as you wish) and tossed in a vinaigrette spiced with a little mustard. Sprinkle with parsley.

Haricots Blancs en Salade
WHITE BEANS VINAIGRETTE

Any dried white beans, freshly cooked (they must not be overcooked), left over, or canned (well drained), may be used. They are first dressed, then placed in the serving dish, and very thin slices of white onion are scattered over them. Sprinkle with parsley.

Poireaux en Salade
LEEKS VINAIGRETTE

Clean the desired number of leeks; cut off most of the green parts and wash the leeks very thoroughly, split if necessary, under cold running water. If they are large, do split them lengthwise; each piece should be about the size of a large stalk of asparagus. Tie them into bundles in two places, put them in boiling salted water just to cover, and cook them slowly for 25 minutes, or until they are tender but not limp. Drain them well (and be sure to save the broth to add to a soup).

The leeks may be presented in a serving dish or arranged on individual plates. Make your vinaigrette in a bowl, adding mustard to taste, and whisk the dressing well until it is almost opaque, or emulsified, and pour it over the leeks. This dish also makes an excellent salad course. (It is, by the way, oddly colorless; be sure to sprinkle with parsley.)

Salade de Champignons

MUSHROOMS VINAIGRETTE

This is an exceptionally delicious salad to make when large, firm white mushrooms are in prime season. It can well be served by itself; if so, make a generous amount.

Trim the mushroom stems close to the caps. Rinse the mushrooms cautiously, so that no water is trapped in the caps, and wipe the tops of the caps with a soft cloth. Slice the mushrooms evenly, thin but not too thin, and toss them carefully in a bowl with a little less vinaigrette than you think you may need, then add a little to taste; there should not be too much. You may leave them to marinate for about 45 minutes, or serve them immediately; this is a matter of taste. Sprinkle with both chopped chives and chopped parsley before serving.

The vinaigrette for mushrooms may be varied by using a little less vinegar and adding a trickle of lemon juice.

Salade de Boeuf

JULIENNE OF BEEF VINAIGRETTE

This is a thrifty classic of the French hors-d'oeuvre tray for which any leftover roast, braised, or broiled (not stewed) beef may be used. It is a given, however, that whenever a *pot-au-feu* has been made (see page 194), the leftovers will appear as *salade de boeuf*, with the best results of all.

Cut the meat into thin julienne strips and place them in a shallow serving dish. Scatter thin slices of white onion and of tender young carrot over the top. Pour over them the usual vinaigrette, but seasoned with mustard. Leave to marinate for 2 or 3 hours. Sprinkle with the obligatory parsley before serving.

Carottes Marinées

MARINATED CARROTS

Carrots, white wine, herbs, seasonings, garlic, olive oil

Scrape 6 to 8 young carrots (about 1 pound) and cut them into quarters lengthwise. In a saucepan combine ¾ cup of dry white wine, 1 cup of water, and a *bouquet garni* composed of parsley, bay leaf, thyme, and a sprig or two of tarragon or chervil, all tied together. Add salt and pepper, 2 teaspoons of sugar, 1 crushed clove of garlic, and 5 tablespoons of olive oil. Bring the marinade to a boil and simmer it for 5 minutes. Add the carrots and boil them until almost done but still quite firm; cool them in the liquid. Arrange them prettily in a dish of suitable size and spoon some of the liquid over them. Chill them briefly in the refrigerator and sprinkle them with finely chopped parsley before serving.

Céleri Rémoulade

CELERY ROOT HORS-D'OEUVRE

Celery root, egg yolks, mustard, tarragon vinegar, olive oil, herbs

This simple, classic recipe does require that you have a very good, sharp vegetable shredder that will cut julienne strips less than ⅛ inch thick. This is the only way the celery root will have the right texture. (Blanching the celery, as some recipes mistakenly advise, does not work well.) Today, the julienne disk of a food processor does this best of all, but you must be careful; you need one of the more powerful machines and the julienne disk must be sharp and not have received too much prior use.

Choose celery roots that are not too large and pare off all the fibrous outside. Cut the roots into manageable chunks and shred as evenly as possible. For 2 cups of shredded celery root, mash together 1 hard-boiled and 1 raw egg yolk. Add 1½ teaspoons of strong Dijon mustard, salt, pepper, and 2 tablespoons of tarragon vinegar. Work the mixture to a smooth paste and add bit by bit ½ cup of cold olive oil, whisking constantly until the sauce thickens like mayonnaise. Mix the dressing and celery root together, chill, and sprinkle with minced parsley and chives before serving.

Oignons à la Grecque

SPICED ONIONS

Onions, butter, stock, vinegar, raisins, tomato paste, olive oil, herbs, spices

Peel 1½ pounds of very small white onions (a quick dip in boiling water helps the process) and trim the root ends. In a skillet brown them on all sides in 2 tablespoons of butter; it does not matter that they do not brown evenly. In a saucepan combine ¾ cup of strong beef or chicken stock, ¼ cup of wine vinegar, ¾ cup of seedless golden raisins, 3 tablespoons of tomato paste, 1 tablespoon of olive oil, a scant 2 tablespoons of sugar, ½ teaspoon of salt, ⅛ teaspoon of crushed red pepper flakes, ¼ teaspoon of dried thyme, 1 bay leaf, and a generous grinding of black pepper. Simmer this sauce for 2 or 3 minutes.

Arrange the browned onions close together in a shallow baking dish and cover them with the sauce. Bake them in a 325° oven for 1 hour, or until they are tender when pricked with the tip of a pointed knife. Serve chilled, as an hors-d'oeuvre or with cold meats.

Oeufs Farcis aux Câpres

STUFFED EGGS

Small eggs, mayonnaise, lemon, capers, parsley, pimiento

For a change, buy the smallest eggs available. Hard boil them and cool them thoroughly under running water. Shell them, cut a tiny slice off each end so the halves will stand up, and then cut the eggs in half crosswise (not lengthwise). Remove the yolks and mash them to a smooth, medium-thick purée together with homemade mayonnaise seasoned with lemon. Add to taste to the purée finely chopped capers and parsley, freshly ground pepper, a speck of sugar, and a little salt. Fill the whites with this mixture and garnish them with a tiny square of canned pimiento or sweet red pepper between two little sprigs of parsley. Arrange in a serving dish.

Large eggs may be prepared in the same way and presented on a perfect leaf of lettuce on individual plates.

Moules Ravigote

MUSSEL SALAD

Mussels, peppercorns, onion, white wine, vinegar, olive oil, capers, fresh herbs

Scrape and wash 3 pints of mussels. Put them in a kettle with a *bouquet garni*, a few peppercorns, 1 sliced onion, and ½ cup of white wine. Steam them, covered, until they open, about 6 minutes (discard any that do not open), and remove the mussels from their shells. Strain the cooking liquid through a colander lined with several layers of cheesecloth into a small saucepan. Simmer this until it is reduced to about ½ cup. Let cool.

Make a sauce with 1½ tablespoons of white wine vinegar, ¼ cup of olive oil, 1½ teaspoons of capers, pepper to taste (no salt until later), and a generous teaspoon each of fresh chopped parsley, chives, and tarragon. Now add the reduced mussel liquid, taste for salt, and add the mussels. Transfer to a serving dish, refrigerate, and serve cool but not cold.

Pâté Maison

PORK AND LIVER PÂTÉ

Pork, chicken livers, shallot, parsley, spices, brandy, Madeira, bacon

An aromatic slice of *pâté maison*, served with French bread, butter, and *cornichons*, is a classic hors-d'oeuvre all over France.

Put 1 pound of fresh lean pork and 1 pound of chicken livers (or ½ pound of chicken livers and ½ pound of calf's liver) several times through the finest blade of a meat grinder. Add 1 chopped shallot, 2 tablespoons of chopped parsley, 2 teaspoons of freshly ground pepper, ⅔ teaspoon of powdered ginger, ¼ teaspoon of cinnamon, 2¼ teaspoons of salt, 1 tablespoon of brandy, and 1 tablespoon of Madeira. Mix all the ingredients together thoroughly.

Line a loaf pan with strips of bacon, pack in the pork-and-liver mixture, and bake the pâté in a 350° oven for about 1½ hours. Cool the pâté under pressure, preferably under another loaf pan containing any handy object heavy enough to pack the meat down to a firm consistency. Refrigerate.

To serve, you may unmold the pâté and remove the bacon. The convenient household way, however, is to cut slices in the loaf pan and serve these on a small platter.

Note: If you use a food processor to grind the meats, read the instructions for using your machine. The pork and liver are to be finely ground, but not pulverized; the pâté is intended to have substantial texture.

Terrine de Viande Mirasol

PORK, VEAL, AND SAUSAGE PÂTÉ

Pork, veal, sausage meat, olive oil, white wine, onion, garlic, shallots, carrot, herbs, spices, bacon

Cut 1 pound each of lean fresh pork and veal into ¼-inch slices and cut the slices into 2-inch squares. Marinate the meat for 24 hours in ½ cup of olive oil and 1 cup of dry white wine, with 1 onion, 2 cloves of garlic, and 2 shallots, all chopped, 1 sliced carrot, 2 sprigs of parsley, 2 bay leaves, ½ teaspoon of thyme, salt, pepper, and grated nutmeg.

Line the bottom and sides of an earthenware *terrine* (an ovenproof dish with a lid) with bacon. Fill the *terrine* with alternating layers of the marinated meat, drained and free of herbs, and fresh lean sausage meat (about 1 pound). Fill the *terrine* with the strained marinade barely to the level of the top layer of meat, and cover the pâté with more bacon.

Make a stiff paste of flour and water, shape it into a narrow roll, and fit the roll around the edge of the *terrine*. Press the lid on firmly and bake the sealed pâté in a 300° oven for 3 hours. Take off the lid and the flour paste, cover the pâté with aluminum foil, and cool it under pressure, using any handy object heavy enough to pack the meat down firmly. Chill the pâté for 2 days before serving it as an hors-d'oeuvre or with salad. Slice it in the *terrine*.

COLD FIRST COURSES

Oeufs en Gelée au Madère

EGGS IN ASPIC

Serves six.

Eggs, gelatin, chicken stock, Madeira, tarragon, ham

Boil 6 eggs for 6 minutes, cool them under running water, and shell them carefully when they are cold. Soak 1 tablespoon of gelatin in ¼ cup of cold water. Heat 1½ cups of clear chicken stock, add the gelatin, and stir until it dissolves completely. Add 2 tablespoons of Madeira (or port or sherry) and set this aspic aside to cool.

Use small molds or ramekins just wide and deep enough to hold 1 egg each with a little space to spare. Trim 6 thin slices of ham just to fit the tops of the molds. Spoon a little aspic into the bottom of each mold to make a layer about ¼ inch thick. When this is almost firm, decorate it with 2 crossed leaves of fresh tarragon or a tiny sprig of parsley. Gently place an egg in each ramekin, spoon aspic over until the molds are almost full, and cover each egg with a circle of ham. Glaze the ham with a final spoonful of aspic and chill the eggs. Serve them unmolded onto individual plates with a garnish of small leaves from the hearts of fresh lettuce.

Aubergine à la Turque

EGGPLANT AND TOMATO HORS-D'OEUVRE

Eggplant, tomatoes, onions, peppercorns, olive oil

A la turque here means a general Mediterranean style. Eggplant is often served this way in the south of France.

Peel a large eggplant and slice it rather thin. Salt the slices, pile them together, let them stand under pressure for a half hour, and drain off the liquid. Peel and slice 6 large ripe tomatoes and 3 or 4 onions. In the bottom of a shallow baking dish arrange a layer of onion slices, put a layer of eggplant over the onions, then a layer of tomato over the eggplant. Sprinkle in whole peppercorns and a little salt. Keep this up until you have used all the vegetables, finishing off with a layer of tomato slices each neatly decorated with a round of onion. Fill *all* the corners and empty spaces well with bits of tomato.

Fill the dish just to the top layer of tomato with olive oil and bake it in a 250° oven for 3 hours or a little more. Baste the juices over the top several times. Serve chilled, and with this dish it is particularly pleasing to have your French bread heated in the oven to be very crunchy.

Tomates Galloise

SARDINE-STUFFED TOMATOES

Tomatoes, sardines, hard-boiled eggs, watercress, seasonings, lemon, olive oil

Cut off the stem ends of tomatoes, remove the center core and the seeds, and let the tomatoes drain, cut side down, for an hour or two. The proportions for the stuffing are about 3 medium sardines to 1 hard-boiled egg to ¼ cup of chopped watercress. Drain the sardines, take off the skin if it is coarse, and mash them with a fork. Chop the whites of the eggs and mash the yolks. Mix sardines, eggs, and watercress together, and season the mixture well with lemon juice, chives, capers, mustard, pepper, and a little salt and olive oil. Stuff the tomatoes and garnish the tops with a slice of hard-boiled egg and 3 or 4 watercress leaves. Serve with French bread and sweet butter.

Maquereaux Marinés

MARINATED BABY MACKEREL

Serves six.
Baby mackerel, onion, olive oil, white wine, lemon juice, herbs, spices

Sauté 3 small thinly sliced onions very lightly in 2 tablespoons of olive oil. Add 1½ cups of dry white wine, the strained juice of 1 lemon, salt and pepper, 10 grains of coriander, and a *bouquet garni* composed of parsley, thyme, 1 bay leaf, 1 clove of garlic, and a stalk of fennel. Boil this *court-bouillon* over a good flame for 10 minutes.

Coat the surface of a shallow, flameproof baking dish with olive oil, and in it arrange side by side a dozen whole dressed baby mackerel or other small fish such as herring, fresh sardines, or smelts. Sprinkle the fish with salt and pepper, cover them with the hot *court-bouillon*, and poach them gently for 10 minutes. Remove the *bouquet garni* and cool the fish in the *court-bouillon*. Serve chilled, as a luncheon hors-d'oeuvre, with quarters of lemon and French bread and butter.

Homard Alexandre

COLD SLICED LOBSTER WITH HERB, EGG, AND
OLIVE OIL SAUCE

Serves four.
Boiled lobster, watercress, herbs, yolks of hard-boiled eggs, seasonings, olive oil, Madeira

Slice the meat of a boiled lobster and arrange it on a small platter. Decorate with stemmed sprigs of watercress. Mix 1 teaspoon each of chopped chervil, parsley, tarragon, and chives with the mashed yolks of 2 hard-boiled eggs. Add salt and pepper, a little Dijon mustard, 1 tablespoon of wine vinegar, and a few drops of Worcestershire sauce. When the mixture is smoothly blended, add gradually about ½ cup of cold olive oil, stirring constantly until the sauce thickens into a sort of mayonnaise. Add a few drops of Madeira or sherry and drop a neat spoonful of sauce on each piece of lobster just before serving.

SOUPS

Potage de Légumes
PURÉED VEGETABLE SOUP
Serves six.
Onion, carrots, turnips, potatoes, celery, parsley, butter, cream

In a large saucepan sauté 1 large sliced onion in 1 tablespoon of butter until it is soft and lightly browned. Add 2 carrots, 2 small white turnips, 3 medium potatoes, and 2 stalks of celery, all cut into small pieces, a sprig of parsley, and salt and pepper. Cook the vegetables for a few minutes in the butter, stirring often. Then add 5 cups of hot water, cover the saucepan, and simmer the soup over a low flame for 1 hour. Pass the soup through a sieve into another saucepan and force through all the vegetables.

To serve this traditional French *potage*, reheat it with a big lump of butter and add 2 tablespoons of extra-heavy cream or *crème fraîche*.

Potage Parisien
LEEK AND POTATO SOUP
Serves four.
Leeks, potatoes, cream

Clean 2 large leeks, remove most of the green tops, and slice the rest very thin. Peel 3 potatoes and cut them into small even dice. Melt 1 tablespoon of butter in a saucepan, add the leeks, and cook them over a low flame for 5 minutes without letting them brown. Add the potatoes and cook another minute. Then add 5 cups of boiling water and a little salt and simmer the soup gently for 30 minutes, skimming off the surface once or twice. The soup should reduce to about 1 quart. Stir in 1 teaspoon of butter and 3 tablespoons of heavy cream and taste for seasoning. Serve with a sprinkling of chopped chives or parsley.

Potage Purée de Crécy

CARROT SOUP

Serves six.
Carrots, onion, butter, chicken stock, rice, croutons

Slice 4 or 5 medium carrots very thin and chop 1 medium onion. Sauté the vegetables in a large covered saucepan over low heat in 2 tablespoons of melted butter for 15 minutes. Season them with a little salt, pepper, and a pinch of sugar. Then add 1 quart of hot chicken stock and ¼ cup of raw rice and simmer the soup for 35 minutes. Strain it through a sieve and force the vegetables through with the liquid. Add 2 more cups of stock, reheat the soup, and add a lump of butter. Garnish with small croutons sautéed in butter.

Soupe à la Tomate

FRESH TOMATO SOUP

Serves four.
Onion, carrot, butter, flour, tomatoes, parsley, sugar, rice

Melt 2 tablespoons of butter in a large saucepan, add 1 onion and 1 small carrot, both sliced, and cook them together slowly without browning until the onion is soft. Stir in 2 tablespoons of flour and blend well. Add 3 large ripe tomatoes, cut coarse, stir, and add 2½ cups of hot water, a large sprig of parsley, salt, pepper, and 2 lumps of sugar. Bring the soup to a boil, cover, and simmer it for 45 minutes. Force it through a strainer fine enough to catch the tomato seeds. Return the soup to the stove, add a little chicken stock or water if it is too thick, and add ¼ cup of cooked rice and a lump of butter.

Soupe à l'Oignon

ONION SOUP

Serves four.
Onions, chicken stock, bread, cheese

When you are left with the carcass of a roast chicken, boil it with seasonings to make a stock. Then try, instead of the usual chicken soup, a Parisian *soupe à l'oignon*.

In a heavy kettle sauté 4 or 5 thinly sliced onions in a generous tablespoon of butter. Cook the onions until they are soft and lightly browned and stir them often, as they may tend to burn. Season the onions with a little salt and pepper (remember your stock is seasoned) and pour in 5 cups of the hot stock. Simmer the soup for 5 to 8 minutes, pour it into a flameproof casserole, and float slices of toasted French bread on top. Sprinkle the bread with plenty of grated Swiss or Parmesan cheese and brown lightly under a hot broiler. Serve from the casserole.

Potage Purée de Céleri

CELERY SOUP

Serves four.
Celery root, celery, onion, butter, milk, chervil, croutons

Peel about ¾ pound of celery root (celeriac) and cut it into thin julienne strips, or grate it coarse. Scrape 5 or 6 outer stalks of celery (remove the leaves) and slice them thin. Chop 1 large onion. Melt 2 tablespoons of butter in a heavy saucepan, add the three vegetables, cover, and simmer them very slowly without browning for 15 minutes. Add 3 cups of hot water and salt and pepper and simmer the soup for 35 to 40 minutes. Drain the vegetables in a sieve, reserving the liquid, then mash them through the sieve into a saucepan. Stir the liquid into the purée and add 1¼ cups of hot milk. Reheat the soup and, off the fire, stir in a lump of butter. Add 1 tablespoon of chopped chervil or parsley and serve with small croutons sautéed in butter.

Purée Saint-Germain

SPLIT PEA SOUP

Serves six to eight.
Split peas, bacon, stock, herbs, croutons

Soak 1 pound of green split peas for 4 hours. Drain them and cook them, covered, in 4 cups of salted water, skimming once or twice, until they are soft. Drain the peas again, reserving the cooking water, and force them through a sieve. In a heavy saucepan sauté 3 tablespoons of finely minced fat bacon. Add the cooking water, 1½ cups of beef or chicken stock, the puréed peas, and a *bouquet garni*. Simmer the soup for 15 minutes, remove the *bouquet garni*, stir in 1 tablespoon of butter creamed with 1 teaspoon of flour, and serve the *purée Saint-Germain* with a sprinkling of crisp brown croutons sautéed in butter.

Potage au Chou

CABBAGE SOUP

Serves six to eight.

Bacon, cabbage, carrots, turnips, celery, leeks, potatoes

Put in a kettle a good piece of bacon, bacon rind, or rind of a ham. Add 1 small head of cabbage (about 1½ pounds), 3 carrots, 3 small white turnips, 3 stalks of celery, and 2 leeks, all cut into slices or diced. Add cold water to cover well and salt and pepper. Cook, covered, very slowly for 2 or 3 hours. Add some sliced potatoes 1 hour before serving if desired.

Potage du Couvent

WHITE BEAN AND VEGETABLE SOUP

Serves six.

Dried white beans, turnips, carrots, celery, onion, cloves, herbs, stock

Cook in salted water to cover well 1 cup of dried white beans (previously soaked), 3 small white turnips, 3 carrots, 1 stalk of celery with its leaves, all cut into pieces, along with 1 onion stuck with 2 cloves, 3 sprigs of parsley with their stems, and a pinch of thyme. Simmer until the beans are very tender, about 1½ hours.

Drain the vegetables, reserving the cooking water, and mash them through a fine sieve into another saucepan. Add to this purée the desired amount of liquid, composed of equal parts cooking water and stock (or *bouillon* from a *pot-au-feu*; see page 194). Thicken a little, if desired, with potato starch. This should be a smooth, creamy purée. Cook all together for a few minutes, add a lump of butter, and serve.

Soupe au Potiron

PUMPKIN SOUP

Serves four to six.

Pumpkin, onion, milk, cream, eggs, butter

Use 1½ pounds of pumpkin, peeled and cut into pieces. Put them in a soup kettle with 1 sliced onion and 6 cups of salted water. Cover the kettle and boil the pumpkin for 15 minutes, or until it is soft. Drain off the water and reserve it, and force the pumpkin through a sieve. Put this purée in the top of a double boiler and add 1¾ cups of milk and ¼ cup of cream. *Soupe au potiron* should be quite rich and thick, but you will probably still need to dilute the pumpkin and milk mixture with some of the reserved cooking water. Add salt and pepper to taste and cook the soup over simmering water for 20 minutes.

Mix a few spoonfuls of soup with 2 beaten eggs. Add the egg mixture gradually to the soup, stirring constantly, and keep stirring until it begins to thicken. Then stir in a lump of butter and serve immediately.

Purée de Lentilles à la Conti

LENTIL SOUP

Serves four.

Lentils, bacon, butter, onion, carrot, herbs, egg yolks, croutons or lemon

Soak 1 cup of lentils in cold water overnight. Drain them and put them in a soup kettle with 6 cups of fresh water and 1 teaspoon of salt. Bring the water to a boil and skim the surface once or twice. Meanwhile, in a skillet, sauté 2 strips of bacon, diced, in 1 tablespoon of butter. Add 1 onion and 1 carrot, both chopped, and a pinch of thyme. Simmer all together over a low flame for 7 or 8 minutes, until the vegetables are golden but not brown. Add 1 bay leaf, 2 sprigs of parsley, and the contents of the skillet to the simmering lentils.

Cover the kettle and simmer the soup for 2½ hours, or until the lentils are thoroughly cooked. Then remove the parsley and bay leaf and force the soup through a sieve; or cool it and purée it in an electric blender.

To serve, mix a little of the soup in the bottom of a tureen with 2 lightly beaten egg yolks. Reheat the soup, taste it for seasoning, and pour it into the tureen. Stir it carefully and garnish it with small croutons sautéed in butter, or with thin slices of lemon.

Velouté Cressonière

CREAMED WATERCRESS SOUP

Serves six.

Potatoes, watercress, cream, egg yolks, butter

Peel and slice 1 pound of potatoes. Cut off about 3 dozen perfect leaves from a large bunch of watercress and put them aside. Chop the rest of the watercress coarse and sauté it in a soup kettle in 1 tablespoon of butter until it is somewhat softened. Add 5 to 6 cups of salted boiling water and the sliced potatoes, and simmer all together for 20 minutes, or until the potatoes are soft. Pour the soup through a sieve into a saucepan and force through as much as possible of the vegetables. Bring the soup back to the boil, add the reserved watercress leaves, and simmer it another 2 or 3 minutes only.

In a small bowl mix together ¼ cup of heavy cream and 2 egg yolks and stir in a few spoonfuls of the hot soup. Take the soup off the fire and slowly stir in the egg and cream mixture. Add a lump of butter, taste the *velouté* for seasoning, and reheat it briefly without letting it boil. Serve immediately.

Note: You may add 1 small thinly sliced onion when you sauté the watercress.

Potage Dame Edmée

FRESH GREEN PEA AND CHICKEN SOUP

Serves eight.

Chicken, stock, peas, butter, onion, lettuce, spinach, herbs, egg yolks, cream

The next time you boil a chicken for a fricassee, reserve some of the white meat and stock for this delectable soup. (Or you may use leftover roast chicken and canned chicken broth.) In a large saucepan put 4 cups of fresh peas, 6 tablespoons of butter, 1 finely minced onion, a tender head of garden lettuce cut into julienne strips, about 15 leaves of fresh spinach, 4 sprigs of parsley, a few sprigs of chervil if you have it, 2 teaspoons of sugar, ½ teaspoon of salt, and 1¾ cups of water. Cover the saucepan, bring the soup to a boil, and cook it over a moderate fire until the peas are tender. Meanwhile, boil 1 cup of fresh peas, in a separate pan, to add to the soup later.

Pass the soup through a strainer, or a vegetable mill, pressing the vegetables through with the liquid. Return the soup to the saucepan, add 3 cups of chicken stock, stir well, and simmer over a low fire for about 15 minutes. Then add the extra cup of peas, drained, and ¼ cup of cooked white meat of chicken, cut into very fine julienne strips.

Mix 3 egg yolks with 1½ cups of light cream and add this gradually to the soup, stirring constantly. Continue cooking until the soup thickens to a creamy consistency, but do not let it boil.

Bisque de Homard

LOBSTER BISQUE

Serves six.

Lobster, chicken stock, white wine, seasonings, cream, egg yolks, sherry

In a soup kettle heat together 4 cups of chicken stock, 2 cups of water, and 1 cup of dry white wine, with 1 stalk of celery and 1 onion, both cut into pieces, 4 crushed peppercorns, 1 bay leaf, a pinch of thyme, and a sprig of parsley. When this *court-bouillon* has simmered for 15 minutes, boil a live 2-pound lobster in it for 20 minutes. Remove the lobster and strain the stock through a fine sieve. Let the lobster cool, remove the meat, and set it aside. Discard the large claw shells, break the rest of the carcass and shell into pieces, and reserve.

Heat 4 cups of the stock in the top of a large double boiler, stir in 2 tablespoons of butter creamed with 2 tablespoons of flour, and add 1 cup of thin cream. Add the reserved shells and cook the bisque over simmering water for 1 hour, stirring occasionally. Shortly before serving, strain the bisque again, return it to the double boiler, and add ¼ cup of sherry and ½ cup of heavy cream mixed with 3 lightly beaten egg yolks. Taste the bisque for seasoning, reheat it, stirring until it thickens a little, and garnish it with pieces of claw meat. (See Lobster Canapés, page 151, for one way to use up the rest of the meat.)

EGGS & CHEESE

Oeufs Brouillés Paul Reboux

SCRAMBLED EGGS WITH ORANGE

Serves two.

Eggs, orange rind, cream, sherry, butter

The witty, unorthodox, and controversial writer Paul Reboux proposed this version of scrambled eggs. The method, however, is classic and produces results that resemble in no way the American breakfast egg.

Break 4 eggs into a bowl and beat them lightly with a fork until well mixed. Mix in the finely grated rind of half an orange, salt, pepper, and 1 tablespoon each of heavy cream and sherry (more or less, according to taste). Now, in a small heavy saucepan or casserole in which a lump or two of butter have been melted, scramble the eggs. This is done over the slowest possible fire, stirring continuously for some 10 minutes with a fine wire whisk until the whole reaches a rich, creamy consistency, whereupon the eggs should be removed instantly from the fire. Serve surrounded by triangles of bread fried in butter or buttered and toasted strips of French bread.

Oeufs Cocotte à la Crème

EGGS POACHED IN CREAM

Eggs, butter, cream, truffle

For each egg use a small ovenproof custard cup or a 3-inch miniature soufflé ramekin. Put a piece of butter in each cup, break an egg over the butter, and add a tablespoon of very heavy cream. Sprinkle lightly with salt and freshly ground white pepper. Put the cups in a large shallow pan and carefully fill the pan with boiling water just to the level of the cream in the cups. Cover the pan, keep the water barely simmering, on top of the stove, and cook the eggs for about 6 minutes, or until the whites are set. Test the edges with a spoon before serving, as the cooking time depends somewhat on the thickness of the cups. Sprinkle each egg with minced truffle and serve immediately.

Note: If you have no truffle, do not substitute anything else; only truffle will improve fresh eggs, butter, and cream in a recipe as simple as this one.

Oeufs sur le Plat Lorraine

BAKED EGGS

Eggs, ham, Swiss Gruyère cheese, cream

Butter individual shirred–egg dishes. In each one put first a thin slice of ham, then a thin slice of Swiss Gruyère. Break 2 eggs into each dish and pour over them 2 tablespoons of heavy cream. Sprinkle sparingly with salt and pepper. Bake the *oeufs Lorraine* in a 350° oven for 10 minutes, or until the cheese has melted, the whites are set, but the yolks are still soft.

Oeufs Bonne Femme

BAKED EGGS WITH MUSHROOMS

Croutons, mushrooms, butter, eggs

Cut slices of firm white bread into circles about 3 inches across. Sauté the circles in butter until they are crisp and brown on both sides. In another skillet, over a low flame, sauté finely minced mushrooms in butter until they are soft and the liquid they give off is reduced. Arrange the sautéed croutons close together in a shallow buttered baking dish, spread them with the cooked mushrooms, and carefully break an egg over each one. Season with salt and pepper and bake the *oeufs bonne femme* in a 350° oven for 10 minutes, or until the whites are set but the yolks are still soft.

Flan d'Oeufs sur le Plat Savoyarde

BAKED FLAN OF EGG WHITES AND YOLKS

Serves three or four.

Eggs, cream, nutmeg, butter, grated cheese

Separate 6 eggs, putting the whites in a bowl and leaving each yolk in half an eggshell. With an egg beater, beat the whites with ¼ cup of heavy cream, a pinch of nutmeg, and salt and pepper until the mixture is frothy. Into a shallow baking dish, over low heat and using an asbestos mat, put

2 tablespoons of butter and add the egg whites as soon as it melts. Cook them, stirring constantly with a whisk, until they are thick and creamy.

Take the dish from the fire and drop the yolks one by one in a circle on top of the whites. Cover the baking dish, put it back on the fire, still using the mat, and cook the eggs for about 6 minutes, or until the whites are puffed and set but still soft. Serve the flan immediately, from the baking dish, with mild freshly grated cheese to sprinkle over it and accompanied by a crisp green salad with a tart dressing.

Epinards à la Chimay

SPINACH PURÉE WITH STUFFED EGGS

Serves six.

Spinach, eggs, onion, shallot, mushrooms, butter, cream, nutmeg, cayenne, bread crumbs

Simmer 1 small onion, 1 small shallot, and 4 large mushrooms, all minced fine, in 1 tablespoon of butter until they are soft and reduced. Season with salt, pepper, and grated nutmeg. Cut 6 hard-boiled eggs in half lengthwise. Remove the yolks and mash them with the mushroom mixture, 2 teaspoons of butter, a little cream, and a touch of cayenne. Stuff the egg whites with the yolk mixture, sprinkle them lightly with fine bread crumbs, dot them with butter, and place in a small buttered baking dish.

Meanwhile, in a covered kettle cook 3 pounds of spinach with ¼ cup of water for 10 minutes, or until it is just soft, and purée it in an electric blender. Reheat the spinach over a good flame to cook away all excess liquid, then add a lump of butter, ⅓ cup of extra-heavy cream or *crème fraîche*, and salt and pepper. Brown the stuffed eggs lightly under the broiler. Put the spinach purée in a deep serving dish, arrange the eggs in a circle on top, and serve immediately.

Crème de Camembert

CREAMED CAMEMBERT CHEESE

Camembert, white wine, butter, toast crumbs

This is not the same thing as Clémentine's special treatment of a fine Camembert in the old days (see page 120). Rather, it is a way to put a little glory into the lesser Camemberts found in our supermarkets — or even in good cheese stores, for a great Camembert has, sadly, become a rarity, even in France. It assists a Brie of routine quality, too.

Carefully scrape off all the skin of the Camembert (to the quick, so to speak) and let the cheese stand in a bowl, covered with dry white wine, for 12 hours. Drain it and cream it well with a fork or a spatula with 5 tablespoons of unsalted butter. Shape the Camembert cream into the form of the original cheese and coat it lightly on top and all around with very fine toast crumbs. Or you may, of course, use Clémentine's ground toasted almonds. Chill before serving.

SHELLFISH & SNAILS

Palourdes à la Bretonne

BAKED CLAMS

Serves two.

Clams, butter, shallot, parsley, white wine, lemon, cayenne, bread crumbs

Remove a dozen small hard-shell clams from their shells, saving some of their liquor. In a small saucepan melt 1 tablespoon of butter, add 1 chopped shallot, 1 teaspoon of minced parsley, 2 tablespoons of white wine, a good squeeze of lemon, 3 tablespoons of the clam liquor, and cayenne pepper (but no salt). Simmer this over low heat until the mixture is thick but still juicy (about 1½ tablespoons).

Brown 2 or 3 tablespoons of coarse bread crumbs lightly in plenty of butter and combine them with the reduced sauce. Replace each clam on a half shell, put some of the bread-crumb mixture on each one, and brown them briefly in a very hot oven.

Coquilles Saint-Jacques au Gratin   page 76.

Huîtres aux Amandes

BAKED OYSTERS WITH ALMONDS

Oysters, almonds, butter, brandy, cayenne

Allow about ½ cup of dressing for each dozen oysters. Cream together equal parts of finely ground blanched almonds and unsalted butter. For each ½ cup of this dressing blend in thoroughly half a minced and crushed clove of garlic, 1½ teaspoons of brandy, and a cautious sprinkling of cayenne pepper. Pour off most of the liquor from oysters on their half-shells and cover each one with about 2 teaspoons of dressing. Bake them in a 450° oven for 5 minutes and serve immediately.

Moules à la Marinière page 79.

Salade Japonaise Dumas

POTATO AND MUSSEL SALAD

Serves six as a separate course.
Mussels, white wine, shallots, new potatoes, herbs, truffles,
French dressing

This salad is expensive, because of the truffles, and not easy to shop for,
because of the fresh mussels. But if you can manage to collect the ingredients it is incomparable. If you must do without the truffles, it is still
wonderful.

Brush, scrape, and wash thoroughly 3 quarts of fresh mussels. Put
them in a soup kettle with ½ cup of dry white wine and 2 minced shallots
and cook them, covered, over a brisk flame until the shells have opened,
about 6 minutes. Remove the mussels from their shells when they are
cool enough to handle.

Peel and slice 2 pounds of small boiled new potatoes while they
are still warm. Combine the mussels and potatoes and add ¾ cup of French
dressing made with 2 parts white wine vinegar, 5 parts olive oil, and salt
and pepper to taste. Add 2 teaspoons each of minced fresh parsley and
chives, toss the salad gently so as not to break the potatoes, and put it in
a serving bowl.

Drain a 2- or 3-ounce can of truffles (save the juice to flavor the sauce
of some other dish), slice them thin, and spread them over the salad.
Cover the serving dish and chill the salad for 1 hour, no longer; or serve
it warm.

Crabe à la Diable

DEVILED CRAB

Serves four.
Crab meat, butter, onion, shallot, brandy, mustard, cream,
bread crumbs

In 2 tablespoons of melted butter sauté lightly, over low heat, 1 small
onion and 1 shallot, both minced fine, until they are soft and translucent.
Stir in 1 teaspoon of brandy and 1 teaspoon of Dijon mustard, and remove
from the heat.

Make a cream sauce with 2 tablespoons of butter, 2 tablespoons

175

SHELLFISH
&
SNAILS

of flour, and 1 cup of light cream. Season with salt and pepper. Add the cream sauce to the first mixture and then add 1¼ cups of cooked flaked crab meat. Mix all together, taste for mustard, and spoon the mixture into 4 small individual ramekins (or crab or scallop shells). Sprinkle with bread crumbs, dot with butter, and bake in a 350° oven for about 15 minutes, or until the crumbs are delicately browned.

Homard à la Crème

LOBSTER IN CREAM

Serves two.

Lobster, butter, brandy, seasonings, egg yolks, cream, sherry

Slice the meat of a 2-pound boiled lobster and heat the pieces in 2 tablespoons of hot butter for 1 or 2 minutes. Add salt, pepper, and a little paprika. Pour on 1 tablespoon of warmed brandy, set it aflame, and shake the pan back and forth until the flame dies. Beat 2 egg yolks together with ¾ cup of cream, add 2 tablespoons of sherry, and pour this sauce over the lobster. Keep the lobster over a low fire, stirring constantly, until the sauce thickens, but do not let it boil.

Serve in individual ramekins or shirred-egg dishes, with buttered and toasted strips of French bread.

Homard Grillé à l'Ail

GARLIC-BROILED LOBSTER

Lobster, olive oil, snail butter

Split live lobsters lengthwise and remove the veins in the tails. (If your fish market does this for you, don't allow it to be done more than 3 hours before you cook the lobsters.) Crack the claws, lay the lobsters flat, shell side down, in a broiler pan, and paint the cut sides, end to end, with olive oil.

Broil the lobsters under a high flame, but not too close to it, for 8 to 12 minutes in all, depending on their size. As soon as the tail meat begins to pull away from the shell, 4 or 5 minutes, spoon a little Snail Butter with Garlic (see next recipe) into either side of each shell and over the meat. Serve the lobsters immediately when they are done. To test, the meat in the tails should be resilient but not yet firm to the touch. Fifteen minutes is probably the limit, even for a large lobster.

Note: The original recipe, from an old cookbook, also calls for a very cold sauce to be served with the very hot lobster. It is made of 3

parts homemade mayonnaise thinned with 1 part *crème fraîche* and seasoned with a touch of minced and crushed garlic, lemon juice, and freshly ground white pepper.

Homard à l'Américaine   *page 31.*

Lobster Delmonico   *page 77.*

Escargots de Bourgogne
SNAILS IN BUTTER AND GARLIC
Canned snails, butter, parsley, garlic, shallots, nutmeg

Providing one is equipped with a taste for garlic and a set of metal snail dishes, shell-shaped clamps, and little two-pronged forks, this famous specialty should present no serious problems even to the amateur cook. The classic Burgundian butter sauce is simplicity itself. The snails are imported in quantity nowadays, with the snails in a can and their shells in a separate package; the shells are reusable.

Allow 6 snails per person for a first course or a full dozen for a main course. They can be prepared well in advance, chilled, and heated at the last moment.

Snail Butter with Garlic: For four dozen snails, cream together 1¾ sticks of butter, ½ cup of minced parsley, 8 to 10 minced and crushed cloves of garlic, 4 or 5 minced shallots, a pinch of nutmeg, and pepper and just a little salt to taste.

Wash and drain the shells. Drain the brine from the canned snails, place one in each shell, and pack the shells brim-full with the garlic butter. Arrange them carefully, open ends up, in the hollows of the snail dishes and heat them in a 450° oven until they are bubbling hot. Serve them in the same dishes, with plenty of French bread for mopping up the melted butter.

FISH

With fish, Clémentine served only small boiled potatoes. Even these were dispensed with if the sauce for the fish was rich. A vegetable followed, as a separate course.

Sole Meunière

SOLE OR FLOUNDER SAUTÉED IN BUTTER
Sole or flounder, flour, butter, lemon, parsley

Small, whole, but rarely obtainable fresh Dover sole are the ideal fish to sauté *à la meunière*. However, the many fine American varieties of sole and flounder, whole or filleted, are also at their best when treated in this perfectly simple fashion. Have your whole fish skinned and tails and heads removed.

Sprinkle the fish lightly with salt and pepper, dip it in flour, and shake off the excess. Over high heat, melt enough butter in a large skillet to coat the surface generously, but not so much that the fish will stew rather than brown. Put in the fish as soon as the butter is hot and sizzling, but before it starts to brown. Lower the heat a little, cook the fish to golden brown on the first side, turn it, and brown the other side. Do not overcook.

The timing, alas, is a matter of experience and depends on the thickness of the fish, which is done when it is just resilient, not too firm, to the touch. For small flounder fillets this may be as little as 1 or 2 minutes of cooking to a side; for a small whole sole, up to 3 or 4 minutes to a side; and more, with caution, for thick fillets. The pieces must lie flat, in one or two skillets, as needed, so they do not overlap.

Remove the fish to a hot platter when it is done, sprinkle generously with lemon juice and finely chopped parsley, and keep it warm. For each serving, add 1 generous tablespoon of butter to the skillet and heat it until it is dark gold and foaming but not brown. Pour the hot butter over the fish, garnish each piece with a slice of lemon dipped in chopped parsley, and serve immediately.

Filets de Sole au Vin Blanc

SOLE OR FLOUNDER IN WHITE WINE

Serves four.

Sole or flounder fillets, white wine, shallot, mushrooms, butter, egg yolks, cream, parsley

Spread 1½ pounds of fillets of sole or flounder in a shallow baking dish. Add 1 cup of dry white wine, sprinkle the fillets with salt and pepper, and add 1 finely chopped shallot and ¼ pound of sliced mushrooms. Dot the fish with butter and bake it in a 350° oven for 20 minutes, or until it is just firm.

With a basting syringe, draw off the liquid in the baking dish and simmer it down to about 1 cup. Mix 2 egg yolks with ½ cup of heavy cream and stir them carefully into the reduced fish stock. Add 1 teaspoon of chopped parsley, pour the sauce over the flounder, and glaze it briefly under a hot broiler.

Clémentine's Flounder   page 76.

Sole Gratinée comme en Gironde

SOLE OR FLOUNDER BAKED WITH MUSHROOMS AND BREAD CRUMBS

Serves four.

Fillets of sole or flounder, mushrooms, shallots, herbs, bread crumbs, white wine, stock

Butter a shallow baking dish with 1 tablespoon of butter creamed with 1 teaspoon of flour. Mix together ¼ pound of mushrooms and 2 shallots, all chopped fine, 1 teaspoon of minced chives, and 1 tablespoon of minced parsley. Spread half this mixture in the baking dish, sprinkle it lightly with fine bread crumbs, and arrange 8 fillets of sole or flounder on top. Cover the fish with the rest of the chopped vegetables, sprinkle lightly again with bread crumbs and with a little grated Swiss cheese, and dot with butter. Add ½ cup each of white wine and chicken stock and bake the fish in a 350° oven for 20 to 25 minutes.

Filets de Sole, Sauce Normande

SOLE OR FLOUNDER WITH NORMANDY SAUCE

Serves four.

Sole or flounder fillets, hard cider or white wine, onion, herbs, butter, egg yolks, lemon

Buy enough whole sole or flounder to make 2 pounds of fillets and save the heads and backbones. In a covered saucepan simmer the rinsed heads and bones for 20 minutes in 2 cups of water and 1 cup of hard cider or dry white wine, with several slices of onion, 1 bay leaf, a sprig of parsley, a pinch of thyme, 4 or 5 peppercorns, and a little salt. Strain the *court-bouillon* and poach the fillets in it for 20 minutes, or until they are firm, keeping the liquid just below the boiling point. Transfer the fillets to a heated dish and keep them warm.

Sauce Normande: Blend 1½ teaspoons of flour into 1 tablespoon of melted butter and add gradually ¾ cup of the fish stock. Season the sauce with salt and pepper, heat it, stirring, until it is slightly thickened, then add 2 egg yolks first beaten with the juice of half a lemon and 2 tablespoons of the stock. Add 1 tablespoon of butter and stir the sauce with a whisk until it is hot and thick; do not let it boil. Spoon over the fish and serve at once.

Haddock au Vin Blanc *page 74.*

Cabillaud à la Bretonne

COD BAKED IN CIDER

Serves four.

Codfish, hard cider, shallots, parsley, mushrooms

Put a 2-pound piece of fresh cod, boned and skinned, in a baking dish first greased with 3 tablespoons of salad oil. Sprinkle the fish with salt and pepper and with 2 shallots, 1 teaspoon of parsley, and 4 or 5 mushrooms, all chopped. Add 2 cups of hard cider. Work 1 teaspoon of flour to a smooth paste with 1 tablespoon of butter and add it to the cider. Bake the codfish in a 350° oven, basting it several times. It should be done in 20 to 30 minutes.

Poisson à la Niçoise

BAKED FISH WITH TOMATOES AND OLIVE OIL

Serves four.

Fish fillets, olive oil, tomatoes, garlic, parsley, oregano, butter

This is a simple way to prepare any fish suitable for baking and it will add flavor to less interesting fish such as the humble haddock.

Coat a baking dish with olive oil and place 2 pounds of fish fillets in it in a single layer. Season them with salt and pepper. Peel, seed, and chop coarse 4 or 5 small tomatoes; mix them with 1 chopped and mashed clove of garlic, 1 tablespoon of minced parsley, ¼ teaspoon of dried oregano, and salt and pepper. Spread the mixture on the fish, sprinkle it with ¼ cup of olive oil, and dot it with 2 tablespoons of butter. Bake the fish in a 350° oven for 30 minutes, more or less, depending on the thickness of the fillets.

Poisson Grillé, Sauce aux Câpres

BROILED FISH WITH CAPER SAUCE

Makes a sauce to serve four to six.

Broiled fish, butter, meat glaze, anchovies, vinegar, capers

Any good broiled fish will be enhanced by this simple sauce.

Melt ¼ pound of butter and add ½ teaspoon of meat glaze (or extract) and 2 chopped anchovy fillets. Stir until these are dissolved but do not let the butter boil. Add freshly ground pepper, a few drops of vinegar, and 2 teaspoons of drained capers. Be sure the sauce is very hot and pass it in a sauceboat.

Maquereaux au Beurre d'Estragon

BAKED MACKEREL WITH TARRAGON BUTTER

Serves four.

Mackerel, olive oil, butter, tarragon, tarragon wine vinegar

Have 4 small tinker mackerel cleaned and split without completely separating the halves. Spread them, skin sides down, in an oiled baking dish, season them well with salt and pepper, and pour a little olive oil over them; let them marinate for an hour before cooking.

Place the fish in a 400° oven, or under the broiler, and cook them for 15 to 20 minutes, or until the meat separates easily from the backbones, which you may now carefully remove.

Meanwhile, mash 1 generous tablespoon of chopped fresh tarragon in a mortar and mix in gradually 4 tablespoons of soft butter, salt and pepper, and about 2 teaspoons of tarragon wine vinegar. Spread the butter on the still broiling-hot fish and serve at once.

Maquereaux aux Olives *page 68.*

Truites Sautées au Beurre
TROUT PAN-FRIED IN BUTTER
Serves four.

This basic method, *à la meunière,* for cooking small whole trout applies, as do the variations, to any small white-fleshed fish, whether from fresh or salt water. (Among them, whiting). Don't insist on trout; buy your freshest local fish.

Have 4 small trout cleaned, the fins trimmed off, and the heads and tails left on. Wash the fish and wipe them dry. At the last minute, dip them lightly in flour seasoned with salt and pepper and shake off the excess. In a large heavy skillet, or two skillets, melt a generous tablespoon of butter for each fish. When it just sizzles and foams, add the fish and brown them over medium heat on both sides. The timing does depend on their size, but when they are nicely browned, they should be properly cooked through. Remove them to a hot platter or individual plates and keep them warm.

Truites aux Amandes: In the butter left in the pan (you may need to add about 2 tablespoons), lightly brown ½ cup of slivered almonds. Sauté them over low heat until they are golden. Spoon the almonds and the browned butter (it must not have been allowed to scorch) over the trout, provide a wedge of lemon for each trout, and serve at once.

Truites à la Crème: Sauté almonds in butter as above and, when they are golden, stir ½ cup (or a little more) of heavy cream briskly into the skillet. Scrape and stir well with a whisk so the cream will take up the brown color of the butter, let the sauce reduce a little, and pour it over the trout.

Truites à la Grenobloise: Once the trout are cooked, in the butter left in the pan (you may need to add about 2 tablespoons), sauté 4 large minced mushrooms and 2 tablespoons of dry bread crumbs. Add the juice of half a lemon and 2 teaspoons of drained capers. Stir the sauce briskly for a few seconds and pour it over the trout.

Saumon Poêlé au Vouvray   page 136.

Saumon Val de Loire

BAKED SALMON VAL DE LOIRE

Serves four.

Salmon, salt pork or bacon, shallots, butter, wine vinegar, white wine

Skin one side of a 2-pound cross-cut piece of a small salmon. Tie a slice of bacon over the skinned side; or, better, with a larding needle run a few fine strips of salt pork into the fish. Butter a shallow baking dish, put in 3 or 4 minced shallots, and place the salmon on top of them, skin side down. Dot the fish with 4 tablespoons of butter and bake it, uncovered, in a 350° oven for 15 minutes, basting several times with the pan juices. Then add ¼ cup each of good wine vinegar and water to the pan and cook the fish another 15 minutes, still basting.

Remove the salmon to a hot platter, discard the bacon, and keep the fish warm. On top of the stove, dilute the pan juices with ½ cup of dry white wine and stir in 1 tablespoon of butter creamed with 2 teaspoons of flour. Simmer the sauce, stirring often, for 2 or 3 minutes, taste it for seasoning, strain it, and pour it over the salmon.

Note: You may use a salmon fillet or steak, which will require less than 30 minutes cooking in all, depending on thickness.

Saumon Poché, Sauce Verte

POACHED SALMON WITH GREEN MAYONNAISE

Serves six.

Salmon; ingredients for a court-bouillon; greens and herbs, mayonnaise and cream for the sauce; tomatoes, cucumbers, French dressing

In 2 quarts of water simmer for 15 minutes 1 carrot and 1 onion, both cut into pieces, 2 sprigs of parsley, 1 bay leaf, ½ teaspoon of thyme, 6 peppercorns, 1 tablespoon of salt, and ½ cup of white wine. Then put in a 3-pound piece of salmon wrapped in a square of cheesecloth. When the liquid returns to the boil, turn the flame very low and poach the salmon, covered, for 25 minutes. Remove the cover and cool the fish in the cooking liquid; then drain and unwrap it, chill it, and skin the top side before masking it with the following sauce.

Sauce Verte: Trim the stems from fresh spinach, watercress, parsley, and tarragon. Measure, quite firmly packed, 1 cup of spinach, ½ cup of watercress, ½ cup of parsley, and ¼ cup of tarragon. Drop all these greens into boiling water and let them boil for 3 minutes, uncovered. Drain them in a sieve, cool them under running water, and squeeze them dry in a cloth. Chop them as fine as possible, add about ¼ cup sour cream or *crème fraîche*, and reduce them to a fine purée in an electric blender. Mix the green purée thoroughly with 1½ cups of homemade mayonnaise.

Use part of this sauce to mask the salmon and serve the rest in a sauceboat. Garnish the platter with watercress and with 6 peeled, hollowed, and well-drained tomatoes stuffed with diced cucumbers seasoned with French dressing and minced parsley.

Mousse de Poisson, Sauce Normande

FISH MOUSSE WITH NORMANDY SAUCE
Serves four.
Cooked fish, egg whites, nutmeg, cream, *sauce normande*

Use 2 cups of boned and skinned freshly poached white fish. Purée it, one quarter at a time, in an electric blender. Return the fish to the blender, one third at a time with the white of 1 egg each time, and blend until the purée is very smooth. Season with salt, pepper, and a good dash of nutmeg and chill the mixture for 1 hour. Then add gradually 1 cup of heavy cream and beat the mousse with a wire whisk until it is light and well blended.

Pour the mousse into a generously buttered fish mold and cover with a piece of buttered waxed paper. Place the mold in a baking pan containing about 1 inch of boiling water and cook the mousse in a 350° oven for 20 minutes, or until it is firm to the touch. Let it stand a few minutes, then unmold and cover with *sauce normande* (see page 180).

Aïoli Provençal

STEAMED SALT COD WITH GARLIC MAYONNAISE
Salt cod, vegetables, garlic mayonnaise

The *aïoli* is a pungent Mediterranean mayonnaise that is served in large quantities, thoroughly chilled, with hot, poached salt cod fillets, hard-boiled eggs, and boiled vegetables: Whole new potatoes in their jackets, small whole artichokes, leeks with the green tops trimmed off, and carrots and white turnips, cut into pieces, are the usual assortment (plus, also, snails and squid!).

Use as many cloves of garlic in the *aïoli* as you dare. The correct recipe calls for 8 cloves per cup of homemade mayonnaise; 3 cloves are about the minimum if the dish is to keep its character. Start with the garlic, minced and mashed to a pulp, in a bowl. With a sauce whisk beat in 2 egg yolks. Add ¼ teaspoon of salt and a little freshly ground pepper; then add, drop by drop, ¼ cup of chilled olive oil, stirring furiously. Pour this mixture into an electric blender, turn the blender on, and slowly add the juice of half a lemon and 1 tablespoon of lukewarm water. Then add gradually 1 cup of chilled olive oil. Do not make more than this amount of *aïoli* at a time in an electric blender. Allow ½ cup, preferably more, per person.

To poach dried salt cod: For an *aïoli* with all the trimmings, 1½ pounds of dried cod is ample to serve eight. Place the cod on a rack in a fish poacher and leave it under a trickle of running water overnight and up to 12 hours, emptying the poacher at least once. This is the best way, though wasteful of water. You may simply soak the cod in water to fill the poacher, changing it 3 or 4 times.

Lift out the cod, rinse the poacher, replace the rack and the fish, and add fresh water to cover well. Bring to a boil, reduce the heat to a simmer, and then poach the cod for 12 to 15 minutes, or just until it flakes easily.

Lift the fish out again, let drain well, and transfer to a large platter. Surround becomingly with some of the boiled vegetables, and serve the remaining vegetables from heated serving bowls.

185

FISH

POULTRY

Poulet Rôti à l'Estragon
ROAST CHICKEN WITH TARRAGON

Roast a chicken in the usual way, but instead of using a stuffing, put a large bunch of fresh tarragon inside, along with a small quartered lemon. Baste the chicken often, every 10 minutes, with its own juices (but stop basting for the last 20 minutes so that the skin may brown).

The tarragon flavors the meat deliciously. If the bird has been well rubbed with butter and is repeatedly basted (you may want to add a small amount of chicken stock to the pan), it will be at its best without any sauce—only with the pan juices skimmed of fat and stirred in the roasting pan with a few spoonfuls of stock to deglaze it. Add a squeeze of lemon.

Poulet Farci Cassini page 92.

Poulet Cocotte
BAKED WHOLE CHICKEN
Serves four.
Chicken, bacon, butter, onions, carrots, seasonings, white wine, mushrooms, parsley

In a flameproof casserole brown 1 strip of bacon, diced fine, in 1 tablespoon of hot butter. Remove the bacon, reserve it, and put a cleaned and trussed 4-pound chicken on its side in the casserole. Brown it on one side, then the other, then breast down, for 5 minutes each time.

Meanwhile, in a skillet sauté a second strip of diced bacon in 1 tablespoon of butter, remove it, and set it aside. To the fat remaining in the skillet add 8 to 10 tiny whole onions, or 3 or 4 medium ones, quartered, and 3 medium carrots, cut into small pieces. Toss the vegetables in the fat, sprinkle them with ½ tablespoon of sugar, and cook them, stirring often, until they are brown on all sides, or about 10 minutes.

Then turn the chicken on its back, and add to the casserole the sautéed vegetables, salt, pepper, ½ cup of hot water, and ¼ cup of dry white wine. Place it, uncovered, in a 350° oven and bake the chicken for 45 minutes to 1 hour. Fifteen minutes before it is done, add the reserved bacon and ¼ pound of quartered mushrooms first sautéed briefly in a little butter.

Sprinkle the *poulet en cocotte* with chopped parsley. Present and carve it in the casserole. Serve with *pommes sautées* (see page 224).

La Poularde Pochée à la Mère Brazier

POACHED CHICKEN WITH VEGETABLES

Serves three or four.
Chicken, chicken stock, carrots, turnips, celery, leeks, bacon, herbs, butter

Heat 2 quarts of chicken stock with 2 carrots, cut into pieces, 2 small white turnips, quartered, 2 stalks of celery, cut into pieces, 4 leeks with most of their green tops cut off, a cube of lean bacon 1 inch square (or 2 slices), a pinch of thyme, 1 bay leaf, and 2 sprigs of parsley. Simmer this *court-bouillon* for 10 minutes, then added a trussed 3-pound chicken, young, tender, and plump. (*Chez* la Mère Brazier the chicken would have numerous slices of truffle inserted under the skin over the breast and leg meat.)

Simmer the chicken, covered, for 20 minutes after the stock comes back to a boil, then turn off the heat and let the chicken stand and continue to poach in the hot stock for 20 minutes. Remove it to a hot platter, carve it, pour a little of the stock over it so it will not dry out, and keep it warm. The vegetables should be tender by this time, but if they are not, continue cooking them while you make the sauce.

In a small saucepan, over a brisk fire, reduce 1¼ cups of stock to ¾ cup. Taste it for seasoning and whip in 2 tablespoons of creamed unsalted butter at the last minute, off the fire. Serve the chicken surrounded by the vegetables and pass the sauce separately.

Note: You may also present the chicken whole and carve it at the table, especially if you have put truffles under the skin.

Poule au Riz   *page 91.*

Poule au Pot Henri IV

KING HENRY IV'S "CHICKEN FOR EVERY POT"

Serves six.

Fowl, bread, ham, shallots, garlic, herbs, nutmeg, eggs, carrots, turnips, onions, leeks, celery

Use a plump 5- to 6-pound boiling fowl. Mix together well a stuffing of 5 slices of stale French bread, crumbled and soaked in ½ cup of milk; the liver, heart, and skinned giblet of the hen, and 1 slice of ham or bacon, all ground together with the finest blade of a meat grinder; 2 shallots and 2 cloves of garlic, all minced; 2 tablespoons of chopped parsley and a pinch each of rosemary, thyme, nutmeg, salt, and pepper; and, lastly, 2 small eggs, or 1 large one, lightly beaten. Stuff the hen, sew it up carefully at both ends, and truss it.

Put the hen in a soup kettle and add 3 small carrots and 2 small white turnips, all cut into pieces; 3 whole onions, one of them stuck with 2 cloves; 2 leeks with most of the green part cut off; 1 small stalk of celery with its leaves; and 1 bay leaf, 6 crushed peppercorns, and 1 teaspoon of salt. Add water to cover the hen, but not more than 3 quarts. Cover the kettle and bring the water to a boil, then simmer the hen over very low heat for 2 hours, or until it is tender.

To serve, carve the hen and arrange the meat on a hot platter. Break open the carcass, remove the stuffing, and slice it. Arrange the stuffing and the vegetables around the meat, pour a little of the broth over the platter, and serve the rest in cups. Coarse salt is passed at the table with *poule au pot.*

Coq au Vin Blanc

CHICKEN IN WHITE WINE

Serves four to six.

Chicken, butter, onions, garlic, white wine, herbs

In a heavy saucepan, sauté 1 sliced onion and 1 minced clove of garlic in 1 tablespoon of butter until the onion is soft. Add the neck, back, wing tips, and giblets of a plump roasting chicken. When these have browned a little, add 4 cups of dry white wine and 1 bay leaf, cover the saucepan, and simmer the mixture over the lowest possible heat for about 2 hours.

About 45 minutes before serving, in an iron skillet sauté the rest of the chicken, cut into serving pieces, in 2 tablespoons of hot butter. When the chicken has browned, strain the white-wine stock and blend into it 1 tablespoon of butter creamed with 1 teaspoon of flour. Pour the wine sauce over the chicken and simmer the *coq au vin*, covered, for about 30 minutes. Serve with rice or boiled potatoes and garnished with the following onions that have been cooked separately.

Glazed Onions: To serve six, in a heavy skillet cook until golden 18 small whole onions in 1 tablespoon each of butter and oil; add salt, pepper, a pinch of thyme, 1 small bay leaf, and ½ cup of chicken broth. Cover the skillet and simmer the onions gently for 45 minutes or more, adding more stock if needed, until they are tender but still whole and the liquid is reduced to a glaze.

Notes: This recipe is no different from the more familiar *coq au vin* made with red wine, but the flavor is more delicate.

To make glazed onions for the red-wine version of the dish, brown them well at the beginning.

Poulet Sauté à la Paysanne Provençale
SAUTÉED CHICKEN WITH WHITE WINE AND TOMATOES

Serves four.

Chicken, olive oil, onion, white wine, tomatoes, garlic, parsley, black olives

Have a 4-pound chicken cut into serving pieces, wipe them dry, season them with salt and pepper, and dip them lightly in flour. In a broad sauté or frying pan brown them on all sides in ¼ cup of hot olive oil. Add 1 tablespoon of finely chopped onion and let it cook slowly until it is golden. Add ½ cup of dry white wine and cook until this is reduced by about half. Then add 4 medium-size tomatoes, peeled, seeded, and chopped coarse, 1 small clove of garlic, chopped and mashed, and 1 tablespoon of finely minced parsley. Cover the pan and cook the chicken slowly for 15 to 20 minutes. Five minutes before it is done, add a dozen pitted black Italian olives. Serve with steamed potatoes.

Poulet Sauté "Bouchard" *page 126.*

Poulet Sauté à la Normande

ESCOFFIER'S CHICKEN SAUTÉ NORMANDY

Serves four.

Chicken, mushrooms, onion, brandy, cream, stock

Have a 4-pound chicken cut into serving pieces, wipe them dry, and season them with salt and pepper. In a broad sauté or frying pan, heat together 2 tablespoons of butter and 1 tablespoon of oil. Sauté the chicken slowly in this, over moderate heat. After about 10 minutes, when the chicken is browned on all sides, add ½ pound of quartered mushrooms, first cooked in butter for about 5 minutes, and 1 generous tablespoon of chopped onion.

Continue cooking the chicken slowly, without letting the onion burn, for about 15 minutes, or until the pieces of white meat are done. Remove these to a dish and cook the dark meat for another 5 minutes. Return the white meat to the pan, add 2 tablespoons of apple brandy (or good French brandy), and cook until it has almost completely evaporated. Then add ¾ cup of heavy cream and 3 tablespoons of hot stock (or hot water in which ½ teaspoon of meat glaze has been dissolved). Taste the sauce for seasoning and simmer all together for 2 minutes.

If you like a thicker sauce, blend 1 teaspoon of potato starch into the cream before adding it. Serve the chicken in a deep hot dish with the mushrooms and sauce poured over it.

Poulet du Cloître   page 108.

Poulet Cintra   page 93.

Farce de Dinde aux Marrons

CLÉMENTINE'S CHESTNUT TURKEY STUFFING

Chestnuts, shallots, onion, sausage meat, bread crumbs, celery, mushrooms, herbs, brandy, Madeira

For a 15-pound holiday turkey, prepare the following stuffing: Peel 2 pounds of chestnuts and boil them in salted water until they are tender but not soft (or use about 1½ pounds of whole canned chestnuts packed in brine, drained).

In a large skillet, sauté 2 shallots and 1 onion, all chopped, in 1 tablespoon of butter. Add ½ pound of sausage meat, heat all together briefly, breaking up the sausage, and pour off the excess fat. Mix in 1½ cups of bread crumbs moistened with ½ cup of hot chicken stock (or turkey stock, if you are already simmering the bird's neck and giblets to make a basting liquid). Add the cooled chestnuts, crumbled by hand; 2 stalks of celery and 6 mushrooms, all chopped; 1 tablespoon of minced parsley, 1 teaspoon of dried thyme, salt and pepper, ¼ cup of brandy, and 2 tablespoons of Madeira.

Mix the stuffing well, cool it completely, and refrigerate. Pack it loosely inside the turkey shortly before you roast it.

Notes: Clémentine's original recipe calls for a 2-ounce can of truffles, chopped, with their juice, rather than mushrooms.

Even the dedicated Clémentine loathed peeling chestnuts. She would be thrilled by the fine frozen fresh chestnuts from Italy, perfectly peeled, that appear in specialty shops today at holiday time. Follow the package instructions for poaching them until tender.

Blanquette de Dindon à la Crème

CREAMED LEFTOVER TURKEY

Serves four.

Cold roast turkey, flour, butter, cream, turkey broth, mushrooms, lemon juice

Cut cold roast turkey into large dice and remove the skin. For 2 packed cups of turkey meat, blend 1 tablespoon of flour into 1½ tablespoons of melted butter and add gradually ½ cup each of cream and turkey broth made from the carcass (or use canned chicken broth). Add salt and pepper to taste and cook the sauce, stirring often, until it is smooth and slightly thickened.

Meanwhile, in a small covered saucepan, simmer ¼ pound of quartered mushrooms for 5 minutes in 3 tablespoons of water and 1 tablespoon of lemon juice. Add the turkey meat and the mushrooms, with their liquor, to the cream sauce, and simmer the *blanquette* slowly until the turkey is heated through. Serve with plain rice, *not* on toast as Fannie Farmer would do!

Canard aux Navets

ROAST DUCK WITH WHITE TURNIPS

Serves four.

Duck, onions, white wine, stock, white turnips, butter, sugar

Put a young duck in a roasting pan with 4 small whole onions, sprinkle it with salt and pepper, and roast it in a 350° oven for 20 to 25 minutes per pound. Prick the skin well to release the fat. After the duck has begun to brown, add ¼ cup each of dry white wine and chicken stock to the pan juices and baste it several times with them.

Meanwhile, peel and cut into pieces 1 pound of young white turnips. Brown them on all sides in 2 or 3 tablespoons of butter, then sprinkle them with 1 teaspoon of sugar. Forty-five minutes before the duck is done, put them in the roasting pan with the duck to finish cooking.

Transfer the duck to a hot serving platter and put the turnips and onions around it. Skim all the fat from the pan juices, deglaze the pan with a little white wine, reheat the juices, stirring briskly, and serve them in a sauceboat.

Caneton Champsaur à la Normande

ROAST DUCK WITH APPLES

Serves four.

Duck, russet apples, bread, cinnamon, white wine, stock, Calvados, cream

Albert Champsaur, a jovial, moustachioed Frenchman, and Gwynn Champsaur, a lively Canadian lady, were the prewar owners of Le Grand Cerf in Les Andelys, close by the Seine in Normandy.

Sauté 1 cup of diced soft white bread in 2 tablespoons of hot butter until it is lightly browned. Peel, core, and chop coarse enough russet or tart apples to make 2 cups and add them to the bread. Cook until the apples begin to soften. Season this stuffing with ⅛ teaspoon of cinnamon and salt and freshly ground pepper. Moisten it with a very little white wine.

Stuff a young duck with this, truss it, and rub it with salt and pepper. Roast it, uncovered, in a 350° oven for 20 to 25 minutes per pound; prick the skin several times to release the fat. Add ½ cup each of white wine and chicken stock to the roasting pan and baste the duck often. When it is done, remove it to a hot platter and skim as much fat as possible from the pan juices. Pour in 2 tablespoons of Calvados or apple brandy and ¼ cup of heavy cream. Reheat the sauce, stirring briskly, and pour it through a strainer into a sauceboat. Follow with a vegetable as a separate course.

Faisan aux Endives

PHEASANT WITH ENDIVE

Serves four.

Pheasant, salt pork, onion, carrot, chicken broth, endives, butter, lemon

Tie a strip of salt pork over the breast of a cleaned and trussed 3½-pound domestic pheasant. In a flameproof casserole brown the bird on all sides in 2 tablespoons of hot butter. Add 1 onion and 1 small carrot, both quartered, and ½ cup of chicken broth, lower the heat, and cook the pheasant covered, for 50 minutes. Put a piece of parchment paper under the lid to catch the steam, discard this liquid occasionally, and add more broth sparingly to the casserole as needed. Ten minutes before the bird is done, turn it breast side down to finish browning.

Meanwhile, slice 8 heads of endive crosswise into ¾-inch sections, separate the leaves, and heat them slowly in a heavy saucepan with 2 tablespoons of melted butter. When they begin to soften, add salt and pepper, the juice of half a lemon, and ½ cup of water and simmer the endive until it is cooked through and the liquid is almost evaporated.

When the pheasant is done, transfer it to a hot platter and discard the trussing strings and the salt pork. You may carve it now, or later at the table. Stir ¼ cup of boiling water into the juices in the casserole, scrape up all the brown scraps, strain this sauce over the bird, and add the endive to the platter.

BEEF

Pot-au-Feu

FRENCH BOILED DINNER

Serves six to eight.
Beef, veal knuckle, carrots, turnips, leeks, onion, cloves, herbs, cabbage, potatoes

In a soup kettle put a 4- to 5-pound piece of rump of beef, free of fat, a cracked veal knuckle, a piece of beef shin bone, 5 or 6 quarts of water, a few whole peppercorns, and 2 tablespoons of salt. Simmer the meat for 2 hours and skim the surface of the bouillon several times. Then add 4 carrots, 2 medium white turnips, and 6 small leeks, all cut into pieces, 1 large onion stuck with 3 cloves, 1 bay leaf, ½ teaspoon of dried thyme, and several sprigs of parsley. Simmer the *pot-au-feu* over a low fire for another 1½ hours.

One half hour before serving, ladle out enough bouillon to cook separately a small head of cabbage, cut into serving pieces.

Traditionally, the strained *pot-au-feu* bouillon, with the fat skimmed off, is served first as a soup course. Then the beef is served sliced, with the vegetables, boiled potatoes, coarse salt, and a pot of French mustard.

Boeuf à la Mode

POT ROAST WITH WINE, CARROTS, AND ONIONS

Make to serve four to six, and serve again cold.
Beef, veal knuckle, salt pork, white wine, herbs, spices, brandy, carrots, onions

Boeuf à la mode is one of the most delicious commonplaces of French cooking. Serve it hot one day and cold the next, when the sauce will have jelled like an aspic.

Remove the fat from a 4-pound piece of beef suitable for a pot roast, such as boneless rump or round. Run a few narrow strips of salt pork through it with a larding needle. In a deep iron casserole brown the meat on all sides in 1 tablespoon of butter. Add 1 cup of hot water, 2 cups of white wine, salt and pepper, a bay leaf, a sprig of parsley, a good pinch of thyme, a pinch of nutmeg, and a cracked veal knuckle. Simmer the beef, covered, over a low flame for about 2 hours, then add 2 tablespoons of brandy, 4 carrots, cut into pieces, and 6 small whole onions. Stick 2 or 3 cloves into one of the onions.

Simmer the *boeuf à la mode* for another 1½ hours, or until it is tender. Remove the veal knuckle and the cloves before serving. The sauce should be fairly brown and rich; if there is too much, pour it into another pan and reduce it over a brisk flame.

Boeuf Bourguignon *page 85.*

L'Estouffat Lamandé *page 24.*

Estouffat de Noël à la Gasconne

CHRISTMAS EVE SMOTHERED BEEF

Serves six.

Round of beef, garlic, ham rind, spices, herbs, bacon, shallots, onions, carrots, brandy, red wine, stock

The tradition in Gascony is to cook this savory dish on Christmas Eve and serve it after midnight Mass.

Make 6 small incisions in a 3- to 4-pound piece of round of beef and insert half a clove of garlic into each one. In an ovenproof casserole place a piece of ham rind about 4 inches square, add the piece of beef, and sprinkle it lightly with salt and pepper and a pinch each of nutmeg and cinnamon. Add a *bouquet garni,* 3 whole cloves, 1 slice of bacon, diced, 4 shallots, cut into halves, 2 medium onions, quartered, and 2 carrots, cut into long strips. Then add ¼ cup of brandy, 2 cups of red wine, ½ cup of beef stock, and enough water almost to cover the meat with liquid. Put a piece of heavy parchment paper over the casserole and tie it tightly around the rim. Put the lid on the casserole and cook the *estouffat* in a 225° oven for about 6 hours.

To serve, remove the beef to a deep platter, surround it with the vegetables, and pour the juices over it, first skimming from them as much fat as possible. Serve with buttered noodles.

Boeuf Farci page 85.

Tournedos et Filets Mignons
PAN–BROILED BEEF TENDERLOIN

Beef tenderloin slices should be cut about 1½ inches thick. The meat is so tender that it tends not to hold its shape, so each slice is tied around the perimeter with kitchen string, which is snipped off just before serving.

For 4 slices, heat 1 to 1½ tablespoons of butter in a heavy skillet and brown the meat in it, over a high flame, for 1 minute on each side. Lower the heat a little and cook the slices for 2½ to 3 minutes per side. The meat should be both well browned outside and rare inside. (To test, it should be just resilient to the touch, not soft and not rigid.)

Though the tenderloin is a choice cut, it is not notable for flavor. Therefore *tournedos* and *filets mignons* (the difference is merely the point at which the slices are cut from the whole filet) are always given some elaboration. The simplest is *steak au poivre*: Generous amounts of finely cracked (not ground) black pepper are pressed into both sides of the slices before they are sautéed. These are often flamed with warmed brandy (about 4 teaspoons for a skillet of 4 slices) before being removed from the pan.

Three more variations follow. Slim, crisp *pommes frites* have always been the traditional accompaniment, but they are not really necessary.

Tournedos Béarnaise
BEEF TENDERLOIN WITH BÉARNAISE SAUCE
Serves four.
Sliced beef tenderloin, egg yolks, cream, butter, vinegar, fresh herbs

Cook four *tournedos* in the usual way and serve with this simplified household version of *sauce béarnaise*:

In a small earthenware bowl mix together well 2 egg yolks, 2 tablespoons of cream, ¼ teaspoon of salt, a pinch of cayenne pepper, and 1 tablespoon of tarragon red-wine vinegar. Fit the bowl into the top of a small pan of barely simmering water and stir the sauce with a wire whisk until it is as thick as heavy cream. Bit by bit add 6 tablespoons of unsalted butter, whisking constantly. When the last of the butter is added and melted and the sauce has become fairly thick, add 1½ teaspoons of chopped fresh tarragon and ½ teaspoon each of chopped parsley and chives. Taste for seasoning; it may need a drop more vinegar. Serve from a sauceboat.

It used to be, in small neighborhood restaurants in Paris, that *tournedos béarnaise* were, without fail, served with shoestring-size French-fried potatoes, half a broiled tomato, and the conventional, and suitable, sprig of watercress.

Note: If you use dried tarragon (a scant teaspoon), mellow it in a small cup with 2 teaspoons of boiling water before adding.

Tournedos aux Champignons

BEEF TENDERLOIN WITH MUSHROOM SAUCE

Serves four.
Sliced beef tenderloin, mushrooms, butter, sherry, brandy, cream, mustard

For four slices of tenderloin: Sauté 16 medium-size mushrooms, sliced, in 2 tablespoons of butter for 5 minutes, or until they are soft and some of the liquid they render has evaporated. Add salt and pepper and 2 tablespoons of dry sherry. Put a match to 1 tablespoon of warmed brandy and pour it flaming over the mushrooms. Shake the pan until the flame dies out, then add 3 tablespoons of heavy cream blended with 1 teaspoon of flour and 1 tablespoon of mild white-wine mustard. Simmer all together, stirring often, until the sauce is slightly reduced.

Meanwhile, cook the filets and transfer them to a hot platter or individual plates when they are done. Pour the mushroom sauce over them and serve at once.

Note: Young green beans, buttered and dusted with finely minced parsley, would be a good accompaniment. Clémentine, however, would have served the beans afterwards as a separate course.

Filets Mignons Flambés à l'Avignonaise

FLAMBÉED BEEF TENDERLOIN WITH GARLIC

Sliced beef tenderloin, garlic, French bread, butter, olive oil, brandy, tomatoes, parsley

Rub slices of beef tenderloin on both sides with a large cut clove of garlic. Season them generously with freshly ground pepper and a little salt.

Cut slices from a large loaf of French bread, or cut on the diagonal if necessary, to make croutons to fit the filets. Sauté the bread in a half-

and-half mixture (not too generous) of hot butter and olive oil, with just a little finely minced garlic, until you have crisp croutons browned on both sides. Do not overbrown, or the garlic will be bitter.

In another skillet, cook the filets. Remove from the heat when they are done and, immediately, in the same pan, slip a crouton under each one. Pour 1 teaspoon of warmed brandy over each filet, put a match to it, and shake the pan until the flame dies out.

Transfer croutons and filets to a hot platter or to individual plates, pour on the pan juices, and garnish with small broiled tomatoes.

Note: Clémentine would have loved cherry tomatoes for this. In a skillet heat 5 cherry tomatoes per serving in a little hot olive oil and butter. Stop cooking just before the skins burst and serve sprinkled with finely minced Italian leaf parsley.

Grillade aux Truffes   *page 39.*

Langue de Boeuf en Gelée
BRAISED JELLIED BEEF TONGUE
Beef tongue, veal knuckle, onions, carrots, garlic, herbs, spices, white wine, brandy, parsley

Boil a well-scrubbed fresh tongue in lightly salted water to cover well for 1 hour, skimming the surface several times. Remove the tongue, skin it, and trim off the roots. In an ovenproof casserole brown lightly 2 onions and 2 carrots, all cut into pieces, in 1 tablespoon of bacon fat. Add the prepared tongue, a cracked veal knuckle, a *bouquet garni,* 1 clove of garlic, 6 whole cloves, 6 crushed peppercorns, 1 teaspoon of salt, ½ cup of dry white wine, and 4 cups of the water in which the tongue was boiled. Cook the tongue, tightly covered, in a 250° oven for 2½ hours, or until it is very tender.

Remove the tongue, cool it, and store it in the refrigerator. Strain the broth through a cloth, reserving the carrots, and simmer it until it is reduced to 3 cups. Cool it and store it also in the refrigerator. Next day, or when the broth has jelled firmly, scrape off all the fat, bring the broth to a boil, add 2 tablespoons of brandy, simmer it another minute, and take it off the heat. Slice the tongue and arrange the slices in a serving dish, sprinkle them with minced parsley, and garnish them with slices of the reserved carrots. Pour on the broth, let the dish cool, and chill it until the broth has jelled again. Serve with crunchy French bread.

Note: A 3- to 3½-pound tongue makes 8 or more servings. If the tongue is larger, parboil a little longer and braise a little longer, checking the level of the liquid and adding water and a little wine so that the cooking liquid remains at least 1½ inches deep in the casserole.

Rognon de Boeuf au Vin Rouge *page 126.*

VEAL

Escalopes de Veau à l'Estragon
VEAL SCALLOPS WITH TARRAGON
Serves four.
Veal scallops, beef broth, tomato paste, tarragon

Use 4 large or 8 small veal scallops cut very thin and pounded even thinner with a wooden mallet or potato masher. Salt and pepper the scallops and dip them lightly in flour. Sauté them briefly in a large iron skillet over a medium flame with 2 tablespoons of hot butter until they are brown on each side. Put the scallops on a platter and keep them hot.

Stir ½ cup of beef broth or juices from a roast, 1 tablespoon of tomato paste, and 1 teaspoon of chopped fresh tarragon into the pan juices. Simmer the sauce for 2 or 3 minutes, taste for seasoning, and pour it over the scallops. Buttered noodles are good with veal.

Note: If you use dried tarragon (¾ teaspoon), it will have more flavor if it is soaked in a spoonful of boiling water before it is added to the sauce.

Côtes de Veau Flambées à la Crème
VEAL CHOPS IN CREAM
Serves four.
Veal chops, butter, oil, brandy, white wine, cream

For 4 veal chops, in a heavy skillet heat together 1½ tablespoons of butter and 1 tablespoon of oil. Wipe the chops dry and brown them in the fat, over a brisk fire, for about 3 minutes on each side; be careful not to burn the fat. Season the chops with salt and pepper, cover the skillet, lower the heat, and continue cooking for 15 to 20 minutes, or until tender. Then pour 2 tablespoons of warmed brandy over the chops, set it ablaze, and shake the pan back and forth until the flame dies. Remove the chops to a hot serving dish and keep them warm.

Add 1 or 2 tablespoons of white wine to the pan and stir in all the brown juices. Blend 1 teaspoon of potato starch with 1 tablespoon of cold water and stir in 1 cup of heavy cream. Add this to the pan, season the sauce, simmer it, stirring, until it is slightly thickened, and pour it over the chops. Noodles will be good with this. A vegetable would best be served as a separate course.

Paupiettes de Veau à la Française

BRAISED VEAL BIRDS

Serves four.
Veal scallops, sausage meat, bread, egg, parsley, white wine, cream, mushrooms

On a chopping board pound 8 veal scallops quite thin with a wooden mallet. Trim them to even rectangles and add the scraps, minced fine, to the following stuffing.

Mix together ¼ pound of sausage meat, ½ cup of crumbled stale bread soaked in hot milk and squeezed dry, 1 beaten egg, 1 tablespoon of minced parsley, and a little black pepper. Spread the stuffing on the scallops, roll them up, and tie them neatly with kitchen thread. Melt 2 tablespoons of butter in a skillet, add the veal birds, and simmer them, without browning too much and turning several times, for ½ hour. Then add ½ cup of white wine or stock and braise the *paupiettes* slowly covered for 1 hour, or until they are glazed brown and tender. Transfer them to a heated platter and cut off the threads.

Deglaze the skillet with a little hot stock and ¼ cup of cream, and stir this sauce briskly over a good flame for 2 or 3 minutes. Pour the sauce over the *paupiettes* and serve immediately with sautéed mushroom caps. A fine potato purée is good with these.

Blanquette de Veau

VEAL FRICASSEE

Serves three or four.
Veal, onions, carrots, mushrooms, egg yolks, lemon

A *blanquette de veau* is a veal stew almost too delicate to be called a stew. Every cook in France knows the recipe well.

Cut 1½ pounds of young, white stewing veal into cubes and put the meat in a bowl with boiling water to cover. Put a lid on the bowl and let the meat stand for 20 minutes. Drain off the water and put the veal in a heavy saucepan with 2 onions and 2 carrots, all cut into pieces, salt and pepper, and a sprig of parsley and cover the veal again with boiling water. (You may use chicken or veal stock that is not highly seasoned.) Simmer the *blanquette,* covered, over a low fire for about 1½ hours. Then add ½ pound of sliced mushrooms and simmer for another ½ hour.

In a separate saucepan melt 1 tablespoon of butter, blend in 1 tablespoon of flour, and stir in gradually 2 cups of the veal broth. Simmer this sauce until it is slightly reduced. Beat 2 egg yolks in a bowl with 1 teaspoon of lemon juice and add the hot sauce gradually. Return the mixture to the saucepan and stir it over a very low flame until it just begins to thicken. The sauce should be almost white. Pour it over the meat and vegetables, which have been drained and kept hot, and serve the *blanquette* with rice.

Veau Sauté Marengo

VEAL MARENGO

Serves three or four
Veal, olive oil, tomatoes, onions, white wine, stock, garlic, mushrooms

In a heavy casserole brown 1½ pounds of tender stewing veal, cut into cubes, in 3 tablespoons of olive oil. Add 4 ripe tomatoes, peeled, seeded, and chopped, and 1 dozen tiny whole onions (2 medium onions, chopped coarse, will do) first browned briefly in butter. Simmer the mixture for 4 or 5 minutes, sprinkle on 2 teaspoons of flour, and blend it in thoroughly. Then add 1 cup of dry white wine, 2 cups of chicken stock, 1 whole clove of garlic, and salt and pepper. Cover the casserole and simmer the veal for 1 hour. Then add 1 dozen mushroom caps, first sautéed for 3 or 4 minutes in butter, and simmer all together for another ½ hour, or until the meat is tender. Serve sprinkled with chopped parsley and garnished with croutons sautéed in butter.

Rôti de Veau Bourgeoise

BRAISED ROAST OF VEAL

Serves six.
Veal, carrots, onions, white wine, bacon, herbs, stock

In an iron casserole or *cocotte* brown a 3½-pound piece of boneless young veal in 2 tablespoons of butter. Add 1 carrot and 1 onion, both cut into pieces, ½ cup of white wine, ¼ cup of water, a *bouquet garni,* salt and pepper, a piece of bacon rind, and ½ teaspoon of meat glaze. Bake the roast, covered, in a 325° oven for 1½ hours, then uncover it and bake it another 30 minutes to brown the meat and reduce the sauce. Serve the *rôti de veau* sliced on a hot platter with the sauce and surrounded by the following vegetables.

Garniture Bourgeoise: In a skillet sauté 3 strips of lean bacon, diced, in 1 tablespoon of butter. Add 18 very small onions and, when these are lightly browned on all sides, add 6 young carrots cut into small pieces, salt, pepper, and 1 teaspoon of sugar. When the carrots begin to brown, add 1 cup of beef stock and simmer the vegetables until they are tender and very little liquid remains. Cover if the liquid reduces too fast.

Foie de Veau Grillé à la Française

PANBROILED CALF'S LIVER

Calf's liver, butter, garlic or shallots, vinegar, herbs

The secret of good calf's liver is to use only young tender liver that is very light in color and then never to overcook it, which, Clémentine rightly said, makes it inedible. Have your butcher slice it *evenly* and not too thin.

Dip the slices lightly in flour and shake off the excess. Cook them briefly in hot butter over a brisk fire; 2 minutes on each side should be plenty. The slices should brown quickly and remain pale pink inside. When the liver is almost done, add for each slice half of a small, finely minced and mashed clove of garlic. (Or use finely minced shallots.)

Arrange the liver on a hot platter. For each slice stir 1 teaspoon of tarragon red-wine vinegar into the pan juices and add butter if the pan is dry. Pour this sauce over the liver. A dusting of finely chopped parsley, or half parsley and half fresh tarragon, is the indispensable final touch. Serve with potatoes (French-fried, sautéed, or boiled).

Foie de Veau Poêlé à la Bourgeoise   *page 115.*

Rognons de Veau au Vin Rouge

SAUTÉED VEAL KIDNEYS WITH RED WINE

Serves three or four.

Veal kidneys, butter, mushrooms, onion, red wine

Kidneys must be cooked only briefly or they will be tough. This simple recipe gives succulent results and will work equally well with cubes of calf's liver.

Remove all the fat and membranes from 2 veal kidneys, split them lengthwise, and with scissors remove the hard center cores. Rinse the kidneys, dry them well with a cloth, and slice them thin. First sauté 5 or 6 sliced mushrooms briefly in hot butter. Now, in another skillet, brown the sliced kidneys for about 3 minutes in plenty of hot butter with 1 small finely minced onion. Season with salt and pepper and add the mushrooms. Sprinkle a scant 2 teaspoons of flour over all, blend the mixture well, and add ½ cup of a good red wine and a little stock or water. Let the liquid simmer down briefly and pour the kidneys into a ring of fluffy white rice. The kidneys should have cooked no more than 5 minutes in all.

Rognons de Veau en Casserole Dijonnaise

VEAL KIDNEYS WITH CREAM AND MUSTARD

Serves four to six.

Veal kidneys, herbs, spices, lemon juice, onion, cream, mustard, mushrooms

Remove all the fat and membranes from 4 veal kidneys and with scissors remove the hard center cores. Rinse the kidneys and dry them well with a cloth. Season them with salt, pepper, a pinch of thyme, and a dash of nutmeg.

Melt 4 tablespoons of butter in an earthen or enameled casserole and, when it is hot but not brown, cook the kidneys in it, over a brisk fire, for 3 minutes, turning them from time to time. Remove the kidneys, let them cool a little, and slice them.

Return the slices to the casserole and sprinkle them with lemon juice, a little grated onion, and 2 teaspoons each of chopped chives and parsley. Into ¾ cup of cream blend 1 tablespoon of Dijon mustard, salt, pepper, and a dash of cayenne. Over the kidneys spread ¾ cup of small mushroom caps, or sliced mushrooms, first sautéed in butter for 3 or 4 minutes. Pour the seasoned cream over all, cover the casserole, and bake in a 350° oven for 10 minutes or a little longer if necessary to reduce the sauce. No accompaniment is needed, but small boiled potatoes would accommodate the flavor of the dish.

Cervelles au Beurre Noir

CALVES' BRAINS WITH BLACK BUTTER

Serves four.

Calves' brains, butter, vinegar, capers

Soak 4 calves' brains in cold water for 1 hour. Drain them, remove the outer membranes, rinse the brains, and drop them into boiling water with a little lemon juice and salt. Simmer them for 15 minutes, drain them again, and let them stand covered with ice water until they are thoroughly cooled. Dry them with a towel.

Dip the brains in a little flour seasoned with salt and pepper. In a skillet sauté them gently in butter until they are lightly browned on all sides and remove them to a heated platter. Add 6 tablespoons of butter to the skillet and, when it takes on a nut-brown color, take the skillet off the fire and stir in 2 tablespoons of vinegar. Heat the mixture until it foams and add 4 teaspoons of drained capers. Pour this *beurre noir* over the brains and serve immediately.

Serve with small boiled new potatoes.

Note: This is Clémentine's method, but it does present problems, first because the calves' brains she bought at the *boucherie* were young and tiny, so that one whole calf's brain per person was quite correct. Second, though Diane and little Phinney were brought up on this dish and find nothing odd in being presented with a whole calf's brain on a plate, to this day not many Americans take to the idea.

Calves' brains in our markets tend to be much larger, and just one may well be enough for two people. This solves the second problem. Cut the brains after parboiling for 15 minutes — with a very sharp knife so as not to crush them — crosswise into slices ¾ of an inch thick (no thinner). Dip these lightly in the flour and proceed with the recipe. Do not overcook. The brains will taste just as good, and the effect is more discreet, so to speak.

LAMB

Côtelettes d'Agneau à la Niçoise

PAN-BROILED LAMB CHOPS WITH SPRING VEGETABLES

Serves four.

Lamb chops, green beans, potatoes, tomatoes, garlic, white wine, tomato paste, tarragon

The mark of a dish from Nice and the Riviera is its Mediterranean aroma of garlic, olive oil, and ripe tomatoes. This particular recipe requires a modest effort in presentation.

Pan-broil 8 small rib lamb chops in 2 tablespoons of olive oil. Start over high heat, brown the chops on both sides, reduce the heat, and remove the chops while they are still appetizingly pink in the center. Arrange them in the center of a hot platter. Around the chops place neat alternating piles of buttered young green beans, small new potatoes browned in butter, and 8 tiny whole tomatoes sautéed in olive oil until just softened.

To the juices in the pan in which the chops were cooked add 1 chopped and mashed clove of garlic, 2 or 3 tablespoons of dry white wine, the same amount of veal or chicken stock, 1 teaspoon of tomato paste, a little butter, and 1 teaspoon of chopped fresh tarragon. Heat the sauce, stirring briskly, and pour it over the chops.

Gigot à la Bretonne

ROAST LEG OF LAMB WITH GARLIC AND WHITE BEANS

Serves six to eight.

Leg of lamb, garlic, dried white beans, onions, herbs, butter, tomatoes

A roast leg of lamb in French households is so automatically served with stewed white beans (*Soissons* or the greener *flageolets*) that the Breton origin of the dish is almost ignored. The combination is perfected by presenting the *gigot* on a large deep platter with the beans, which can then soak up all the juices as the roast is carved. When planning this dish, first put 2 cups of dried white beans (American varieties are just as good as the French) to soak in cold water overnight.

Remove all the fat and the fell (the papery skin on the meat) from a leg of young lamb. Cut 2 cloves of garlic in half lengthwise and insert the pieces next to the bone at both ends of the roast. Spread the lamb generously with butter and give it a good dusting of freshly ground pepper. Roast it in a preheated 450° oven for 15 minutes, then lower the heat to 350° and roast it for 12 minutes per pound in all, about 1¼ hours for a roast of average size, or to a meat-thermometer reading of 140° to 145° for juicy medium-rare lamb.

Just before setting the lamb to roast, drain the water from the beans, cover them with boiling water (about 2 quarts), and add salt, 2 whole peeled onions, and a *bouquet garni*. Cook the beans at a simmer for 1 to 1½ hours, until they are tender but still firm. Do not let them become dry. In another saucepan, melt a generous lump of butter and add the 2 onions from the bean pot and 2 peeled, seeded, and coarsely chopped tomatoes. Cook this mixture down to a purée, stir in the beans carefully so as not to break them, and add a little juice from the roasting pan.

When the roast is done, let it rest for 20 minutes. If necessary, simmer the beans again just long enough to reheat them. Place the leg of lamb on its platter and add the beans along one side to catch the juices during the carving.

Agneau à la Poulette

LAMB FRICASSEE

Serves four.

Lamb, butter, flour, herbs, onions, mushrooms, lemon, egg yolks

Have 2 pounds of good tender lamb cut into 1½-inch cubes. Cover them with salted boiling water and let them stand, covered, for 10 minutes. Drain the lamb and dry it. Put it in a heavy saucepan with 2 tablespoons of butter and, when the butter has melted (do *not* brown the meat), stir in 1½ tablespoons of flour. Blend it in well, then add gradually enough boiling water (or half water and half stock) to cover the meat. Add salt, pepper, a *bouquet garni*, and 6 to 8 small whole onions. Cover the pan and simmer the lamb for 1 hour. Then add 10 or 12 mushrooms and continue cooking for ½ to 1 hour, or until the meat is tender. During this time, add a little hot liquid if the sauce reduces too fast; or remove the lid and raise the heat if it stays too thin.

When the meat is done, taste the sauce for seasoning and add the juice of half a lemon. Mix 2 egg yolks with a little sauce, add this to the stew, and cook gently, stirring, until it is well blended and slightly thickened. Do not let it boil and transfer to a serving dish as soon as it is ready. Serve with boiled, sliced, and buttered potatoes sprinkled with chopped parsley.

Ragoût de Mouton Bourgeoise

BROWN LAMB STEW WITH VEGETABLES

Serves four to six.
Lamb, salt pork, onions, tomatoes, stock, white wine, garlic, herbs, seasonings, carrots, turnips, potatoes

In a large heavy casserole heat 3 tablespoons of finely diced salt pork. Let it melt and brown a little and add 2½ pounds of lamb cut into 1½-inch cubes for stewing. (Breast, shoulder, or shank half of the leg — or a combination. For this dish, the lamb need not be very young, but the recipe is for lamb, not mutton.) Brown the cubes on all sides, turning them often and shaking the pot, then add 2 onions, cut into quarters, and 2 chopped tomatoes. Cook together for a little while, season with salt and pepper, and sprinkle with 1 tablespoon of flour. Mix well to distribute the flour and add enough liquid — equal parts water, stock, and white wine — to more than cover. Add 2 cloves of garlic and a *bouquet garni*. Bring to a boil, skim several times, and then lower the heat, cover, and simmer for about 1½ hours.

In another pan, lightly brown a dozen small whole onions, or 6 larger ones, cut up, in fat — a little salt pork or a mixture of oil and butter — adding also a good pinch of sugar. Have ready a dozen little new carrots, 4 small white turnips cut into quarters, and 6 small new potatoes. (When using winter vegetables you may wish to parboil them for 3 or 4 minutes.)

When the meat is close to tender, with a slotted spoon remove it from the casserole to a bowl. Strain the sauce through a sieve into another bowl, let the fat rise to the surface, and remove most of it.

Return the meat and sauce to the cleaned casserole, add all the prepared vegetables, and simmer, covered, for 35 minutes or more, until meat and vegetables are tender.

Épaule d'Agneau Farcie

STUFFED SHOULDER OF LAMB

Serves six.

Boned shoulder of lamb, bread crumbs, parsley, scallions, herbs, eggs, stock

The point to such a dish is to feed a number of people deliciously and economically. Mrs. Beck asked Clémentine to make it when dinner was informal, for close friends.

On a board spread out a boned shoulder of lamb, cut side up; it should weigh about 3¼ pounds after boning. Season it with salt and pepper and spread on it the following stuffing.

Combine 1 cup of soft bread crumbs (soak in a little milk and squeeze almost dry); salt and pepper; ½ cup of finely chopped parsley; 2 scallions with a little of their green tops (or 1 small onion), chopped fine; ½ teaspoon each of dried rosemary and thyme, well crushed; and 1 chopped hard-boiled egg. Mix the ingredients lightly but thoroughly with a fork and bind with 1 beaten raw egg.

Roll the meat into a cylinder and tie it with kitchen string at rather close intervals to hold it in shape. Roast it to your taste (or about 18 minutes per pound in a preheated 350° oven for medium rare).

Remove the roast to a hot platter, let it rest for a few minutes, and cut off the string. Use watercress or parsley to decorate. Skim the fat from the pan juices, add ½ cup of hot stock to the pan, and stir in all the brown scraps. Reheat this sauce, strain it if you prefer, and serve it in a sauceboat.

Cut the rolled shoulder into slices 1 inch thick and serve with a potato purée.

PORK, HAM & SAUSAGE

Côtelettes de Porc aux Navets

PORK CHOPS AND WHITE TURNIPS

Pork chops, butter, white turnips, white wine, parsley

In a large heavy skillet, brown well-trimmed pork chops on both sides in a little hot butter. For each chop, add 1 young white turnip, peeled and quartered, and 2 or 3 tablespoons of white wine or chicken stock, and season with salt and pepper. Cover the skillet, lower the flame, and cook, shaking the pan occasionally, for 40 minutes, or until the turnips are tender and browned on all sides; turn the chops once. If you are making this dish for more than four, use two skillets, as the chops and turnips should fit into the pan in one layer. Serve sprinkled with chopped parsley.

Côtes de Porc à l'Auvergnate

PORK CHOP AND CABBAGE CASSEROLE

Serves four.

Pork chops, cabbage, cream, white wine, sage, grated Parmesan cheese

Remove the outside leaves of a small young cabbage, slice it fine, and boil it for 7 minutes in salted water. Drain the cabbage thoroughly, add salt and pepper and 1 cup of cream, and simmer it, covered, for 30 minutes.

Meanwhile, in an iron skillet sauté 4 well-trimmed pork chops, covered, in butter for 30 minutes, or until they are brown and cooked through. Turn at least once. Remove the chops and season them with salt and freshly ground pepper. Stir ½ cup of white wine briskly into the pan juices, add a good pinch of sage, and simmer the mixture for a couple of minutes. Stir this juice into the creamed cabbage.

Spread half the cabbage in the bottom of an ovenproof casserole. Add the pork chops, cover them with the rest of the cabbage, sprinkle with grated Parmesan and a little melted butter, and bake the casserole, uncovered, in a 350° oven for 20 minutes, or until the top is golden brown.

Rôti de Porc Campagnarde

ROAST PORK WITH HERBS

Serves four.

Boned pork roast, herbs, spices, white wine

This is a standard method applicable to any cut of pork suitable for roasting. The piece need not be boned, but the herbs are more effective if it is. Cuts with a heavy layer of fat should be partly trimmed and scored with a sharp knife.

For a roast weighing 2 pounds after boning, crush together to a powder, preferably in a mortar, 2 tablespoons of coarse salt, ½ teaspoon of dried thyme, ¼ teaspoon each of powdered clove, cinnamon, and nutmeg, 1 bay leaf, and a dozen peppercorns. Rub the meat well on all sides and in every crevice with this powder, then roll and tie it if necessary. Let it stand in a cool place for 24 hours.

Roast the pork, uncovered, in a 350° oven for 1½ hours, turning it occasionally and basting it often, first with a little hot water and later with the accumulated pan juices. When the roast is done, remove it to a hot platter and garnish it with watercress.

Skim as much fat as possible from the pan juices and stir into them ⅓ cup each of hot water and dry white wine. Scrape up all the brown scraps, simmer the sauce for 2 or 3 minutes, strain it, and serve it in a sauceboat. Mashed potatoes are the natural accompaniment.

Filet de Porc Lorraine

BAKED PORK TENDERLOIN

Pork tenderloin, butter, bread crumbs, onion, shallot, garlic, parsley, stock, vinegar

In a small roasting pan, on top of the stove, brown a boned pork tenderloin on all sides in 2 tablespoons of butter. Cover the tenderloin with a generous layer of fine bread crumbs mixed with salt and pepper. Mince 1 onion, 1 shallot, 1 clove of garlic, and 2 or 3 sprigs of parsley and sprinkle them on the meat.

Put the roast in a 450° oven to brown the layer of crumbs, basting several times with melted butter. Once they are brown, lower the oven temperature to 350°, add 1 cup of stock to the pan, cover it, and bake the meat until it is done but not dry, about 50 minutes. Uncover the pan, raise the oven temperature, and brown the crumbs again for another 10 minutes.

Place the roast on a hot platter and stir 1 tablespoon of wine vinegar, or to taste, into the pan juices before serving them in a sauceboat. Carrot and potato purée (see page 224) is very good with this.

Note: Allow ⅓ to ½ pound of boned loin per person. A small piece of loin will need almost as long a cooking time as a large one, as it is the circumference, not the overall weight, that dictates the timing.

Saulpiquet Montbardois Belin

BRAISED HAM WITH MUSHROOM SAUCE

Serves eight.

Half a ham, carrot, onion, white wine, stock, mushrooms, cream, peas, brandy, lemon

Trim the fat from a 5-pound half of a processed ham. (Or use half a smoked ham, but simmer it in water first, allowing 15 minutes per pound.) In a heavy saucepan or kettle, brown lightly in butter 1 small carrot and 1 onion, both sliced. Put in the prepared ham, a *bouquet garni*, and 2 cups each of dry white wine, chicken stock, and water. Braise the ham, covered, at the lowest possible simmer, allowing 15 minutes per pound, and turn it once while it is cooking. When it is done, let it rest in the liquid for 15 minutes, then remove it and keep it warm.

Skim all the fat from the broth and simmer it briskly until it is reduced by about one third. Sauté ¾ pound of sliced fresh mushrooms in 2½ tablespoons of butter for 5 minutes. Dissolve 1 tablespoon of potato starch in a little of the reduced ham broth, then add enough broth to make 1¾ cups. Add this to the mushrooms, add 1¼ cups of heavy cream, and simmer the sauce for 5 minutes, stirring often. Then add 1 cup of cooked young green peas, 2 tablespoons of brandy, and the juice of half a lemon and simmer another 2 or 3 minutes. Serve the ham carved into thin slices with the sauce poured over them. This needs no accompaniment, but steamed new potatoes would not intrude.

Jambon, Sauce Madère

HAM WITH MADEIRA SAUCE

Serves four.

Baked ham, onion, butter, flour, tomato paste, chicken stock, Madeira, spinach

In a heavy saucepan sauté 1 small minced onion in 1 teaspoon of butter until it is soft. Blend in 1 teaspoon of flour and brown it lightly, stirring briskly. Stir in 1 teaspoon of tomato paste, add 1½ cups of chicken stock, and simmer the sauce over a low flame until it is reduced to about 1 cup.

Just before serving, heat but do not brown 8 thin slices of baked ham in a skillet with a little butter. Spread a bed of well-drained purée of spinach on a hot platter or individual plates and arrange the ham on top. Add 2 tablespoons of Madeira to the hot sauce, strain it, pour over the ham, and serve immediately.

Jambon Persillé

JELLIED HAM WITH PARSLEY

Serves eight.
Ham, chicken stock, herbs, shallots, white wine, gelatin, vinegar, parsley

This is a family version of a Burgundian specialty that is usually presented by chefs, elaborately molded and made of pieces of a whole ham.

Cut enough leftover ham into small chunks to make 4 cups of lean meat. Simmer 3 cups of chicken stock with 1 teaspoon of minced fresh tarragon, a *bouquet garni*, 2 chopped shallots, and 1 cup of dry white wine for 20 minutes. Strain the hot stock through cheesecloth and stir in 2 envelopes of gelatin, first dissolved in ½ cup of cold stock, and 1 tablespoon of tarragon vinegar.

Put the ham in a glass serving bowl and pour over it just enough of the stock to half cover it. Put the remaining stock in the refrigerator and when it just begins to thicken stir in a generous ¼ cup of finely minced parsley. Pour the stock over the ham and chill the *jambon persillé* thoroughly.

Present as a first course, with French bread, or later in the meal with a green salad.

Jambon à la Crème   page 109.

Mousse de Jambon   page 109.

Croque Monsieur   page 109.

Crêpes Parysis   page 99.

Crêpes

FRENCH CRÊPES

Eggs, milk, flour, oil, butter

Beat 2 eggs, add ¾ cup of milk, then add ½ cup plus 1 tablespoon of flour, 1 teaspoon of oil, and a pinch of salt. Beat well with a rotary beater until the batter is perfectly smooth. Or mix everything in an electric blender and you have a perfect batter in an instant. These amounts will make 8 to 10 *crêpes* and are the maximum you should mix in the blender at one time. Let the batter rest at least 1 hour before using.

Heat a 6-inch frying pan, grease it with a few drops of oil and a dot of butter, and pour in 2 to 2½ tablespoons of batter. Cook over a moderate flame until the bottom is lightly browned and the top is dry. Turn and brown the other side. Add a very little oil and butter as needed to make succeeding *crêpes*. Spread the *crêpes* on a board as they are done.

Note: These are used with ham, Parmesan, and béchamel sauce (next recipe) for *crêpes Parysis* (see page 99). Clémentine used to let Diane and Phinney have a couple of warm *crêpes* for dessert, with currant jelly, when they weren't invited to have dinner with the grown-ups.

Sauce Béchamel

WHITE SAUCE

Milk, seasonings, butter, flour

Sauce béchamel was at one time a complicated affair. Today it is made according to the simple formula for white sauce known to almost anyone. But there are still refinements reminiscent of the elaborate old recipes. Here is a typical home cook's way of making a plain white sauce flavorful.

For 2 cups of béchamel sauce, pour 2½ cups of milk into a heavy enameled saucepan and add 4 peppercorns, half a bay leaf, half a small white onion, sliced thin, 4 or 5 thin slices of carrot, and a few parsley stems. Heat just to a simmer and cook over very low heat (do not let it boil over!) for 15 minutes. Strain the milk and clean the saucepan well.

In the same pan, over low heat, melt 2 tablespoons of butter and stir in 3 tablespoons of flour. Cook the *roux*, stirring constantly with a wooden spatula, for 2 to 2½ minutes, until it is smooth and thickened. Remove from the heat, add 2 cups of the seasoned milk, all at once, and beat well with a whisk. Return the pan to medium-high heat and simmer, whisking almost constantly, for 1 or 2 minutes, until you have a medium-thick sauce. Season with a little salt and white pepper and finish the sauce with 1 tablespoon of butter.

Note: This is the basic sauce to use for gratinéed dishes and for creamed vegetables. It is called for in the recipe for *crêpes Parysis.*

Tomates Farcies

BAKED TOMATOES STUFFED WITH SAUSAGE

Tomatoes, sausage meat, bread crumbs, onion, garlic, butter, parsley

Slice off and reserve the smooth ends of 4 firm tomatoes. Scoop out the centers of the tomatoes, reserve them, and discard the seeds. Mix together a stuffing of ¼ pound of fresh sausage meat; ½ cup of bread crumbs moistened with 2 tablespoons of stock; 1 small onion and 1 small clove of garlic, both minced and sautéed together in butter until soft; the tomato centers, chopped; and 2 tablespoons of chopped parsley.

Stuff the tomatoes, sprinkle them with more bread crumbs, dot each one with a small piece of butter, and replace the caps. Bake the tomatoes in a lightly oiled baking dish in a 325° oven for 35 minutes.

Note: Very fatty sausage meat should be heated in a skillet to render the fat. Pour it off, but don't overdo this; this economical stuffing is meant to be rich and delicious.

Saucisses au Vin Blanc

SAUSAGES IN WHITE WINE SAUCE

Serves three or four.

Country sausage, butter, shallot, herbs, white wine

Use fresh pork sausages of the kind generally known as country sausage. Brown the sausages slowly in a skillet, pricking the skins well so they will not burst. Remove the sausages when they are done and drain them on brown paper. Pour off all the fat in the skillet.

For 1 pound of sausages, melt 1 tablespoon of butter in the skillet and add 1 minced shallot. Sauté the shallot for about 30 seconds, then blend in ½ tablespoon of flour and cook the mixture for 2 or 3 minutes. Then add a *bouquet garni* and 1½ cups of dry white wine and simmer the sauce for 20 minutes. Remove the *bouquet,* return the sausages to the skillet, and reheat them in the sauce. Serve with mashed potatoes.

VEGETABLES

To Clémentine, any preparation of a vegetable more elaborate than simple poaching and buttering was a separate dish — independent and an intrusion were it to be served with the main course of the meal. (And, when a perfect vegetable in season appeared in the market, it, too, might well be buttered and parsleyed and served alone.)

The Becks, of course, had not the slightest trouble accommodating themselves to this. What stunned their New England friends was the lavish changing of plates for separate courses (long before the now ubiquitous automated dishwasher), including more plates for salad, cheese, and dessert (a fresh plate, knife, and fork for the presentation of a ripe peach to end a meal were routine).

Among this small group of vegetable recipes are some clearly designed as separate courses. Others are real recipes, but very simple. Their savor served entirely alone is something to be considered, in the old-fashioned way that Clémentine took for granted.

Artichauts Farcis Maison

STUFFED ARTICHOKES

Serves four.

Artichokes, lemon, bread crumbs, Parmesan cheese, parsley, onion, garlic, olive oil

Soak 4 artichokes in water with the juice of a lemon. When you remove them, shake and squeeze them well to get rid of the water. Cut about ½ inch off the tips of the outer leaves. Now, in each circle of leaves, well down toward the base, insert a little of the following mixture (which you must augment if the artichokes are large): ⅓ cup of bread crumbs, ⅓ cup of grated Parmesan cheese, ⅓ cup of finely chopped parsley (it needs plenty of parsley), and 1 finely chopped onion. In the center of each artichoke put a peeled clove of garlic.

Place the artichokes in a casserole just large enough to hold them close together, pour 2 tablespoons of olive oil over each one, and pour water, about 1 cup, to a depth of 1 inch into the casserole. Bake, covered, in a 325° oven for 1 to 1½ hours, depending on the size of the artichokes, until outer leaves can be easily pulled away. Serve as a separate course.

Asperges Vinaigrette

ASPARAGUS WITH MUSTARD FRENCH DRESSING

Asparagus, parsley, chives, vinegar, olive oil, mustard

Our own fresh green asparagus are delicious served cold with a not too strong French dressing, but the large tender white asparagus of Europe are a particularly distinguished vegetable that responds well to seasoning with mustard. Though they are expensive imported fresh, in cans, or in jars, they are well worth the price for a special occasion.

Present the asparagus as a separate course, arranged on individual plates with minced parsley and chives sprinkled on the tips. Pass in a sauceboat the usual vinaigrette (adjusted to taste) made of 1 part red-wine vinegar, 3 parts olive oil, and salt and pepper, and season it quite highly with Dijon mustard. Just before serving, beat the dressing well with a whisk until it is almost opaque, or emulsified, before pouring into the sauceboat.

Note: Asparagus vinaigrette used to be served quite often freshly cooked and hot rather than cold. In that event, lemon juice might be substituted for part of the vinegar. For green asparagus, do use part or all lemon.

Carottes Vichy

BRAISED CARROTS

Serves four.
Carrots, sugar, butter

Scrape a bunch of young carrots (6 or 8 small ones) and slice them paper- thin. Cook them over a very low flame in a heavy pan with ¼ cup of water, a pinch of salt, ½ teaspoon of sugar, and a good lump of butter. In about 20 minutes the water should be completely evaporated and the carrots should be cooked and just beginning to glaze. Do *not* cover the pan, or the carrots will steam rather than glaze, though you may start them off with a lid for a few minutes so that the liquid does not reduce too soon. (Little Phinney is against using a lid, ever.)

Carottes aux Oignons Campagnarde

GLAZED CARROTS AND ONIONS

Serves four to six.

Carrots, onions, bacon, butter, seasonings, parsley

In a heavy saucepan brown 2 strips of lean bacon, diced, in 1 tablespoon of butter. Remove the bacon scraps and in the fat remaining in the pan brown 12 tiny whole onions lightly on all sides. Then add 6 young carrots, cut into small pieces. Season the vegetables with a little salt, pepper, and ½ teaspoon of sugar. When the carrots are lightly browned add ½ cup of water. Simmer the vegetables, covered, over a very low flame for about 30 minutes, or until they are tender and the liquid is reduced to a glaze. Remove the lid if necessary. Sprinkle with parsley before serving.

Champignons à la Crème

MUSHROOMS IN CREAM

Serves four.

Mushrooms, onion, butter, heavy cream

A pristine dish designed for the very best large, firm white mushrooms.

In a skillet sauté 1 small minced onion in 2 tablespoons of butter until it is soft but not brown. Add 1 pound of fresh mushrooms, trimmed and sliced not too thin, and cook them over a medium flame until almost all the liquid they render has evaporated. Season them with salt and pepper and blend in 1 teaspoon of flour. Add 1 cup of warm heavy cream and simmer the mushrooms for 2 or 3 minutes, or until the sauce thickens slightly. Serve on buttered toasted French bread or with rice.

Note: The original recipe calls for *crème fraîche*, of which ¾ cup would be enough. No herb is needed.

Champignons Farcis

STUFFED MUSHROOMS

Mushrooms, butter, garlic, parsley, bread crumbs, olive oil

Use 1 pound of large mushrooms to serve as a first course for four people, or use ¾ pound of very small ones to serve as cocktail hors-d'oeuvre for six to eight.

Rinse the mushrooms and wipe dry. Remove the stems from the caps, trim off the root ends, and chop the stems. Sauté these briefly in 3 tablespoons of hot butter. After 2 or 3 minutes, add half a clove of garlic, chopped and mashed, salt, pepper, and 2 tablespoons of minced parsley. Cook together for another 2 minutes, remove from the fire, and mix in about ½ cup of bread crumbs, or enough to make a light stuffing. Fill the mushroom caps with this, and put them in a shallow well-oiled baking dish. Pour a few drops of olive oil over each mushroom and bake them in a 350° oven for 10 to 15 minutes; they must not be overcooked.

To serve as a first course, arrange immediately on heated individual plates, with a sprig of parsley and a seeded segment of lemon. To serve with apéritifs, place on a warmed platter with an attractive small jar of wooden toothpicks.

Chou Farci Aristide

CABBAGE-STUFFED CABBAGE

Serves four.
Cabbage, butter, onion, parsley, bread crumbs, eggs, nutmeg

Discard any wilted outside leaves of a 1½-pound cabbage and peel off 5 or 6 perfect leaves and reserve them. Core the cabbage and slice and chop the rest of it fine. In a heavy casserole melt 6 tablespoons of butter, add the cabbage, and cook it, uncovered, stirring often, over very low heat for 30 minutes, or until it is soft and golden. Add 1 medium onion, minced, and 2 tablespoons of chopped parsley, and simmer all together for 10 minutes. Let the cabbage cool, add 3 tablespoons of bread crumbs, 2 lightly beaten eggs, a pinch of nutmeg, salt, and pepper and mix well.

Put a clean cloth in a bowl, leaving the edges hanging over the side. Arrange the reserved cabbage leaves in the bowl, overlapping and stem ends up, to form a large cup closed at the bottom. Spoon the cabbage into this cup, pull the cloth up around it, and tie it tightly, like a pudding in a bag. Drop the "pudding" into boiling salted water to cover generously and cook it at the lowest possible simmer for 1 hour, turning it once. Unwrap it, drain it, and put it in a serving bowl, stem end down, with a little melted butter poured over it. To serve, quarter the cabbage with a sharp knife.

Note: This is an astonishingly good dish and may well be served, French style, as a separate course. It also works very well with an American baked ham. If you want to double the recipe for eight, duplicate it with two 1½-pound cabbages; a larger cabbage "pudding" is most unwieldy.

The preparation time is considerable. For convenience, let the ingredients of the "pudding" cool, assemble, and refrigerate. Begin the final cooking a little more than an hour before serving.

Choux Rouges à la Flamande

RED CABBAGE AND APPLES

Serves four to six.

Red cabbage, onion, bacon fat, apples, brown sugar, clove or nutmeg, red wine

Soak 4 cups of finely shredded red cabbage in cold water for 1 hour and drain it. Chop 2 medium onions and sauté them in a heavy saucepan in 2 tablespoons of bacon fat until they are golden. Add 2 tart apples, peeled, cored, and sliced, and simmer together for 5 minutes. Then add the cabbage, 2 tablespoons of brown sugar, salt, pepper, and a pinch of either powdered clove or nutmeg. Add ½ cup each of water and red wine, cover the pan, and simmer the cabbage gently until it is very tender, or for at least 1 hour. Add a little red wine if the liquid cooks away too fast.

Courgettes au Four   *page 69.*

Endives Braisées

BRAISED ENDIVE

Endive, butter, onion, parsley

For each serving, use 2 plump heads of endive, 1 tablespoon of butter, and 3 tablespoons of water, reducing the amount of water if cooking a large quantity. Place the endive close together, in no more than two layers, in a heavy saucepan with the butter, water, a few slices of onion, a sprig of parsley, and a sprinkling of salt and freshly ground pepper. Cook them, tightly covered, over a low flame. The liquid should be absorbed and the endive should be cooked through and just beginning to glaze in about 30 minutes. Serve them with a dusting of finely chopped parsley.

Note: Many recipes for braised endive specify blanching first, a strong stock for the liquid, and long cooking. This is all nonsense. Clémentine's quick household version is fresher and better. You must be sure, however, that the liquid in the pan is completely reduced and the endive are tender.

Epinards à l'Italienne

SPINACH ITALIAN STYLE

Serves three or four.

Spinach, butter, olive oil, onion

Wash 2 pounds of tender young spinach, remove the stems, break the leaves into 2-inch pieces, and dry them well. Melt 3 tablespoons of butter in a large heavy saucepan and add 3 tablespoons of olive oil and 1 small sliced onion. When the oil and butter are hot, put in the spinach, several handfuls at a time, turning and stirring the leaves to coat them, and adding more as they wilt. Simmer the spinach over low heat, uncovered, stirring occasionally, until all the liquid is absorbed. Season to taste with salt and pepper before serving.

Epinards au Madère à la Germaine

CREAMED SPINACH WITH MADEIRA

Serves three or four.

Spinach, mushrooms, nutmeg, cream, Madeira, croutons

Epinards au madère is no ordinary vegetable. It deserves to be eaten as a separate course.

Over medium to low heat, cook 2 pounds of spinach leaves, covered, with very little water for about 10 minutes, or until just soft. Drain thoroughly and put through the finest blade of the meat grinder. Drain the spinach again, add 1 tablespoon of butter, a dash of nutmeg, salt and pepper, and ¼ cup of heavy cream.

Sauté ¼ pound of sliced mushrooms in 1 tablespoon of butter for 4 or 5 minutes, add them to the spinach, and stir in 2 tablespoons of Madeira. Sauté 1 cup of diced white bread in 2 tablespoons of butter until the croutons are crisp and golden brown. Reheat the spinach and sprinkle it with the croutons.

Note: The meat grinder was Clémentine's accepted weapon; now we have blenders and processors. The trick is not to overpulverize the spinach.

Haricots Verts à la Lyonnaise

GREEN BEANS AND ONIONS

Serves four.

Green beans, onion, wine vinegar, parsley

Lyon is famous for its wonderful food. Most *lyonnais* recipes have a characteristic savor of sautéed onion.

Snap off the stems and tips of 1 pound of young green beans. Leave the beans whole, boil them in a minimum of salted water until they are tender but still firm, and drain them thoroughly. In a heavy pan sauté 1 chopped onion in 2 tablespoons of butter until it is soft and golden. Add the green beans, mix them well with the onion and butter, and reheat them over a low flame for a few minutes. Add salt and pepper to taste and ½ teaspoon of wine vinegar. Sprinkle the beans with finely chopped parsley before serving.

Navets à la Bordelaise

BRAISED TURNIPS

Serves six.

White turnips, butter, garlic, shallot, bread crumbs, parsley

Peel 2 pounds of young white turnips and cut them into pieces each about the size of a walnut. Melt 3 tablespoons of butter in a heavy pan and add the turnips, salt and pepper, and a very small amount of water. Cover the pan and cook the turnips very slowly; from time to time remove the lid and shake the pan to turn the turnips and cook them evenly on all sides. When they are done and tender, the liquid should be almost entirely absorbed.

Mix together 2 cloves of garlic and 1 shallot, all minced very fine, ½ cup of coarse dry bread crumbs, and 1 tablespoon of minced parsley. Add 1 tablespoon of butter to the pan of turnips, sprinkle with the bread-crumb mixture, and brown briefly over moderately high heat, shaking the pan often.

Note: These turnips, cooked independently, are designed to be served with roasts or broiled meats.

Petits Pois à la Française

SIMMERED GREEN PEAS

Serves three or four.

Green peas, lettuce, onion, butter, sugar, herbs

Here is the incomparable French method for preparing fresh green peas, which can also make frozen peas almost indistinguishable from the fresh.

In a covered pan, over a low flame, simmer 3 cups of green peas in 2 tablespoons of water (frozen peas need no water) with 5 fine green lettuce leaves, 1 small sliced onion, 2 sprigs of parsley, a pinch of sugar, a pinch of thyme, and, when the peas are nearly done, salt and pepper to taste. The peas should be tender and the liquid almost absorbed in about 20 minutes.

Poireaux Braisés au Beurre

BRAISED LEEKS

Serves six to eight.
Leeks, butter, salt

Trim off the roots and cut off most of the green tops of 16 to 18 large fresh leeks. Split the remaining tops of the leeks lengthwise to within about 2 inches of the bottoms and wash them thoroughly under cold running water. Place the leeks in a flameproof casserole just large enough to hold them in roughly 3 layers and add water up to the second layer, ¼ pound of butter, cut into pieces, and 1½ teaspoons of salt. Bring to a boil over fairly high heat, and cook, partially covered and over low heat, for 30 minutes, or until the leeks are tender when pricked with a pointed knife. Transfer them to a shallow baking dish, arranging them this time in one layer, and cover them with cooking liquid. Reserve any extra liquid to add to a soup.

Fifteen or 20 minutes before serving, reheat the leeks, covered with a lid or aluminum foil, in a 325° oven until they are bubbling hot and beginning to glaze.

Salade Normande

GREEN SALAD WITH CREAM AND LEMON DRESSING

Lettuce, heavy cream, lemon juice, salt, white pepper, fresh herbs

Dress tender green lettuce, washed and very well dried, with the following *sauce normande.*

Mix together 5 parts of heavy cream, 1 part of strained lemon juice, and salt and white pepper to taste. Add a generous sprinkling of chopped fresh chives, parsley, tarragon, and chervil, or as many of these as are available. Dried herbs are not successful in this dressing. Make the dressing at the last minute, as the lemon juice will curdle the cream if it is allowed to stand.

Truffes et Marrons en Cocotte   *page 38.*

Truffes sous la Cendre   *page 39.*

POTATOES

Pommes Sautées
SAUTÉED POTATOES
New potatoes or potato balls, butter, oil, salt

Use tiny peeled new potatoes, as far as possible all the same size or trimmed to be so, or potato balls cut from boiling potatoes with a 1½-inch ball cutter. Allow six per person and cook them in a skillet large enough to hold them in a single layer, or use two skillets.

Dry the prepared potatoes well in a towel (this is important). In the skillet, heat equal parts of butter and oil—enough to coat it well, but less than ⅛ inch deep. Add the potatoes and, over medium heat, cook them, shaking the pan often to roll them in the fat, for 5 or 6 minutes without letting them brown. When they are pale gold, sprinkle them with salt, turn the heat very low, and cook them, uncovered, shaking the pan often, for 15 minutes or more, depending on their size, until they are tender and browned on all sides. Add a little butter if needed to prevent them from sticking, but they must brown, not "stew," in the butter.

Purée de Carottes et Pommes de Terre
CARROT AND POTATO PURÉE
Serves eight.
Carrots, potatoes, butter, cream

Peel and cut up 4 large winter carrots and 10 medium potatoes. Boil the vegetables separately until they are tender, drain them, and mash them separately through a colander; there should be about twice as much potato as carrot. If the carrot purée is watery, simmer it with a lump of butter until the excess water evaporates. Combine the two purées and beat them well with a wooden spoon, adding more butter, a little cream, and salt and pepper.

Note: This is a light purée, good to serve in a multicourse feast at

Thanksgiving or Christmas. But it is originally just a homely dish; make it with 1 large carrot and 2 small potatoes, add parsley, and serve with lamb chops just for two.

Pommes de Terre Alsacienne

BAKED GARLIC POTATO PURÉE

Serves four.

Potatoes, butter, eggs, garlic, parsley, nutmeg

Mash 2 pounds of boiled potatoes and beat in 2 tablespoons of butter and 2 beaten eggs. Mix in thoroughly 2 tablespoons of flour, 2 or 3 minced and crushed cloves of garlic, 2 tablespoons of very finely chopped parsley, a pinch of nutmeg, and salt and pepper to taste. Transfer the potatoes to a buttered baking dish and bake them in a 350° oven for 15 minutes, or until the top is lightly browned. Pour a little melted butter over the crust before serving.

Gratin Savoyard

SCALLOPED POTATOES WITH SWISS CHEESE

Serves four.

Potatoes, nutmeg, Swiss cheese, butter, stock

This potato dish is famous in the French frontier province of Savoie.

Slice 4 large potatoes thin and arrange a quarter of the slices in a buttered baking dish. Season sparingly with salt, freshly ground pepper, and freshly grated nutmeg, then sprinkle a few tablespoons of grated Swiss cheese evenly over the potatoes. Continue in the same way for three more layers, ending with cheese. Dot generously with butter.

Moisten the *gratin* with *bouillon* (homemade beef or chicken stock; you may also use canned broth, but then do not use salt in the initial assembly) to just below the top level of potatoes. Bake in a slow (275° to 300°) oven for 1¼ to 1½ hours, until the potatoes are tender (test with the tip of a pointed knife), the liquid is almost entirely absorbed, and the top is browned.

Pommes Gratinées à la Normande

SCALLOPED POTATOES WITH LEEKS

Serves four.

Potatoes, leeks, onion, butter, bay leaf, chicken stock

In a skillet sauté the white parts of 2 leeks and 1 medium onion, all sliced thin, in 2 tablespoons of hot butter until they are soft and golden but not at all brown. Slice 4 large potatoes thin, arrange a third of the slices in a buttered baking dish, spread half the sautéed vegetables over them, put in another third of the potatoes, then the rest of the vegetables and 1 bay leaf, and finish with the rest of the potatoes. (Sprinkle a little pepper between layers; add salt only if your stock is low in salt.)

Fill the dish just to the level of the top layer of potatoes with chicken stock, dot the *gratin* generously with butter, and bake it in a slow oven (275° to 300°) for 1¼ to 1½ hours, or until the potatoes are done, the liquid is absorbed, and the top is delicately browned.

Pommes de Terre à l'Ardennaise

STUFFED BAKED POTATOES WITH MUSHROOMS

Serves six.

Potatoes, butter, cream, egg yolks, grated Parmesan, nutmeg, parsley, mushrooms

Slit the tops of 6 baked Idaho potatoes lengthwise and scoop out the pulp. Mash the potato and beat in 2 tablespoons of butter, ¾ cup of cream mixed with 3 egg yolks, and 2 tablespoons of grated Parmesan. Add salt and pepper to taste, a pinch of nutmeg, and 1 tablespoon of minced parsley. Parboil 6 mushrooms in salted water for 4 or 5 minutes, drain them, chop them fine, and add them to the potatoes. Stuff the potato skins with this delicious purée, sprinkle them with more grated Parmesan, dot them with butter, and return them to a 350° oven for 15 minutes, or until the cheese is lightly browned.

RICE, BEANS, MACARONI & SEMOLINA

Riz à la Basquaise

BASQUE RICE

Serves four.

Rice, butter, chicken stock, onions, sweet pepper, olive oil

Heat 1 cup of raw rice in 2 tablespoons of melted butter, stirring often, until every grain is coated and it begins to turn golden. Add 1 cup of chicken stock and bring it to a boil, then lower the flame and cook the rice, covered, for 15 minutes, or until all the liquid has been absorbed. Add another 2½ cups of hot chicken stock and continue cooking the rice very slowly, still covered, until all the liquid has been absorbed, or another 18 to 20 minutes. Do not overcook and do not stir the rice while it is cooking.

    Meanwhile, in a skillet, sauté 3 medium onions, chopped, and 1 sweet red or green pepper, diced, in 3 tablespoons of butter or olive oil until they are cooked through and golden. Mix the vegetables and rice together with a fork and add a little freshly ground pepper.

Salade de Riz

RICE AND VEGETABLE SALAD

Serves four.

Rice, green beans, artichoke bottoms, celery, eggs, radishes, French dressing

Boil 1 cup of rice in plenty of salted water until it is done but still quite firm. Drain it thoroughly and while it is still hot add ¼ cup of tart French dressing made of 2 parts wine vinegar, 5 parts olive oil, and salt and pepper to taste. When the rice has cooled, mix with it ¾ cup of diced cooked green beans, 3 cooked and diced artichoke bottoms (canned if you must), 1 small stalk of celery with its leaves, chopped fine, and the whites of 3 hard-boiled eggs, also finely chopped. Turn the salad into a glass bowl, sprinkle the top with the sieved yolks of the 3 hard-boiled eggs, and decorate it with thinly sliced red radishes and a circle of minced parsley. To serve, add another ¼ cup of the French dressing and toss the salad again at the table. This is excellent with cold chicken, ham, or cold boiled lobster.

Poule au Riz   page 91.

Haricots Blancs à la Moustierenco

STEWED WHITE BEANS

Serves six.

Dried white beans, herbs, celery, onions, olive oil, tomato, meat juice, garlic

Soak 2 cups of dried white beans overnight in water to cover. Drain them, cover them with boiling salted water, and add a *bouquet garni*, 1 stalk of celery with its leaves, and 1 small onion stuck with a clove. Cook the beans slowly until they are tender but still firm; drain them and remove the onion, celery, and herbs.

In a skillet sauté 1 medium onion, chopped, in 1 tablespoon of olive oil until it is golden. Add 1 large tomato, peeled, seeded, and chopped, and simmer together for 4 or 5 minutes. Add a little brown juice from a roast, or 1 teaspoon of meat glaze dissolved in ¼ cup of the water in which the beans were cooked. Then add the beans, cover, and simmer them for 20 minutes. A few minutes before serving, taste for seasoning and add a very finely minced half clove of garlic. The beans should be very tender but not mushy.

228

RICE,
BEANS,
MACARONI
&
SEMOLINA

Purée Ali-Bab

KIDNEY BEAN PURÉE

Serves six to eight.

Kidney beans, red wine, herbs, bacon, butter

Wash 1 pound of dried kidney beans and soak them overnight in water to cover well. Bring them slowly to a boil in the same water and simmer them for 1½ to 2 hours, or until they are tender. Add salt shortly before they are done. Drain the beans, reserving the cooking water, and force them through a sieve. This is a smooth purée, so you may use a food processor, adding a little cooking water. However, "pulse" the machine and do not overprocess the beans. To purée in a blender, also add cooking water and purée in batches.

Meanwhile, simmer 1½ cups of dry red wine with a few slices of carrot and onion, 1 bay leaf, a sprig of parsley, a pinch of thyme, and salt and pepper until the wine is reduced by half; strain it and discard the vegetables. In a skillet brown 3 slices of bacon until they are crisp. Drain on absorbent paper and pour off all but 1 tablespoon of the fat in the skillet. Blend 2 teaspoons of flour into the remaining fat and gradually add the reduced red wine. Simmer this sauce, stirring often, until it thickens, then stir it into the puréed beans.

Before serving, reheat with a good lump of butter and salt and pepper, and add a little of the cooking water, if necessary, to give the purée a good consistency. Serve the purée with the bacon crumbled over it. This is a good accompaniment for grilled meats, particularly game.

Macaroni à la Crème

MACARONI IN CREAM

Serves four as a separate course.
Macaroni, butter, ham or truffles, egg yolks, cream, Swiss cheese, nutmeg

This simple dish is delicious, but it can become miraculous if 2 or 3 chopped truffles are substituted for the ham.

Boil ½ pound of elbow macaroni in salted water for 12 minutes and drain it. Melt 3 tablespoons of butter in a saucepan. Add the cooked macaroni, ¾ cup of ground ham, 2 egg yolks mixed with 1 cup of cream, and ¾ cup of grated Swiss cheese. Season with freshly grated nutmeg, pepper, and salt if necessary. Reheat over a very low flame, stirring constantly, and serve immediately. A salad of finely cut bitter salad greens is good with this, but if you use truffles, serve alone.

Gnocchis Italiens

BAKED SEMOLINA WITH CHEESE

Serves six as a separate course.
Semolina, eggs, Parmesan or a sharp American cheese, butter

Cook 1 pound of Italian semolina (or use Cream of Wheat) in 6 cups of liquid, half water, half milk, adding a little salt. When cooked and quite thick, remove from the fire and, with a wooden spoon, beat in gradually 3 beaten eggs. Add about ½ cup of grated Parmesan (or a little more sharp American cheese—Clémentine's *fromage de Coon*) and several grindings of black pepper and mix thoroughly. Spread this on a bread board in a layer about ½ inch thick and let cool.

When cold and firm, cut the semolina into squares. Place these in a shallow buttered baking dish, dot with butter, and sprinkle with more grated cheese. Bake in a 375° oven until just sizzling and golden brown. If you prefer, cover with a cream sauce containing grated cheese before baking.

RICE,
BEANS,
MACARONI
&
SEMOLINA

DESSERTS

Fruits Rafraîchis du Cardinal

RIPE FRESH FRUITS WITH STRAWBERRY SAUCE

Pineapple, strawberries, peaches or nectarines, oranges, sugar, kirsch or brandy

This is not a *macédoine*, but rather a bowl of ripe fruits cut into serving pieces. The fruit is not meant to be marinated, but adding the strawberry sauce soon after the bowl is assembled will protect the peaches from discoloring.

In a crystal bowl, place alternate layers of pineapple slices, halved and cored; handsome whole strawberries, hulled; quarters of small peeled peaches or nectarines; and slices of navel oranges, seeded and all the white membrane cut away. Add the juice that escapes from the oranges to the bowl. Refrigerate for 2 hours.

Cut up and mash well, but do not purée too fine, more ripe strawberries with sugar and a few spoonfuls of kirsch or brandy to taste. You need quite a lavish amount of sauce. Cover the fruits in the bowl completely with the sauce and keep refrigerated until 15 minutes before serving.

Coupe Jacques

FRUIT CUP WITH SHERBET AND CHAMPAGNE

Pineapple, bananas, strawberries, oranges, grapes, kirsch, sherbet, mint, champagne

Half fill large stemmed wine glasses with a *macédoine de fruits* made of diced fresh pineapple, bananas, strawberries, oranges, and seedless grapes that have all been marinated and chilled together with a little sugar and kirsch. On the fruit place a scoop of fresh fruit sherbet, preferably lemon or raspberry, and decorate it with a tiny sprig of mint. At the table open a bottle of chilled dry Champagne and pour a little over each *coupe*. Needless to say, one drinks the rest of the Champagne with *coupe Jacques*.

Pêches aux Framboises Antoinette

POACHED PEACHES WITH RASPBERRY SAUCE

Serves four or eight.

Fresh peaches and raspberries, sugar, vanilla bean, kirsch, almonds

Blanch 8 small ripe peaches, preferably white clingstone peaches, in boiling water for 1 minute, peel them, and leave them whole. In a saucepan, boil together 3 cups of water, 1 cup of granulated sugar, and a vanilla bean for 3 or 4 minutes. Remove the vanilla bean, poach the peaches in the syrup over low heat, a few at a time, for 5 minutes, and remove them to a bowl.

In an electric blender, purée 3 or 4 cups of fresh raspberries and strain out the seeds through a fine sieve. Sweeten the sauce to taste with peach poaching syrup and add 2 or 3 teaspoons of kirsch. Pour the sauce over the peaches in the bowl, refrigerate, covered, and turn the peaches over several times in the sauce before serving.

Depending on their size, serve 1 or 2 peaches per person, in dessert bowls, mask with the raspberry sauce, and garnish with slivered blanched almonds. Dessert knives and forks, as well as spoons, are needed for whole unpitted peaches.

Fraises Chantilly

STRAWBERRIES WITH WHIPPED CREAM

Strawberries, cream, powdered sugar, vanilla

Hull a basket of ripe strawberries and cut them in half. Stir them into a bowl of fluffy whipped cream flavored with a little powdered sugar and vanilla. The cream should not be too stiff and there should be enough of it to smother the strawberries completely. Let the *fraises Chantilly* stand in the refrigerator for 2 hours before serving them. They will be nicely chilled and the cream will be streaked with pink strawberry juice.

Abricots Chantilly

PURÉED APRICOTS AND CREAM

Serves six to eight.

Dried apricots, sugar, almonds, whipped cream, vanilla

Rinse 1 pound of dried apricots, put them in a saucepan with water to cover well, and simmer them very slowly, uncovered, for 25 minutes.

Then stir in ½ cup of granulated sugar and cook them another 5 minutes. Force the stewed apricots through a colander, or cool them and purée them in an electric blender. Taste again for sugar. Mix ¼ cup of blanched slivered almonds into the purée, spoon it into a glass serving bowl, and chill.

Just before serving, whip 1 cup of cream, flavor it with a little sugar and vanilla extract, and spread it over the apricots. Or the whipped cream may be mixed into the cooled apricot purée along with the almonds, making a sort of mousse that may be chilled and served in individual *pots de crème*.

Bananes Flambées   *page 127.*

Figues Flambées Boulestin

FLAMBÉED FRESH FIGS

Serves four or six.
Figs, Curaçao, brandy, heavy cream

Peel carefully 12 ripe purple figs, leave them whole, and put them in a chafing dish with 3 tablespoons each of Curaçao and brandy. Light the alcohol lamp and in a few seconds put a match to the liqueurs. Prick each fig with a silver fork and shake the pan gently until the flame dies. The figs should be warm and a little softened and the liqueur reduced. Serve immediately and pass a pitcher of heavy cream separately.

Poires Joséphine

CARAMEL BAKED PEARS

Serves six.
Anjou pears, sugar, butter, cream

Arrange 6 firm Anjou pears, peeled, quartered, and cored, in one closely packed layer in a shallow baking dish. Sprinkle them generously with granulated sugar and dot them with 4 tablespoons of butter cut into small bits. Put them in the hottest possible preheated oven and bake them until the sugar is brown and caramelized. Then add ¾ to 1 cup of heavy cream, spoon the caramelized juice and the cream over the pears to blend the sauce, and serve them warm, from the baking dish.

Note: Be sure the pears are firm. If the variety is too juicy, the sugar may not caramelize.

Beignets de Pommes à la Francine

APPLE FRITTERS

Serves four.

Apples, rum, sugar, a batter of flour, water, oil, egg, and oil
for frying

In a small bowl blend 3 tablespoons of flour smoothly into ¼ cup of
lukewarm water. Stir in 1 lightly beaten egg yolk mixed with 1½ tablespoons of oil and a pinch of salt. Add a few drops of water if the mixture
is too thick and set it aside to rest at room temperature for 2 hours. The
batter should just coat the spoon like heavy cream. (It can be used, incidentally, for almost any fruit or vegetable of your choice.)

Shortly before serving, peel and core 2 medium apples, slice them
into rings ¼ inch thick, and sprinkle the slices lightly with rum and sugar.
Beat 1 egg white stiff but not dry and with a spoon fold it very gently
but thoroughly into the batter.

Heat vegetable oil ½ inch deep in a large frying pan. It will be the
right temperature (about 360°) when a 1-inch cube of bread browns in it
in 60 seconds. Dip the slices of apple in the batter, coating both sides,
drop them in the hot oil, and fry them, turning them once, until they are
golden brown on both sides. Drain the fritters on brown paper, sprinkle
them with sugar, and serve them immediately.

Tarte aux Fraises

STRAWBERRY TART

Serves six.

Pastry, strawberries, raspberry jelly

Use your own favorite pastry recipe. Line a 9-inch pie pan (or a straight-
sided tart ring) with a thin layer of the pastry dough. Prick the bottom
of the dough well all over with a fork. Press a sheet of aluminum foil
over it and fill with dried beans. Bake the pastry shell for 10 minutes in
a preheated 400° oven. Remove the foil and beans and lower the oven
heat to 350°. Bake the shell for another 7 to 10 minutes, or until it is
lightly browned.

Cool the shell and fill it just before serving with neat circles of raw
hulled strawberries, stem ends down. Have ready 1 cup of raspberry jelly
stirred thoroughly with 2 tablespoons of water. Spoon this over the strawberries and heat the tart for 5 minutes in a hot oven. Serve immediately.

Tarte aux Petits Machins Bleus   page 69.

Tarte Tatin

UPSIDE-DOWN APPLE TART

Serves six or eight.
Apples, butter, sugar, pie pastry, whipped cream

Use a large round glass baking dish about 2 inches deep. Butter it very generously and cover the bottom with a ¼-inch layer of sugar. On the sugar, arrange a layer of neatly overlapping slices of tart apples, peeled and cored. Then fill the dish to the top with more sliced apples, sprinkle them with sugar, and dot them lavishly with butter.

Cover the dish with a circle of flaky pie pastry and bake the tart in a 375° oven for about 30 minutes; it is ready when the apples are golden and the sugar is beginning to caramelize. Loosen the crust all the way around, put a serving platter upside down over the baking dish, turn the whole thing over, and remove the baking dish. Serve the *tarte Tatin* hot, with a bowl of chilled whipped cream.

Crème Renversée

CARAMEL CUSTARD

Serves four to six.
Sugar, eggs, vanilla, milk

In a heavy metal charlotte mold, over moderate heat, heat together ½ cup of sugar and 2 tablespoons of water until the sugar melts and browns; rotate the mold back and forth constantly instead of stirring the sugar. When it is a good caramel color, tilt and turn the mold to coat all the inside, then let the caramel cool and harden on the mold. (Or, the caramel may be made in a small saucepan and poured into a warm china or glass ovenproof mold.)

Beat together in a bowl 2 whole eggs, 3 egg yolks, ¼ cup of sugar, a pinch of salt, and 1 teaspoon of vanilla extract. Stir in gradually 1½ cups of hot milk and pour this custard into the mold. Set it in a shallow pan of hot water and bake the custard for 1 hour in a 250° oven; it will be done when a knife inserted in the center comes out clean. Cool, then chill in the refrigerator.

Serve turned out onto a chilled platter; the caramel will cover the custard like a sauce.

Crème Brûlée à la Jeanne

CRÈME BRÛLÉE

Serves six.

Cream, eggs, dark brown sugar

Scald 2 cups of heavy cream in the top of a double boiler. In a bowl with an egg beater beat together 4 eggs, a pinch of salt, and 3 tablespoons of dark brown sugar. Pour the hot cream slowly into the beaten eggs, stirring constantly, and return the mixture to the double boiler. Cook the custard for exactly 3 minutes over simmering water, beating constantly with the egg beater.

Pour the custard into an ovenproof serving dish and let it cool completely. Then cover the top with a ¼-inch layer of finely crumbled dark brown sugar and put the custard under a hot broiler, leaving the door open, until the sugar melts and glazes. Chill the *crème brûlée* for several hours and serve it ice cold.

Mont-Blanc

CHESTNUT PUDDING

Serves eight.

Chestnuts, milk, sugar, vanilla, butter, egg yolks, whipped cream

Slash the shells of 2 pounds of chestnuts on the flat side. Put the chestnuts in a frying pan with a little hot oil and heat them until the shells begin to loosen. Let them cool, peel them, and boil them in salted water for 10 minutes; drain them and remove the remaining bits of the inner skin.

Cover the chestnuts with 2¼ cups of milk, add ½ teaspoon of vanilla extract and 6 tablespoons of sugar, and boil them gently until they are soft. Force the mixture through a colander or ricer and add 2 tablespoons of butter and enough hot milk to give the purée a moderately thick consistency. Mix it thoroughly and let it cool. Then add 2 egg yolks and chill it in the refrigerator.

Shape the chestnut purée into a low pyramid on a serving platter and cover it with sweetened whipped cream.

Note: You may use frozen peeled chestnuts. Canned chestnuts packed in brine should be drained and rinsed; these will require less cooking.

Mousse au Chocolat

CHOCOLATE MOUSSE

Serves eight.

Bittersweet chocolate, eggs, rum or vanilla

In the top of a double boiler over simmering water, melt ½ pound of bittersweet chocolate, broken into pieces, with ¼ cup of water. Stir until it achieves a beautifully smooth consistency. Remove the top of the double boiler from the heat and stand it in cold water to cool, stirring occasionally.

Beat well the yolks of 5 eggs and add these to the chocolate, together with 1 teaspoon of rum or of vanilla extract. Transfer the chocolate mixture to a large bowl and carefully but thoroughly fold in 5 stiffly beaten egg whites. Put this delectable substance into a serving bowl or individual ramekins and chill at least 2 hours before serving.

Note: This is the simplest recipe for chocolate mousse you are likely to find and also very likely the best. You must, however, use chocolate of the finest quality. Also, use very fresh eggs, or the mousse may separate.

RECIPE INDEX

· D ·

244

245

ABOUT THE AUTHOR

SAMUEL CHAMBERLAIN adopted the pen name of Phineas Beck* in 1941 to write his one book of first-person narrative—about the gastronomic education of the Chamberlain family. The story of Clémentine, their French cook, was published as a series of articles beginning that year in the second (February) issue of the newly founded *Gourmet* magazine. The cast of characters is quite real: Mrs. Beck is, of course, the author's wife, Narcissa Gellatly Chamberlain ("Biscuit," to whom the book is dedicated); Diane is his elder daughter, Narcisse; and son, little Phinney, stands in for his younger daughter, Stephanie. Clémentine's real name was Germaine. *Clémentine in the Kitchen* appeared in book form in 1943, under the Phineas Beck by-line, and remained in print until 1985.

Samuel Chamberlain attended the Massachusetts Institute of Technology as an architecture student, but his major work proved to be as an artist and printmaker. The comprehensive catalogue of his drypoints, etchings, and lithographs was compiled and written by Narcissa G. Chamberlain and published under the title *The Prints of Samuel Chamberlain, N.A.* by the Boston Public Library in 1984. He was known to a wider public for his photographic books, many of them on New England subjects; from the first, *A Small House in the Sun* (1936, reissued in 1971) to, many volumes later, his finest collection, *The New England Image* (1962), and *New England Rooms* (1972), all were published by Hastings House Publishers, which also issued his annual *New England Calendar* from 1939 to 1984.

246 The Chamberlains lived for more than a dozen years in France, where the story of Clémentine begins, but before World War II they established themselves permanently in Marblehead, Massachusetts. Mr. Chamberlain served overseas in the United States Air Force during the war as an officer in photographic intelligence. At the earliest possible

---

*A Franco-American play on words: *Fin bec* is the French argot for a more sedate expression, *fine bouche*—meaning a gastronome with a discriminating palate. *Clémentine*'s narrator, needing a name with a New England flavor, became Phineas Beck through a bit of phonetic invention that has mystified readers for decades.

moment, in 1949, he and Mrs. Chamberlain returned to France for the summer, and for many European summers thereafter, to produce more articles for *Gourmet*. These culminated in a series of lavishly illustrated and very successful books — *Bouquet de France: An Epicurean Tour of the French Provinces* (1952, 1966); *Italian Bouquet* (1958); and *British Bouquet* (1963) — in all of which Mrs. Chamberlain participated as co-author and as translator and tester of the many recipes included in each book.

Etched in Sunlight, Samuel Chamberlain's illustrated autobiography, was published by the Boston Public Library in 1968. In it, he remarked of the articles that became *Clémentine in the Kitchen*: "It was great fun to write them because they were ninety per cent true."

CLÉMENTINE IN THE KITCHEN

was set on the Linotron 202 in Bembo, a design based
on the types used by Venetian scholar-publisher Aldus
Manutius in the printing of *De Aetna*, written by Pietro
Bembo and published in 1495. The original characters
were cut in 1490 by Francesco Griffo who, at Aldus's
request, later cut the first italic types. Originally adapted
by the English Monotype Company, Bembo is now
widely available and highly regarded. It remains one
of the most elegant, readable, and widely used
of all book faces.

Composed by Crane Typesetting, Barnstable,
Massachusetts. Printed and bound by Arcata Graphics/
Halliday, West Hanover, Massachusetts on Glatfelter
Offset Eggshell. Designed by Richard C. Bartlett.